BOY GONE FERAL ON BUNNY HILL
BY
SAM HUMPHREY

Dedications

This book is dedicated to my parents who are sadly not with us anymore, but without their courage and sacrifices I would not have had a story to tell.

It is also for my children Mark and Emma who have continued the family tradition of successfully making a living working with horses. I am very proud that they have both excelled in their chosen Equestrian professions.

Finally, it is for my three beloved granddaughters Katherine, Florence and Georgina so that they will know their roots and some of their family history.

For me the jury is out as to whether or not we live in a better world today, with all the fantastic technology, or was it the quieter days before computers and mobile phones and less government regulation. I will leave that decision to my grandchildren to decide at a later date

My Thanks

Writing a book is not easy and without the help and support of others I would not have managed to write this book.

First a big thank you to everyone who has contacted me about my first book, "The Knights Errant".

When you finally get to the point of clicking "Publish Book" it is with great trepidation. How will my work be received? The joy and relief that I have had from your comments both verbal and by email is just amazing. Thank you all so much. Without those comments and encouragement, I would not have started this second book, let alone finished it.

Writing a book is just a small part of actually getting a book published and I cannot express my gratitude enough to the unsung heroes who have worked behind the scenes to get this book into print. My thanks to Louise Proudman for editing this book and the laughs that we have had over her misunderstanding of old country and horsey phrases used by me.

To Lynn Benson for reading every chapter as I wrote it and making helpful comments, and to her husband Dick, who is sadly no longer with us, for inspiring and mentoring me for so many years.

To Jackie Clarke, Vanda Craig and Rex Staples for proofreading and my wife Louise, who has had to put up with my reclusive writing habits for another two years and her stalwart support throughout.

Finally, even though this book has been read and checked by the above people several times, plus with Microsoft editing tools, I am sure there are a few typos still hiding out there. Also, when the manuscript is converted by Amazon to printable book format, strange things happen such as extra spaces or commas turning into hyphens some of these have been beyond.my digital skill to correct. If you find a typo or something strange please let me know and I will try and correct it in a later edition.

My heartfelt thanks to you all.

Forward

People are always asking me, how do you know how to do this or that, who taught you? My answer is always I don't know, I just learnt it growing up on Bunny Hill and this often then leads onto more probing questions about what it was like all those years ago in the fifties and sixties.

I was born just six years after the end of the Second World War. There was still food rationing, the country was bankrupt, and money was very short. Everyone still had to have an identity card and I still have mine to this day.

Telephones in the home were still a novelty, with most people still relying on the red phone boxes in the centre of villages to make urgent calls. We got our first telephone in 1955 just after we moved to Bunny Hill because the nearest red call box was in Costock, over one mile away. Our telephone number was East Leake 366.

Other everyday commodities such as fridges and televisions were also a rarity. It was well into the Sixties before we had a fridge or television.

Although we had a car, it was used by Dad every day for work, so we were reliant on the hourly bus service to travel anywhere, or we walked. Again, it was not until the sixties that my Mother learned to drive and much later before she had her own car.

When our children were born in the late seventies there were no personal computers but by their early teens, they were playing with Sinclair Spectrum computers with 1kb of internal memory, not enough to even save the smallest photo.

Nowadays super-fast personal computers and smart phones are the norm, and everything is going digital. This is a story of life before the computer and mobile phone. A much slower paced life where people communicated by letter and were happy to wait a week or more for a reply.

CONTENTS

Glossary

It has come to my attention that many words that I use in this book are old words specific to the Rural or Horsey World. Other words have just dropped out of use during my lifetime whilst others could be local slang that has gone out of fashion. Below are words that have been brought to my attention, if you come across any other words that mystify you please Email me samhumphrey2@gmail.com and I will add them to the Glossary in a later edition.

Chaff.   Hay or straw chopped into short lengths to add to horse hard feed to bulk it out.

Clenches.   The bent over horseshoe nails on the outside of the horses hoof.

Hard feed.   Oats or barley in whole grains or rolled. Also, pelleted feeds such as horse nuts

Helm.   Correct name for a knight's steel helmet

Plant   When a horse refuses to move

Mi' Duck.   Notts. Derby greeting, my friend

Serry.   A midlands greeting like "Hello", Mate

Skipping out   Removing droppings from a stable to keep bed clean

Skit   When a horse suddenly jumps violently sideways. Horses that do this are referred to

                        as skittish

Scimitar.   A curved wide bladed sword used by Arabian warriors

Shufftie   A sneaky look or preview

Sur-Coat   A garment worn by knights over their armour bearing their coat of arms

Swab.   Young birds not fully fledged

Twitchel.   An Alleyway

Willow wand.   A straight thin piece of Willow wood like a thin stick

Chapter 1

Early Life

I was born at my grandparent's house, 65 Edward Road in West Bridgford, just south of Nottingham, in May 1951. It was a quiet leafy suburb with a twitchel opposite the house that led to two parks which were only a few yards away. A few hundred yards further on was the main shopping area called The Avenue. Not long after my birth, my Mother and Father moved about half a mile away into a semi-detached house on Eltham road that was owned by my grandmother.

My father, Robert Humphrey, was a welder and he had moved from the small Northamptonshire village of Ravensthorpe up to Nottingham because he was offered work on Wilford power station. The power station was being expanded and upgraded after World War II. It was situated on the banks of the River Trent opposite the village of Wilford, which was another well-to-do southern suburb of Nottingham.

My mother, Freda, was the daughter of Harold Holloway, my maternal grandfather, who owned a very successful painting and decorating business that painted all the Players Cigarette factories that were based in Nottingham.
Grandad Holloway was to become my role model in later life and to this day I aspire to be just like him.

I used to love visiting him in his office, it was tucked away, just off Castle Boulevard in Nottingham, right below the towering rock of Nottingham Castle. The office and his works premises were in a builder's yard that backed onto a canal. The yard had two large double gates with spikes on the top of them. They were always padlocked but you could gain access on foot through a small door built into one of the larger doors, very exciting for a small boy. His office was on the first floor of a large wooden building known as the paint shop. It was accessed by a double flight of wooden stairs that made a hollow sound as you slowly **tromped** up them.

As well as Grandad's office, there was a small scruffy kitchen scattered with opened tins of evaporated milk and tall thin bottles of sterilised milk sealed with a crown top, like a beer bottle. The evaporated milk was used as a sweetener in tea. There was also a signwriting studio where a very talented artist called Jimmy worked. Jimmy was an alcoholic and always had a bottle of whiskey and a tin mug by his side on the bench. I asked Grandad why he allowed him to drink while he was working, he explained that if he didn't drink his hands shook so badly that he couldn't paint. There was also another larger room where things such as doors were painted before being fitted.

My grandmother was a kindly woman but also very ill and the thing I remember most, was visiting her in a dark bedroom with the curtains closed. I can't remember anything about my **Dad's** parents until much later in my life because they lived in a village called Ravensthorpe near Northampton and didn't visit us until I five or six years old.

My memories of Eltham Road are scant. I remember that there was a back garden with a toilet and outhouse at the bottom of the garden. I also remember the strong aroma **of ammonia** from the washing and drying of nappies that belonged to my baby sister Jan. One day there was a lot of commotion and people were dashing about screaming and then I was taken to my grandparent's house. It was some years before I found out and comprehended the true horror of that day. My baby sister Jan had choked to death on a soft jelly sweet given to her by our neighbour whilst she was in her pram outside the back door of our house. She was just nine months old! It was a terrible trauma, and the reason we moved to Bunny Hill.

I have no strong recollections of this period at Eltham road, only vague shadows, but I know from talking to my parents it was an awful time. My grandfather realised that my parents needed to get away from Eltham road and make a fresh start. With his help, mum and dad were able to raise enough deposit to purchase a seven-acre smallholding called Roslyn, complete with a substantial number of chickens on Bunny Hill Top.

Bunny Hill Top is eight miles south of Nottingham on the A60, which is the main Nottingham to Loughborough road. I clearly recall my first visit to Roslyn early in May 1955. We turned off the main road and up a steep and rutted track. One side fell away to the main road; the other side was dense woodland. What really stood out was the number of wild rabbits that covered the track and scattered as we slowly bumped our way up. I learned later that the path was the original main road, which these days is now a smooth tarmac road maintained by the council.

By the time we moved to Bunny Hill, I had a new sister called Dawn and she was just four weeks-old when we moved, not the best age to move into a farm with fairly basic amenities. Early May on Bunny Hill can still be cold and the only heating that we had in the bungalow were two open fires, one in the kitchen and one in the lounge. We did however have mains water which was a fairly recent addition. The original water came from a well situated in the conservatory that can still be accessed to this present day. There was no refrigerator, only a perforated metal meat safe fixed to the outside of the north facing wall. It was not until the sixties that we were able to afford a fridge. In the cold mornings, you had to scrape the ice off the inside of the windows to see outside. As you can imagine, this was not the best place to bring a recently born baby.

The layout of the property was very different to what it is today. The front of the property used to be a fruit and vegetable garden, but it is now a turning circle for cars and lorries. The fruit and veg garden flowed seamlessly into the orchard that still exists at the side of the bungalow. The entrance to the farm was on the opposite side of the property to where the entrance is now. The car park we have today was a grass field. Also, the area around the club bar, the indoor school, the ménage, the lorry park and all the hay barns were further fields with hedges and willow trees.

The house was a small square bungalow, in the common 1930's style consisting of a small lounge, a dining room, two bed-rooms, a bathroom with toilet and a small box room. The lounge and dining room had open fires, which was the only heating. The dining room fire heated the two ovens and the hot plate of the cast iron range cooker. There was also a very narrow galley kitchen that had an electric stove, sink and storage cupboards. In all, this was about eight feet long and the working area about three feet wide. At one end, there was a door leading to the dining room and at the other end a sliding door that led into a large conservatory.

Outside there was a long narrow shed which doubled as a garage at one end and a workshop at the other. On the house side of the shed was another vegetable garden and a pig sty, behind which was an open cesspool that collected the sewerage from the house. It was covered by rusty corrugated roof sheets that were slowly disintegrating into the foul-smelling mire below. It was not a safe place for a young child to be around but luckily it was surrounded by a dense bed of stinging nettles. The nettles and fierce warnings from my parents kept me at bay from this lethal steaming pit. This was our sewage system which was emptied once a year by a council tanker creating a nauseous stench that pervaded into the house and choked the other residents of the hilltop.

The most impressive building was a relatively new deep litter hen hut. It was about 100ft long and 30ft wide and was divided into two sheds by a wall with a sliding door and had external nesting boxes running down the long sides. This was my new world and for a boy who had come from a small semi in West Bridgford it was like moving from England to America.

Mum and Dad both loved horses, and it was this love that had brought them together at a local riding stables in Wilford village. By the time they moved to Bunny Hill, they already owned a horse and that was a key factor in choosing the property at Bunny Hill as it had seven acres of land which was enough to keep several horses but that would be in the future. For the first few years we had two income streams, Dad continued working for various engineering companies in Nottingham gaining a reputation as a highly skilled welder capable of welding the new alloys that were being used in post war Britain. Mum looked after the chicken side of the business feeding the chickens, collecting, washing and packing the eggs ready for collection by the egg marketing company. I was fascinated by the chickens and spent hours in the chicken house studying them. One day I woke-up covered in small red spots. Mum suspected measles and took me to the doctor, who after examining me declared that they were flea bites, after which I was banned from spending my days with the chickens.

The other trauma I suffered in my early days at Bunny Hill was to electrocute myself. Dad had been mending a lamp and left the bare wires connected to the mains and, being an inquisitive youngster, I picked up the wire. I must have held onto the wires for some time as I had severe burns to the palm of my right hand. It took a long time to heal and I had to visit the doctor several times to have the dressing changed. I was lucky not to have been killed and I still have three scars in the palm of my hand to remind me of that traumatic day.

It was during a trip to the doctor that I took my first steps to independence at an early age. The doctor's surgery was at Ruddington about four miles away, but as Mum didn't drive, we had to catch the bus and as it was an hourly service it was often a three-hour round trip. With Dawn still very young, this was a major expedition. One of my appointments was on a Saturday morning and Mum insisted that Dad face up to his responsibility as a father and take me in the car. The surgery was very busy, so there was a long wait because in those days you just turned up and waited your turn. Dad was renowned for falling asleep anywhere and everywhere. He was also very bad tempered if you woke him up and would rant and rave. It wasn't long before Dad fell soundly asleep in the waiting room, so when my name was called out, I didn't dare wake Dad and went in to see the doctor on my own saying Dad had just popped out to the shops. The doctor examined me and gave me a prescription and I woke Dad up on the way out. When Mum heard about this, she was furious. Mum rarely raised her voice, but she certainly gave Dad a good roasting for his little nap in the surgery.

We were a one-horse family for the next year and a half, with both Mum and Dad sharing the one horse that they had brought with them and occasionally I would be slapped on its back and led around to get used to the movement of a horse. This changed in the autumn of 1956 when I was informed that I was going hunting. The Quorn Hunt were meeting at Costock Manor and Dad had acquired a pony to take me on the lead rein. He had also managed to get a riding cap, jodhpurs and tweed jacket. I think that they were borrowed as we had no money to spare for luxuries at that period of time and I think my cap (the fee you paid to the Hunt) was waived as Dad had become friends with a local farmer who hunted regularly and owned land that the Hunt would cross on that particular day.

The meet was overwhelming. We were squashed into a corner by huge horses ridden by men in top hats and scarlet tailcoats. The ladies were riding on side-saddles, again wearing top hats or bowler hats and a strange net veil over their faces, which I found frightening. Added to this, they all spoke very loudly and didn't sound like the people that I had known in my short life. Drinks on silver trays were being handed around by smartly dressed waiters but none came anywhere near our corner. I got the distinct feeling that I was not welcome: the riders looked down their noses at me as if they had nearly stepped on a freshly steaming dog turd. Their huge unruly horses backed into us wedging us ever tighter into our little corner. They would then turn around and shout, "Get that bloody pony out of my way you have no bloody business being here!"

At last the hounds moved off and we were able to escape from our corner. Dad dragged me along at the trot at the back of the Hunt as it made its way along the road towards the next village of East Leake before turning right towards the back of Bunny Hill. It was at this point that my legs started to go wobbly and I asked if we could go home now! This caused my Dad to explode, shouting that I was an ungrateful little brat, and did I not realise all trouble that he had gone to, for me to have this very special day. I thought, but didn't dare say, that I had not actually asked to go hunting or in fact, if I even wanted to ride a pony. By the time, we got to Bunny Hill I was in tears, but things suddenly got a lot worse, we left the bridleway and set out over some grass fields and the horses in front started to jump the hedges. We managed to find gateways that kept us moving in the right direction at first but then there were no more gateways I now realise that we had come to a boundary hedge and luckily that hedge had been obliterated by the time we got there leaving a convenient hole for us to go through. Unfortunately, the ditch was far more resilient. To a small child with little to no riding experience, the ditch might as well have been the Grand Canyon and there were also the remnants of the hedge to contend with. I just balled my eyes out saying, "I can't do it Daddy, I will fall off." Dad just shouted at me for being such a wimp and making him look a fool. Eventually, we jumped the fence, I fell off in the mud and got scratched all over by the thorns. I vowed never to go hunting again!

In the autumn of 1956, I started school at Costock C of E Primary School. My arrival at the school was a great relief to the teachers and parents as it took the total number of children at the school to twenty thereby lifting the imminent threat of the school being closed down due to lack of numbers. My only memory of that first day was arriving at the entrance to the school room holding my mother's hand and seeing a crate of small milk bottles, one for each child in the school. I had heard about this daily treat for school children and couldn't wait to get my hands on one of these little bottles of milk, it was so exciting. I was looking forward to school as there were no other children on Bunny Hill and I was keen to find some friends to play with. This proved harder than I had imagined as Costock, at that time, was a small insular farming village and about five surnames accounted for most of the children on the register. Added to this, these five families were all related in one way or another to each other. I was a townie outsider who was not going to be immediately accepted into this close-knit community.

Money was very tight and buying school clothes was yet another unwelcome extra strain on the finances. I was repeatedly told not to scuff my shoes and take great care of my school clothes. I was accompanied on the bus by my mother for my first day, after which caught the 8.30 Trent bus every day on my own to Costock Crossroads and then walked the quarter odd mile to the school at the other end of the village. My trip involved crossing the A60 twice every day! I loved my walks to and from school as the times of the buses allowed me to meander slowly through the village looking at the houses and gardens. There was always a strong smell of cow shit that was deposited on the road twice daily by milking herds that were slowly walked up Main Street by the farmers for milking. I do think it is a shame that farms have been moved out of the villages to pander to the sensitive noses of rich townie interlopers. When I visit my brother-in-law, who lives in rural Germany, the farms are still in the centre of the villages and the smell of silage and cow shit takes me back to those blissful walks to and from school.

In the late fifties, Costock boasted two pubs: The Generous Britain and the Red Lion, a Transport Café at the crossroads, plus a village shop, bakery and Post Office. It also had a resident Doctor called Dr Brown. Each year Dr Brown hosted a garden party for all the children of Costock school and their parents. It was a very formal affair and the teachers taught us about manners and how to behave in the company of adults for several weeks before the big event.

Although I was an outsider when I started at Costock School, there has been a Humphrey at the school for sixty years almost continually since that day in 1956. The school that I attended is now the Village Hall and the playground that seemed so big as a child now looks tiny. Thankfully the village is still very similar to that of my childhood with the exception of one small estate opposite the school that was built on the village cricket pitch and was also used for our school sports day. The rest of the housing development has been in-fill, mainly in the large gardens of the older houses of the village. Sadly, as the population grew the services diminished so that all we have left now is the Generous Britain pub. They call it "progress", but I do not see losing all those local services as progress.

You may wonder why I went to school in Costock and not Bunny. It was a simple line drawn on a map that put us and most of Bunny Hill in the parish of Costock. In fact, we were the last property in Costock Parish as the border was the northern edge of our property along the southern edge of Bunny New Wood. This line like so many lines drawn on maps had a profound influence on our lives and our way of thinking in those early days. Being in Costock Parish gave us a Loughborough-Leicestershire postal address and an East Leake telephone number. Our next-door neighbour had a Nottingham postal address and Nottingham telephone number. To confuse matters even more, the Nottinghamshire Leicestershire border was two parishes further south some four miles away. Even to this day, people who live in Costock Parish tend to shop in East Leake and Loughborough, whereas people on the other side of the hill gravitate towards Ruddington and Nottingham. I know and interact with far more people to the south of Bunny Hill than the north and when meeting people in the equestrian world I always say I live in Leicestershire rather than Nottinghamshire as it's like saying you live in Chelsea rather than Tower Hamlets.

So, this was to become my early new world, Costock School, Bunny Hill and the occasional visit to see my Grandparents in West Bridgford. At school, I gradually made some friends. However, to play with anyone out of school hours they had to be within walking distance of our house as dad had the only car and could not waste time or money taking me to Costock for frivolous activities such as play. The bus was only every hour at peak times and every two hours the rest of the time; again, the family budget could not stretch to unnecessary bus fares. My first friend was David Pycroft who lived at the far end of Ash Lane. It was a long walk to his house but well worth it as the family owned a television, a rare commodity in the 1950s. It was the highlight of my week to go and watch a swashbuckling pirate series called "The Buccaneers". It is hard to comprehend how magical a huge TV-set with a tiny low resolution 11-inch screen in black and white could be today, as we are surrounded by our multi-platform high resolution colour devices. Annoyingly, after the long walk and a week-long anticipation, the TV signal often disappeared during the program leaving us with just a white speckeldy screen to look at. We still have similar problems with broadband and mobile phone signals on Bunny Hill today but thankfully they are slowly getting better bit by bit.

The Ash Lane of the 1950s was very different than that of today: it truly was an ash lane with deep potholes. There were a few brick houses, but the majority were single room wooden shacks with a small veranda at the front, similar to shacks in Deep South states of America. Most didn't have mains water and still relied on water drawn from a well. The people who lived in the shacks were all elderly and had moved to Bunny Hill after the First World War when the scrub land was divided up into small lots to provide small holdings for returning war veterans. I think one of the shack owners told me the plots cost £25 each. None of the shacks had electricity or gas and relied on wood burning stoves for cooking and heating. The lighting came in the form of oil burning lamps.

The people who lived in these shacks were lovely friendly people and when I started to deliver newspapers on the Hill Top, I would stop and listen to their tales. One old gentleman told me that he had to dig four wells before he managed to find water. Another had an amazing collection of bird's eggs all labelled and stored in cotton wool. I spent hours studying these eggs and he would tell me exciting tales of climbing cliffs and travelling to remote places to obtain some of the eggs. It was studying these eggs that first got me interested in the countryside and the environment of Bunny Hill. Although I can't remember all the different eggs, I can still identify most of those which belong to birds that reside on the hill. Today it is illegal to collect bird's eggs but in those days most country kids had a collection. I started my own and was promised the old man's but sadly his hut burnt down. The firemen thought it was caused by an overturned oil lamp. I can't remember if he was killed in the fire or survived but I never saw him again after the fire. Strangely, although all the other huts have been replaced by up market houses, that plot has been refused planning as there is no building to replace. The plot backs onto my land and is now an overgrown wilderness, a reminder of a time gone by.

My next friend was a farmer's son, Jonathan Proudman. They had a small farm on the Nottingham side of the hill with the fields running down to the edge of the brickworks that was at the bottom of the hill just before Bunny. I think that much of their land must have been rented from the brickworks, as every year their farm got a little smaller, as the quarry for the red Keuper Marl that the bricks were made out of got larger. Jonathan's family lived in a large wooden house which probably started out like the ones down Ash Lane but had been extended so that it had two bedrooms a small kitchen and an entrance porch. Like our family, they lived a hard life living from their small farm milking a few cows and keeping a small flock of sheep. His father dealt in all types of farm animals buying from farmers and markets and then selling them on at a profit. You never knew what animals would be at the farm from one week to the next. Jonathan's mother was a lovely kind and welcoming lady who was always making cakes and biscuits for us to eat after school.

At the age of seven Jonathan was allowed the have a 4.10 shotgun which I was very jealous of and although I campaigned hard, I wasn't allowed one until I was nine. We roamed the farm and local woods shooting wood pigeons and rabbits. Because of its small bore, we had to get close to our quarry before firing. This required developing stalking skills, including a lot of patience, as cartridges were expensive, and we were expected to bring home food for the table. Both of our families never had any spare money and from a very early age we were expected to contribute to the family budget by looking after animals and doing general chores. Both our fathers were hard strict taskmasters and anything, but work was frowned upon. However, our mothers conspired to give us treats and give us time to enjoy ourselves when they knew our fathers would be away for a safe period of time.

Mr Proudman was even more scary than my dad, shouting and

waving his stick, threatening to beat the living daylights out of us for being lazy good for nothing children. Thankfully he never did. We were always made to help him load cattle and sheep into the cattle wagon and as he was a short rotund man who had difficulty moving at speed, we were required to herd the animals while he stood at the bottom of the ramp ranting and raving at our attempts to get the animals up the ramp. It was always our stupid fault if any escaped and again much shouting and stick waving would occur. I used to dread the summons to help with loading the stock.

One of the great bonuses of Proudman's farm was fresh milk straight from the cow and still warm. It bears no resemblance to the pasteurised, homogenised watered-down stuff that they call milk today! The downside of the farm was that Mr Proudman was also a part-time knacker-man and a strong smell of dead flesh always pervaded the farmyard.

The brickyard was always a lure for us and although we were under strict instructions not to go near the very dangerous quarry, we of course did! The cliffs were about eighty feet high and very dangerous as the clay face would dry out causing big cracks to appear at the top and then suddenly a large section of the cliff face would break away and go crashing down to the base of the quarry. We used to climb down the cliffs after the brickworks had closed for the day and play in the quarry. As we got older and stronger, we would try and start avalanches by using old fence posts as a lever in the cracks at the top. This was highly dangerous as very often a much larger piece fell away than we expected, and we were very nearly swept into the quarry with the cliff fall on several occasions. We soon started to get the feel of when the cliff was going to fall and would give one last big pull on our fence posts before running like hell for safer ground. I don't know whether they suspected foul play with the cliff falls or it was the beginning of health and safety, but they started to fence off the cliff edge and put up warning notices saying, "Keep Out!".

It was down at the Proudman's farm that I was first introduced to hay making. They had wonderful paddocks of sweet-smelling grass that were full of a wide range of herbs. The grass of old Bunny Hill was a strange thin spiky grass that has all but disappeared now due to reseeding and spraying to improve the yield. Sadly, we needed to improve the quality and the productivity of our grassland, so our family has been partly responsible for its demise. However, the loss of the old meadows is such a shame. Our horses would always leave expensive seed hay to eat the so-called lower quality Bunny Hill hay. You have to ask, "Do they know more about equine nutrition than we do?" There was always much excitement as the time to cut the hay approached. The mowing machine, hay turner and baler were all dragged out of the barn or nettles and oiled and greased ready for the big day.

The 1950s were a period of great transition in farming. During the Second World War, the need for Britain to feed itself forced farming to change from horsepower to tractor power and also to change what we grew. Most of the farm implements that I grew up with in the fifties were horse drawn machines that had been converted by removing the horse shafts and fitting a tow bar for the tractor to tow it. All the power came from the implement's wheels turning a gear box that drove the mechanical action of the particular implement. You could easily tell if it was an old horse drawn machine if it had a metal seat on it where the driver of the horse team would sit. The old machines made the best hay as they were slow and gentle on the grass and helped keep the seed attached to the grass. In my early years, much of the hay was gathered in loose and stacked in the barn loose using pitchforks. We even turned fields of hay by hand, again using only pitchforks. The first tractor that I came across was a Standard Fordson that ran on petrol to start with and when the engine got hot enough you changed over to TVO (tractor vaporising oil, which was a type of paraffin). TVO has a very distinctive smell and when I see vintage tractors parading at agricultural shows the smell transports me back to the hay fields of my childhood. Although I paint an idyllic picture of hay making, it took another two to three days longer to make the hay, even though the crops in those days were much lighter in yield. Getting five or six dry sunny days together in an English summer takes some luck, so many years, much less top-quality hay was made, and it was all hard back-breaking work.

At Costock school, we were treated to a constant viewing of the development of agricultural machinery as our playground ran down from the school to the edge of the busy Costock to East Leake road. The boys from the local farms were very knowledgeable about all types of farm machinery and the main pastime at breaks was tractor spotting. The most exciting was a huge green Field Marshal tractor. It was one of the first that was powered by a diesel engine. It had a single cylinder engine and a massive exposed fly wheel that was more akin to the steam powered traction engine than a tractor. You always knew when it was coming by its sound, which was a very loud "Booup – Booup" sound and all the children would run down to the roadside fence just to get a close look at it. Besides a wide variety of tractors, there were binding machines that cut and tied the corn into stooks that allowed the corn to dry before being fed into the threshing machine. I feel very lucky to have been part of a generation that saw the stooks of corn stood in little groups all over a corn field as depicted in so many old landscape paintings.

Another treat for us in my latter years at Costock School was hearing jet fighters break the sound barrier. We never saw the jets as they were so high, but the enormous rolling boom was a sound I will never forget. Although we never saw the supersonic jets, Hawker Hunter and provost jets that were based at the local RAF Wymeswold Airfield were a common sight over the school and always caused great excitement. Life was very "gung-ho" in those days and I remember visiting the workshop of two old pipe smoking engineers called Jack and Mervyn at the village of Hoton. Their workshop was only yards from the Wymeswold Airfield and the fighter jets were so low that they seemed as if they were going to land right on top of it. On this occasion, my namesake Mervyn, who was the taller member of this Laurel and Hardy duo, was sitting in an old armchair smoking his pipe with a huge mug of tea balanced on an old five-gallon oil drum. In his hands was an air rifle which he was using to take pot shots at the jets as they came into land. Dad enquired "What on earth are you doing Merv?" to which he replied after a mandatory puff on his pipe "Noisy bastards, a man can't hear himself think. I'm just trying to annoy them like they annoy me!" He methodically placed his gun down, took a swig of his tea and another puff on his pipe before enquiring how he could help us.

My world and my parent's world gradually expanded as we made new friends. Dad's welding skills brought him into contact with several farmers who became long term friends, notably the Craig family who farmed at the very end of Ash Lane almost at East Leake; the Sheppard family who had a dairy farm halfway down Bunny Hill towards Costock; and the Sim's family who also had a milking herd but also grew some cereals and did some contracting for other farmers. More will be told about these families later. Personally, I made friends with Steve Amos who went to school at Costock and also delivered the newspapers to the residents of Ash lane and the Hill Top. Steve was a bit older than me. His uncle had a large farm on the outskirts of Costock with land that ran up to the top of Rempstone Hill. Steve's family lived in one of the council houses close to the Shepherd's farm only half a mile from our house. This friendship saw me start to explore the southern side of our hill and in particular the brook that ran along the edge of Costock, known as the Kingston Brook. Steve and I spent days catching newts and other small fish and later building rafts. These hobbies caused us to explore the brook for about a mile either side of Costock, much of which had to be done covertly, as many of the land-owners did not take kindly to two young boys wandering on their land getting up to mischief. We soon became very adept at watching for enemy movement and hiding in the undergrowth to avoid detection. We became so good at this that on several occasions people passed within a foot of us without finding us. I also used this newly acquired skill to hide from my father when I was in his bad books, which was most of the time. Dad was al-ways giving me jobs to earn my keep. My tactic was to get the jobs done as quickly as possible and then run into the woods and hide before he could give me anymore. The woods were my sanctuary, and although I had Jonathan and Steve as friends, I rarely got to meet up with them more than once a fortnight as Dad did his best to keep me gainfully employed.

In the woods, my vivid imagination ran riot. I was the hero sol-dier out of the small cheap war story books that were so popu-lar with boys of my era, mowing down thousands of the enemy with my stick "Sten-gun" that never needed to be reloaded. Sometimes I was a shot down airman avoiding capture in the jungle by Japanese soldiers on a remote island in the Pacific.
In the woods, I discovered the secret tracks of wild animals. These tracks led to holes into what looked like impenetrable brambles but for a small boy it was a secret way through some-thing that was impassable for adults. One day, very early on a winter's morning, I ran into the woods. It was very early, and a damp mist hung in the undergrowth. As I explored this eerie landscape, I came to an abrupt halt when I came to a cleared area where the power lines ran through the wood. Strange nets on poles had been erected and birds were hanging from the nets. Fascinated, I followed the line of nets. Suddenly a man appeared out of the bushes, frightening me to death and causing me to freeze on the spot. Obviously, I was not the only person to be skilled in the art of concealment.

I had never met the owners of the wood or had any permission to enter these private woods, so I thought I was in serious trouble. My fears were unfounded, and the man explained that he was a birdwatcher and that he was catching migrating birds to ring them, so he could understand where they had migrated from. He showed me how to safely remove the birds from the nets, identify them and how to fix a ring to their leg before gently throwing them into the air so that they could fly off and continue their journey. I spent the whole morning with the ornithologist, absolutely fascinated, and could not understand the wrath of my mother when I returned several hours later. Nowadays, as a father and grandfather I can understand that disappearing off early in the morning, not telling anyone where I was going and spending half a day in the woods with a strange man would be cause for great concern, but my childhood naivety shielded me from all these 'what ifs'.

Our next-door neighbour Stan Clarke kept pigs and one day came around to see if I would have one. It had been born blind and would need more attention than he could afford to give it. The gift was accepted, and I became a pig owner. I think my parents thought it might give me a sense of responsibility and maybe curb my wanderlust. We kept the pig in an old chicken shed until it was ready for market (I think that meant the butchers, but I was only six or seven years old, so it was easier to tell a small fib). What this little pig did was to kindle an interest and love of pigs in both me and my mum. Dad also saw the possibilities of a business more profitable than the hens, so gradually we got more and more pigs. To start with our pigs were free range in the paddock that is now the main car park for the riding stables. We used to sow chicory in the field as a feed crop for them. Even to this day we get random chicory plants popping up and they remind me of how much has changed both to the property and in my life.

The free-range pigs were kept in by an electric fence which

zapped me on several occasions. In those days, the electric wire was thick galvanised wire which really gave you a whack if you touched it. I found it great fun to electrocute my young sister Dawn and when she got wise to the "just hold this piece of wire" trick I had to devise more cunning ways to zap her. I discovered that dried dead grass didn't conduct electricity, but wet green grass did, so I would demonstrate with the dry grass and then give her wet grass. She soon got wise to all my tricks and my last attempt ended up hurting us both. I found out that if you wore rubber wellingtons you insulated yourself from the ground (first physics lesson at age of seven) so with my wellies on I grabbed the wire to show her it was switched off. However, I had tricked her to many times, and she was having none of it. Suddenly, I hatched a cunning plan and said, "Quick Dawn give me your hand!" I thought I was insulated but that I could shock her, but of course when the electricity went to ground it shocked us both. The most unexpected thing that happened was as the electricity passed down my arm and up her arm it caused the muscles to contract violently first throwing our hands up in the air and then very forcefully down hurting us both and almost dislocating our shoulders. Dawn went off screaming to mum and I was confined to my bedroom to await dad coming home and receive my punishment. Oh well all playful fun must come to an end at some time.

As the family pig herd increased, the hen flock decreased and soon one half of the large hen hut was converted into a pig breeding unit. The floors had to be insulated to help keep the new-born piglets warm. This was done by placing hundreds of empty glass bottles all touching each on the floor before pouring concrete over them. It was a very effective form of under floor insulation and with a heat lamp above it the piglets were nice and cosy. I suppose this was the beginning of recycling and on Bunny Hill a lot of things got recycled. If a sow farrowed in really bitter winter weather, we often had to bring the piglets into the kitchen and put them in front of the fire to warm up for a few hours. **They** were all put into a hessian sack with the end tied up. You knew when the piglets had revived when the bag started to tumble across the kitchen floor. In extreme cases, we would make a little nest in the bottom oven of the range and pop the odd one in there. It was not a hot oven but slightly warmer than on the floor and it saved the lives of many a new-born piglet.

All the boy piglets had to be castrated when they were just a few weeks old. Dad did this himself with a scalpel and no anaesthetic; I had the unenviable task of dangling the piglet's upside-down, **holding** their back legs so that dad could perform the quick piece of surgery. The piglets kicked like hell and I struggled to hang onto their legs. All the time dad was constantly shouting at me to hold them still so that he could make the cuts. You could not perform my task if you were squeamish as the procedure entailed making two cuts in the scrotum and then putting your fingers inside to pull out the testicles so that the cords could be cut to remove them. After a year or so of holding, dad would let me operate on a few myself. I was always being egged on by local farmer friends to do it the traditional **way, which** they claimed to be much quicker. However, this involved making the cut and then putting your mouth over the cut, sucking out the testicle into your mouth and then biting through the cord before spitting out the testicle. As you can imagine, I was not keen to try this traditional way and never did. People seemed to be fascinated by the procedure and were always asking if they could watch. Many a well-dressed man or woman woke up covered in pig shit after passing out as soon as dad made the first incision.

Life at Roslyn was a bit like the television series "The Darling Buds of May" in that although we lived a very simple **life, people** seemed to want to be part of it. First it was my uncles that came to stay helping out developing the place, mending fences or building pigsty's, in exchange for free board and lodging but later on other friends and customers would also come and give their services for nothing. I think a lot of this came from the war mentality where everyone helped each other survive and never thought of monetary gain. In the fifties, Nottingham still had a lot of bomb damage and a chance to escape to the peaceful countryside was well worth a few hours free labour.

My father was the second eldest of six children, four boys and two girls. Due to the pressures of fitting six children into a small house and his mother being rather overwhelmed by very young children, dad spent part of his childhood living with his Uncle Tom. Uncle Tom was a "Nags Man", which probably means nothing to most people who read this book as they now seemed to have disappeared from the English vocabulary, but I met several Nags Men as a young boy. They were what we would now call Horse Trainers or maybe a Stud Groom, which is another title that has almost disappeared from the equine vocabulary. Uncle Tom was employed by a wealthy man to buy, break-in and train horses for the hunting field. He was a very kind soft-spoken man and I visited Great Uncle Tom and Great Auntie Renee many times at their house in the village of Long Bennington which is situated just off the A1 road about seven miles south of Newark in Lincolnshire.

It was originally part of the A1 Great North Road and its pubs were at the ideal point between Newark and Stamford for travellers to stop and refresh themselves when travelling by horse or coach. The village was bypassed in 1968 and it became just another quiet sleepy village. Although it is in Lincolnshire, it is very close to the fox hunting mecca of Melton Mowbray where the famous hunt countries of the Belvoir, Cottesemore, and the Quorn all converge. It would have been a good base to access both the Belvoir and Cottesemore hunts and it was not totally out of reach the Quorn. I remember my Great Uncle Tom telling me how on one occasion in the 1920s his master had asked him to take two of his horses to the Quorn meet at the Red Lion at Costock. This was a trip of 26 miles. He had to ride one and lead the other mainly at walk so that the horses still had plenty of energy for the days hunting. The trip took five and a half hours which meant leaving at 5.30am. He then had to walk the second horse to the designated place where the field would change onto their second horse and then follow on the tired horse by road until the end of day at approximately 4.30pm. Finally, he had to walk the tired horses the 26 miles back to Long Bennington. You can see why horses were a lot fitter in those days than the horsebox delivered horses of today. It was with his Uncle Tom that dad developed his love of riding and gained the valuable knowledge of horsemastership that would eventually lead him to becoming the owner of his own equestrian centre but more of that later.

I had three uncles who featured in my early life on Bunny Hill. My mother's brother, Ron, was the youngest of three children. My mother was the eldest and then there was my auntie Sheila, known to everyone as "Ding". Ron was only ten years older than me and our relationship was more like I was a younger brother than a nephew. I could talk to Ron about anything and I spent a lot of time with him at West Bridgford, where he lived with my grandfather, and at weekends up at Bunny when he came to stay with us.

Dad's younger brother Keith, known as "Clod", spent a lot of time living with us and worked in Nottingham for a period of time. Clod was a jovial giant with a deep voice and jet-black hair, which was different from the majority of the Humphrey family who were in the main all blond. Clod was immensely strong and would often carry me on his shoulders whilst carrying a spade and fence posts in his hands. He dug endless post holes and concreted in large fence posts to make a boundary fence single handed. It stood for over thirty years until the bases of the posts rotted in our wet clay soil. Clod was nearer to dad's age, so I never had the close relationship that I had with Ron. I can see in my mind to this day, Clod scrubbing himself clean, shaving with great precision and combing his dark bryl-creamed hair to perfection every Saturday evening. I often asked him if he was going to a dance or somewhere special, but his answer was always the same, "No boy, just off to explore the taverns of Nottingham and see what the pretty young ladies might have to offer." Then with a wink and broad grin, he was off to catch the bus into Nottingham.

Finally, there was my father's youngest brother, uncle Ian, known as Jonny within the family circle. Uncle Jonny as I knew him was a less frequent visitor and like Uncle Ron, he was much younger than Dad and again I felt much more at home in his company. Like most of the Humphrey family, he was very softly spoken, and this was accentuated by the Northamptonshire drawl. Uncle Jonny always had time to talk to me and over the years has given me great advice. My overriding early memory of him was when he took me rabbit shooting. He had borrowed dad's .22 rim fire rifle and we crawled on our bellies up our top field in the evening sun to where there were several rabbits feeding. It was a successful foray and he showed me how to gut and skin the rabbit. Mum cooked it and it was served with great ceremony. Unfortunately, I didn't like the earthy taste of the rabbit and still do not enjoy it to this day. The only time I did enjoy rabbit was in Belgium at Horst Castle when it was stewed in a thick, dark and very herby gravy.

So, my three uncles were my early mentors and my maternal grandfather, along with great Uncle Tom, were my role models. I hardly knew my dad's father. I vaguely remember meeting him and being shown his vegetable garden on a visit to Ravensthorpe and him shooting a crow off the power lines with dad's rifle on a rare visit to Bunny Hill. Sadly, he died shortly after that visit from a thrombosis in his leg. This early life was to have a strong influence on me for the rest of my life and not even Dawn, who is four years younger than me, can remember that bygone period of the early to mid-fifties

Sam Humphrey

Chapter 2

My hatred of Horses and Riding.

I have already mentioned my first day's hunting which did not go well at all and started my dislike of horses and all that went with them. Over the next few years my parents unwittingly went out of their way reinforce my view that horse riding was an unpleasant painful pastime and should be avoided at all costs.

My parents to their defence were well meaning, as all parents are, and it was beyond their comprehension that I didn't want to ride. When I tried to tell them, mum would say, "Don't be silly, riding horses is lovely, you will have lots of fun."
Dad's response was, "Get on that bloody pony and do as you are bloody well told!" so I suffered.

The next thing they came up with to humiliate me with was lead rein pony showing. How could anyone in their right mind could think that a boy would want to do this is beyond me. To this day I cannot bear to look at a showing class.

Dad's knowledge of horses soon became well known and through his work in engineering, he came into contact with some wealthy people that kept horses as a hobby. One of these families was keen on showing ponies and somehow, I got put forward as a lead-rein rider. To become a lead-rein rider, I discovered that you had to be scrubbed clean in the bath and then I was dressed in smart riding clothes that I was told to keep spotlessly clean under pain of death. The smart riding clothes included a thick black jacket, usually worn for hunting in the depths of winter; however, for showing you had to wear it mid-summer in 80 degrees Fahrenheit. I also had to wear a white shirt and a tie. The tie was constantly retightened to the point where I could not breathe, and it made my neck sore. The final insult was I had to wear a rose in my buttonhole.

Even when I was on the pony, I was still being brushed to remove specks of dust from my clothing and having my shoes re-polished for the tenth time. However, I think the most painful and degrading thing was people taking out their handkerchief, spitting on it and then scrubbing my mouth or nose and saying, "There you are dear, just making you look spic and span." Finally, we got to enter the ring along with twenty or more other poor souls and were led or should I say dragged around the arena, whilst a man in a suit and bowler hat accompanied by an overdressed woman who sported a large hat bedecked with feathers that was enough to frighten the quietest of ponies let alone put the fear of God into the poor riders. After much pointing and debating from the judges, one by one we were called into the centre of the ring to line up. We were then inspected, and both the riders and ponies were poked and prodded as we came under intense scrutiny. We then had to do a show one by one, which involved being dragged around the arena in various directions and at various speeds. Finally, after more debate they reshuffled the line and slowly gave out the prizes. I always seemed the be at the wrong end of the line to get a nice red, blue or yellow rosette and always got a pale pink one that said commended or sometimes even highly commended. The entire process felt like it had taken half of my short lifetime. As soon as I got out of the arena, I was dragged off the pony and discarded whilst the adults debated how blind and biased the judges were and wasn't the winner somehow related to one of the judges.

Unfortunately, although I never won anything for the owners, the next year I was promoted to the first ridden which meant I was out there on my own. Nobody explained why I had to do the set of walk, trot and canter movements and as I never saw the pony except on show days, I never got the opportunity to practice them. Luckily, I was never asked to go first so I just copied what the others did. I hated it and sulked all through the ordeal and slouched when sitting in line but still they wanted me to ride the next week.

Thankfully, there was a new craze sweeping the horse-show world and this would save me from further ordeals in the show ring. The craze was Gymkhana games. It attracted enormous numbers and the games ran quickly with many separate age groups. They were very exciting to watch and as showing was less exciting than watching paint dry it soon started to push showing off the schedule of many smaller local shows. However, showing still continues to this day at the large agricultural shows. Finally, the best thing about gymkhana games was that it made lots of money for the organisers and for kids who were good at them, as each class gave generous prize money down to fourth place.

Suddenly, there was a quantum leap from the sedate showing classes dominated by wealthy families to these brash working-class games competitions. The other tremendous change was that it was not primarily private owners competing, but the majority of the owners were from riding schools or horse dealing yards, and these people were also making good money out of hiring ponies to the competitors taking part in the new craze! The riding school owners would bring lorry loads of games ponies to the shows along with their riders who were generally stuffed into an overcrowded cab and the Luton part of the lorry that protruded over the top of the cab. What went on in those Luton's cannot be written in this book, except to say a lot of teenagers gained their first sexual experiences in a horsebox either going to or returning from a gymkhana.

The other equestrian sport that was becoming very popular was show jumping. So, by the early sixties the traditional showing classes were fading away and the new format for shows was games and show jumping classes. During the late fifties and early sixties, most show jumping competitions were B.S.J.A affiliated but, like games, as its popularity grew, cheaper unaffiliated club-based competitions started to spring up which undermined the viability of small local shows to put on top class show jumping events or games competitions giving large prize money. We are starting to see the same thing happening today to the latest "In" sports of Dressage and Eventing. During the late fifties and early sixties, most of the villages would hold a gymkhana every year, often combined with a fete or a vegetable show. Many of these started to die out as the sixties progressed and were replaced by the riding schools running their own shows and eventually riding clubs being formed to run shows for people in a specific area. However, with the shows becoming more prolific, the class numbers dwindled, and clubs started to stop giving prize money for games in order to reduce the entry fees and to only give rosettes. This well-meaning decision brought about the end to the heyday of gymkhana games because, without the prize money to fund the keeping of ponies, both the top riders and the riding schools lost interest and started to look for other avenues to make money from their horses.

I had two gymkhana ponies but as we were still struggling financially from expanding the business, my ponies were cheap, and both came with a quirk. Omo was my first. He was about 13.2hh and a flea bitten grey and his quirk was that you couldn't catch the little bastard. Some days you could walk up to him and catch him no bother at all but on important days, like show days, he would trot around you in a circle about 10 yards away just taunting you. Other times he would just gallop off as soon as you entered the field and you just knew that you didn't have a cat-in-hells chance of catching him that day. This meant my planned weekend of games competition never happened on a fairly regular basis. We tried hobbling his front legs (a leather version of the old convicts' leg irons that restricts the movement of the front legs). This failed spectacularly after a week or so when he learned to bound like a kangaroo and travel at a similar speed as a gallop. Our next trick was to tie a long rope around his neck and attach a large car tyre to the other. He could drag the tyre around grazing, but I could sneak up and grab the tyre before he realised that I was close enough to catch him. Sadly, it didn't take long for him to work this out as well and I discovered that he could gallop just as fast dragging a tyre behind him as without one. In fact, it didn't even make any difference with me attached to the tyre! I would often return cut and bruised after being dragged on my belly through nettles and thistles like an Indiana Jones film. On the upside, he was a good games pony and won a lot of prizes if you could actually manage to get him to the event. Eventually, I would catch him midweek and then tether him in the orchard until the weekend.

My next pony was the best games pony I had, but again she had some flaws as most products from the bargain basement do. Her name was Pigeon and she was a black mare, slightly larger than Omo. She tended to rear and sometimes to go over backwards. She was also hopeless when she was in season as she would refuse to start and either rear or plant herself and urinate. Despite her faults, she was brilliant on her day and was picked for the Quorn Hunt Pony Club Prince Philip Cup Team. The PPC, as it was known, is still a very prestigious national games competition for branches of the Pony Club that culminates in a final at the Horse of the Year Show. The team successfully progressed through the area competition, but we were beaten by the Atherstone Pony Club in the regional finals. There was some consolation in that the Atherstone won the cup at the Horse of the Year Show that year, which in those days was held at Wembley Pool in London.

I had one other problem with Pigeon. Because she was much bigger than most games ponies, I struggled to vault on her. I have never excelled at vaulting on, unlike my two younger brothers who were very adept at all the differing types of vault. In the games that you had to dismount to pick something up and then vault back on at the gallop my success rate was about fifty percent. If I missed the vault, I would be pulled over flat on my face at the gallop. Although I was now about eleven years old and enjoying the camaraderie of the games circuit, there was not a lot going on, to change my view, that horses and riding was something to avoid if at all possible.

In my early days of riding I had one other pony that I was allowed to call my own and his name was Robin. He was a very pretty 12.1hh bright bay gelding very similar to the pony that my granddaughter has at the time of writing this book. Robin was very sharp and prone to whipping around. One day when he whipped around, I was ejected very violently, and my foot got hung-up in the stirrup. This panicked Robin and he shot off at the gallop with me being dragged along bouncing around his hind legs. Luckily, he didn't kick me as so often happens in these situations, but I was pretty battered and very shaken. This experience really convinced me that there was nothing to like about horses or riding and it was only strong words and threats from my father that got me back in the saddle. Robin introduced me to another flaw that horses and ponies have and that was their ability to injure themselves. I was riding in our home field when Robin did a buck and a skit sideways. The next moment a fountain of blood was spurting out of his lower front leg. It made me go very weak and wobbly, but I knew I had to get him back to the yard and quickly. Dad quickly stemmed the fountain of blood by making a pad of cotton out of an old bed sheet, but the cut was very deep so reluctantly the vet was called to stitch up the wound. I of course got the blame and a strong lecture about how expensive it was to have a vet come out and stitch a horse and that I would be expected to do extra jobs to help cover some of the cost.

My riding career continued along many different avenues, none of which encouraged me to love the sport. I think I was about ten when I had Omo and one day dad announced that he was taking me cub hunting with the Quorn Hunt. We were cub hunting because we couldn't afford to hunt in the proper hunting season and in those days, children could go cubbing for free and it was only a minimal cap (fee) for adults. This was an excellent way for dad to showcase horses that he wanted to sell. I had a sneaking suspicion that he wanted to showcase Omo in the hope that someone would want to buy him. Although I had many ponies during my early life, I only mention three because these stayed with me long enough to remember them and that was only because they had quirks and were difficult to sell.

All went well to start with. We worked well into the evening preparing our steeds and then got up in the early hours to do more preparation. Whenever we went hunting dad was at his worst. Nothing was ever right, and he would rant and rave at everyone and everything including the dog. My mother, Dawn and I dreaded hunting days. This particular meet was at Ragdale, which is ten miles from Bunny and a place I had never been to or heard of but I'm sure there was an ulterior motive on dad's behalf for the choice of that particular meet. It must have been late in the cubbing season because after about an hour or so of standing around several coverts and tapping our saddle flaps, the hounds were allowed to go away and hunt a fox which caused great excitement from everyone and we all set off at a mad gallop. Dad turned to me and said, "Push your hat down hard and follow me." This was an order rather than fatherly advice

At first it was genuine fun, we galloped across several grass fields and I managed to jump a broken post and rail fence. Dad turned several times and shouted at me to keep up and then we came to a hedge! Dad kicked-on hard and sailed over it, never to be seen again that morning, Omo stopped and slid into the hedge causing both of us to come out of it scratched and bleeding. I made several attempts to get him to jump it, but he was having none of it and I was soon exhausted trying to force him to jump. Thankfully, I was not alone and a group of us tried in vain to find a non-jumping way to follow the hounds but to no avail. It was then that people started to notice me and that I didn't appear to be accompanied by anyone who was looking after me. I explained my predicament and enquired where we were. Apparently, we had run towards Leicester and were close to a village called Thrussington another village I had never heard of! A kindly lady took pity on me and suggested that I accompany her back to where the hounds had met earlier that morning. Along the way she asked my name and where I lived. It was very worrying when she told me that she had never heard of a place called Bunny Hill. When we arrived back at the meet field, there was not a sight or sound of the hunt. The lady apologised that she could not stay with me but was sure my father would come back to find me. I was not so sure so asked for directions home. As she didn't know where Bunny Hill was, she started to ask about other villages that I had heard of. After saying the names of many villages, she mentioned Wymeswold, which I was sure we had passed through on our way to the meet. She gave me directions to there and suggested I then asked my way again.

I started the greatest adventure I had ever had in my short lifetime. I set off from near Ragdale Hall, I turned left when I got to a road and this took me to the Fosse Way Road crossroads at the Durham Ox Pub. Thankfully the Fosse Road was only a single carriageway road in those days and was not the busy high-speed dual carriageway that it is today. I had been told to cross the Fosse and stay on the lane which the lady thought would take me to Wymeswold. A short time, after passing the Durham Ox, I came across a signpost that had half fallen over with the paint peeling off which made it hard to read but I was pretty sure it said 'Wymeswold'.

The lane was very narrow and there was grass growing up the middle of the road. The lane twisted and turned constantly. The sun had come out and it became stifling hot due to the high overgrown hedgerows and I suddenly felt very thirsty in my thick jodhpurs, tweed jacket and tie. There seemed no sign of Wymeswold and I started to wonder if I had misread the sign. As I rounded a bend, I came across two people standing in a gateway, they were a man and a woman and dressed very strangely. They both wore wide-brimmed straw hats similar to those worn by beekeepers and strange clothes that looked like they came from another century. I was going to ask them if I was on the right road for Wymeswold but lost my nerve as their strange dress scared me to death. I murmured good day to them, but they just stared silently at me, so I kicked Omo into a sharp canter and put as much distance as I could between them and me. Writing now it reminds me of a scene from the film Deliverance. I rode on and eventually started to see wisps of smoke rising in the distance; my mood cheered!

Riding down a hill I came to a cottage on my right and a brook on my left. A small sign said Brook Street. I had found civilisation at last but had no idea if I was in Wymeswold or some other village. I rode along Brooke Street until I came to a grass triangle where the road split three ways. I didn't know which road to take so I stopped and let Omo graze whilst I pondered what to do. As I rested, the church bell sounded and that made up my mind; I headed towards the sound. After only a few yards, I saw a shop, a pub and a main road. When I arrived at the main road, there was a signpost that said Rempstone. I knew Rempstone was near Costock, so I followed the sign. Riding through the village on the main road was very scary as it was very busy, and cars were parked at the side of the road forcing me into the middle of the road. Thankfully as I left the village there was a wide grass verge and as I looked back towards the village, I saw a sign that said Wymeswold, so I knew I was on the right route.

I later found out that the wide grass verges that surrounded Wymeswold dated back to the days when livestock was herded on foot from Ashby-de-la-Zouch market to Melton Mowbray market. Wymeswold was one of the overnight stops and herds or animals would be rested and grazed overnight on the wide verges. Apparently herding livestock was very thirsty work as Wymeswold boasted nine thriving pubs during the late 1800s.

I rode on and after a while was cheered up to see Rempstone Garage that lay on the edge of the village: the garage was well known to me as dad often stopped there for fuel and, better still, they sold ice creams. Sadly, I didn't have any money with me because an ice cream would have gone down very well at that moment in time. The road dropped steeply from the Garage into the village and my ride became quite scary as there were steep embankments either side of the road leaving me nowhere to go when I met traffic. Thankfully at the bottom of the hill another signpost pointed to the villages of Costock and Wysall, so I turned right and was soon on another quiet country lane with wide verges. Now that I knew I was getting into home country; I decided to have a canter and soon came to a farm that I recognised from earlier in the year when we had collected the grass that the council had cut on the roadside to save as winter feed for our horses. Another forty minutes and I was home.

It was after lunch when I arrived home and mum was horrified to see Omo and myself covered in scratches and dried blood. These superficial wounds always look worse on grey horses. When I told her my story, she was furious that dad had left me to my own devices. When dad arrived back sometime later, he just shrugged off her complaints by saying, "I knew he would be alright, he's home safe isn't he?" End of story.

On another occasion dad announced that he was taking me for a ride in the woods. This sounded fun until he informed me that I was riding the new pony he had just bought. As usual I was the test pilot to see if the pony was safe for clients to ride it. All went well to start with but as soon as dad got into the wood he suddenly kicked on and shouted back his famous instructions, "Follow me!" The pony shot off like a rocket. In those days, the track was not straight as it is today but constantly twisted and turned around trees and there were many low overhanging branches. The path was just natural earth and even in the summertime there were deep bogs along its way that had to be circumnavigated with great care. The speed we were going terrified me, and I pulled hard on the reins to try and get some control but to no avail. When I pulled on the reins, it felt like they were attached to an iron girder that was securely concreted into the ground. I soon became exhausted and shouted to dad to pull-up, but dad was deaf to my pleas. I knew a bog was coming up and so I started to consider my options because I definitely did not want to hit that bog at full gallop. I considered bailing out, but the trees and brambles put me off that idea. It was then I remembered my favourite stunt that was regularly used in the television series 'The Adventures of Robin Hood' starring Richard Greene. It was my must watch program of the week. Whenever hotly pursued by the Sheriff of Nottingham, Robin would grab a low branch at the gallop and deftly swing up off his horse and hide in the tree whilst the hapless Sheriff galloped on in pursuit of a riderless horse. Perfect! That was my plan. I saw a low branch coming up, I kicked my stirrups away and grabbed the branch. I was whipped from the saddle and there was a moment of elation that lasted about one second. It's amazing what can go through your mind in a second at times like this. I was Robin Hood, I had out foxed the Sheriff, I was a stuntman, this would even impress dad. At the end of that wonderful one second, the rotten branch that I had grabbed snapped, depositing me in a bramble bush with some large stinging nettles thrown in for good measure. I was scratched and stung all over and feeling very sorry for myself; tears welled in my eyes. I was just thinking that at least my ordeal was over and was starting to feel a little bit better about things when dad appeared! To say he was angry was an understatement. I'm sure he had steam coming out of his ears and there was a tirade of expletives coming out of his mouth which roughly translated was that I was a stupid little b******d and if I didn't catch that f*****g pony immediately he was going to thrash the living daylights out of me!

Miraculously all pain and sorrow disappeared, and I ran faster than I had ever run before after my pony. Thankfully I found it grazing in a small woodland glade not far away. It had stood on its reins so was easy to catch. Dad grumbled at me all the way home despairing at how he had managed the breed such an inept creature and so ended another enjoyable day out with dad!

When I talk about the relationship between myself and my dad, people from later decades after the fifties might think him very harsh and even cruel by today's standards but he was no different to the farming fathers of most of my friends. They considered children as free labour but except for giving them chores they saw very little of them, leaving the day to day bringing up of their children to their wives. I think they were uncomfortable in their presence and felt it was their duty to bring them up strictly. Children of the fifties and sixties were definitely in the category of seen but not heard and preferably not seen as well. If asked to describe dad, I would say he was very like the character of Siegfried Farnham in the television series 'All Creatures Great and Small.'

To give an example of the autocratic nature of men in those days, my mother would place an empty cereal bowl and spoon on the table and the moment dad sat down, she would fill his bowl with cornflakes, then pour milk over them and finally sprinkle sugar over them. One morning, as mum prepared to fill dads bowl with cornflakes, he shouted that he didn't want cornflakes ever again. Perplexed, mum enquired "Why?" as cornflakes were always his favourite. The reason he gave was that she had put too much sugar on the cornflakes the day before.

I remember one day overhearing my parents talking about sending me to a boarding school. I was horrified and told my mother exactly so, saying I would run away if sent there. I never dared mention it to my father. However, knowing my roaming wanderlust I think my mother took my threat seriously. Thankfully I passed my Eleven-Plus exam and the ever-present shortage of money meant the idea of boarding school was thankfully quietly forgotten.

Sam Humphrey

Chapter 3

School Days

These days if you could go to a school with class sizes of eight children you would consider yourself very privileged and I suppose in some ways I was. The two teachers of Costock school were kindly and good at teaching the basics of reading writing and arithmetic but I was blissfully unaware of any shortcomings in my education until I moved up to secondary education. Costock school had three sections, infants, juniors and seniors. The infants and juniors shared a large main classroom, one group at each end facing each other. The teacher sat at a desk in the gap between the two groups. The other senior group were in a small second classroom and had a separate teacher.

Outside there was a small tarmac playground, the boys' and girls' toilets were also situated outside at opposite ends of the main building. At the edge of the playground was the caretaker's cottage. The interior of the large room had three major features, two large cast iron stoves, one at either end of the room, and the other feature was large wall clock with a mahogany surround that was positioned at the far end of the room. This clock was the focus of my attention, the teacher probably thought I was staring at her, but it was always the clock above her head. I tracked its movement to morning playtime on to lunchtime, afternoon playtime and finally that magical time of 4pm - home time!

The two cast iron stoves were huge and burnt coke. They stood about four feet high and were the only heating for the large main room. During the bitter winters of the fifties and early sixties, the caretaker would stoke them up until the metal glowed red hot. The stoves were completely unguarded, and we used to huddle around them to thaw out after playing in the snow. Just before I left Costock school, they fitted guards around the stoves after someone was badly burnt. In those days, it was short trousers every day of the year, whatever the weather. It was not until secondary school that I got to wear long trousers and that was in the second term after much pleading to my parents that I was the only boy in short trousers. That was a lie as I think there were two others in my year that still wore shorts. Costock school was like a large family and when the weather was very cold the teachers would make us all hot chocolate to warm us up when we came in from playtime and we would stand around the hot stoves sipping our chocolate until we had thawed out.

PE, or PT as it was called then, now takes place on a regular basis in schools but back in the fifties we only did it a few times a year on warm sunny days in the playground and it mainly consisted of waving our arms around and touching our toes. The latter is something I have never been able to do despite various PE teachers forcing me down, causing excruciating pain at the back of my knees. We never played any games like football or cricket but a few times a year we had to do country dancing which I and most of the other boys hated with a vengeance.

Nowadays, when I go and pickup my granddaughter, Katherine, from Costock school, I am horrified and saddened by the security. I completely understand why it is necessary in these messed up times, but the school looks more like a prison than a place of learning. The children just don't seem to have any freedom to develop life skills and independence. During my time at Costock School, many children went home for lunch. They just went and came back, nobody collected them or checked them out, they just came and went. We had no supervision in the playground and if a fight got too bad somebody would go and fetch a teacher. We just looked after ourselves!

When I was in my last year at Costock, Steve Amos, who by then had moved up to the secondary school at East Leake, came back with tales of a small civil war skirmish that had taken place near Costock on the hill towards Rempstone around an old graveyard and a marsh. The Royalists had ambushed a parliamentarian convoy traveling from Leicester to Nottingham and four soldiers were killed in the skirmish. Their bodies had been buried in East Leake graveyard. After many expeditions, we finally found the old graveyard and the marsh. The marsh was caused by a natural spring and we soon found the source, we took immense pleasure in kneeling down to drink the cool sweet water that bubbled from the ground. The marsh was very dangerous, and you had to leap from one grass tussock to another to cross it. We had tested the depth of the marsh with a long stick which convinced us that it was bottomless.

It was a very eerie place: the gravestones were leaning at all angles and some had sunk down so that only the tops were visible. If you visited in the early morning or the evening, a low mist clung to the ground over the marsh and around the gravestones. It was like a scene from the old black and white Sherlock Holmes film "The Hound of the Baskervilles". The gravestones were heavily pocked with what looked bullet marks which convinced us that we had found the battle site. It was not until several years later when I revisited the site with a greater knowledge of history that I realised that the earliest dated gravestone was a hundred years later than the English Civil War and perhaps we had got a little carried away with our imaginations.

One of the bonuses of finding the spring was that there was an abundance of watercress growing all over the marsh. After taking some home for our mothers we discovered it was hard to buy and commanded a high price. We soon had a thriving business selling bunches of watercress to friends and neighbours. I soon worked out that if I went during school lunchtimes, I was a mile closer to the site. I would only have my main course at lunchtime and then slip out of the back of the playground through a loose fence-pale that could be swung to the side creating a hole just big enough to squeeze through. I had to run the half mile or more to the marsh, quickly pick a bag full of watercress and then run all the way back. I was late getting back once but easily explained being late for afternoon register by saying I had a poorly tummy and had been in the toilets that, which as I mentioned earlier, were outside.

After my unexpected success in the eleven-plus examination I left Costock and went to the new technical grammar school in West Bridgford called Rushcliffe. It had only been open a year when I started and was still not completely full. There was no sixth form and the fifth form were actually bused in from Mansfield every day which was an hour's bus trip each way. Mansfield was a thriving coal mining town in the sixties and these lads were tough and rough. I say lads as Rushcliffe was an all-boys school. Its sister school for girls opened the year that I started and was adjacent to our school. Any fraternising was strictly forbidden!
 Again, as with Costock school, I was not in tune with most of my classmates. There was only me and one other lad who came from a farming/country background. We had nothing in common with the other lads who came mainly from West Bridgford. The other lad was called Rick Hortor and I have heard he and his family now have a successful horticultural business at Kinoulton. We talked about tractors and livestock and the rest of the class thought we were a bit weird!

My first couple of years were difficult and I quickly realised that attending a small village school had its drawbacks. For the first few months, I got lost on a daily basis, turned up late for classes and got detentions. Homework was another problem: we never had any at Costock, so it was completely new to me and dad thought it to be a low priority, especially at weekends. Work came first, and I could do my homework after that if there was any time left. We had two hours homework every night and three hours at weekends! Also, the commute to school was over an hour each way. There wasn't a school bus and the scheduled Trent bus stop was at the top of Wilford Hill, over half a mile from the school. The bus was very slow as it also carried pupils from several other Nottingham schools as well as regular passengers, so it was constantly stopping to drop them off at every stop.

At weekends, I would do my homework Sunday evening but on one Sunday evening a friend of dads turned up with a huge lorry load of hot tarmac that was excess to requirements on some roadworks. It had to be laid quickly before it set, and we laboured very hard for three hours raking it level. It was well worth doing as it was a fortune's worth of Tarmac for free and was the floor of our top yard for the next thirty years. We finished at about 10:30pm, totally exhausted and I still hadn't done my homework or had an evening meal. Mum insisted that I go to bed and dad would write a note as to why I had not done my homework. Even with the note, I got two hours after school detention which meant I didn't get home until after seven in the evening. I hated the school and our riding school - it just wasn't fair.

The only two things that I enjoyed at school were rugby and long-distance running. I played rugby for the school for two years, mainly on the wing but also as a scrum half and at fullback until dad put a stop to it as it took up most of Saturday and cost a fortune in bus fares. Each member of the team had to make his own way to the away matches which often meant catching several buses and this often took well over an hour each way. However, for long distance schools such as Mansfield the school provided a coach but at a cost. When I played an away match, it was usually mid-afternoon before returned home. Dad hated me playing away matches as they were costly and deprived him of a day's free labour. I dreaded the Mansfield matches as the opposition were all from mining families, the teams were hard as nails and they really did kick the s**t out of you. The reason I took up rugby was down to my total lack of knowledge of any games, having never ever played any at Costock school. Yes, we kicked a ball around in the playground but there were no rules or teams and it was very much rough and tumble.

During our first games lesson, the games teacher Mr Trevor Lawless, who was an ex-Notts County player, pointed to me as we all lined up on the playing field. "You boy come and stand in front of me." I dutifully did as I was told. He was gently tapping a football from side to side with his feet. He was a big, strong, imposing man. "Right boy, now I want you to try and take this ball off me. Don't hold back, give it all you've got." It seemed a simple but silly request. I kicked him on the shin with all the force I could muster, after all he had said don't hold back! I was amazed the he didn't even try to avoid the kick. I took the ball off him and was just starting to think that I had a future in football having robbed an ex-professional of the ball with such ease. My euphoria was short lived, halted by a deafening bellowing roar followed by a whack around my ear. I was banned from ever playing football again at the school and was immediately sent off the playing field and told to get changed out of my games kit. I tried to explain that was the way we always took the ball off each other at my previous school but it was to no avail. I did however become instant class hero!

My long-distance running was good enough to get me into a county trial at Wollaton Park. However, my hapless PE teacher never mentioned that I should not eat a huge lunch before attempting to run several miles around a hilly course. Unfortunately, on the day of the trial it was my favourite pudding, steamed jam pudding, and I had three portions. My trial, which was straight after lunch, ended after about one and a half miles with me doubled up with stomach cramp. I foolishly thought if you ate more, you got more energy!

My performance at school for the first two years was mediocre to say the least: I was always in the bottom third of my class with report comments such as "Must try harder". But in my last two years, I did try harder and raced up the rankings to third in the out of twenty-eight and passed seven O levels. The school wanted me to stay on for A levels, but I couldn't get away fast enough. I remember being seen by the careers master who seemed at a total loss when I said I wanted to work outdoors in the countryside and after much stuttering and pondering suggested my only option was forestry work. "Thank you and goodbye!" and anyway I already had a job which I was starting the very next day!

I never looked back or saw any of my classmates again: we had nothing in common. Their lives revolved around shopping and hanging out in the local park. Mine was work, riding, shooting and mending engines. It was a chapter in my life that I was glad to close. I do still see one class member even to this day, his name is Stef Jacques, who lived in Bunny and he travelled on the same bus to school with me. He still lives locally and drinks in the local pub. We say hello and pass the time of day but that's all. He once came up to me in the pub and asked me if I was going to the school reunion for our year. I was amazed that anyone could come up with such an idea. I replied, "Absolutely not, I can't think of anything worse!" He looked quite shocked, stating that he was really looking forward to it. He turned and wandered back to his pint.

Sam Humphrey

Chapter 4

Pony Club Days

I joined the Quorn Hunt Pony Club when I was six, not because I wanted to but because mum and dad thought it was the thing to do now that we were land owning horse owners. As with most early riding activities, I was not keen. I was taken to random fields around the county and balled at by junior army officers or people who thought they were sergeant majors. All we ever did was trot circles whilst someone in the centre bawled sit up straight, heels down, keep your chin up, put your lower leg back. It didn't matter who was instructing, they all shouted and said the same thing. The instructors never explained anything, they just shouted orders. I think those days were the divining moments that were to form my style of teaching riding in later years. If instructors had explained the reason why we had to change the way we rode, I could have accepted their instructions more readily. The problem was nobody's fault, as everything to do with riding was so closely linked to the army and in the army, you gave and obeyed orders without question. When the British Horse Society was formed in 1947, their manual of horsemanship was virtually a carbon copy of the military cavalry handbook and throughout the fifties and early sixties cavalry officers dominated teaching, judging and sitting on equestrian committees. It was the same within the hunting world where Masters of Foxhounds often carried a military title. Thankfully, things are much more enlightened these days.

My pony club days of rallies in fields moved on to training for the Prince Philip Cup Team. This took place in Gaddesby, early on Sunday afternoons, and was run by a lovely kind lady who never balled or shouted at us. There were only ever about six of us and it was great fun practising bending and jumping off our ponies at the canter. The downside of these days was that towards the end of the practice sessions, the lady's husband would return from the pub. It was obvious that their marriage was not in a happy place. It was very clear by his manner that he had always had a lot to drink and he had a very florid complexion. He would stagger into the field and start screaming and shouting at our instructor, using the vilest and most degrading swear words, wanting to know as to why she was wasting her time with stupid children and not at home cooking his Sunday lunch. Their screaming matches could go on for thirty minutes or more and very often heralded the end of our games practice. It seems unbelievable that events such as this could happen in front of children these days but happenings such as these were commonplace in the fifties. I don't know whether it was the war or our society still clinging onto Victorian values, but women were still very much second-class citizens and were expected, like children, to be seen but not heard. Looking back, I can see that there was a real battle going on. Men wanted things to go back to how they were before the war, whereas women had been empowered during the war, proving that they could do the jobs that had been considered only suitable for men and perform them equally as well.

Each Pony Club had a DC (District Commissioner) at its head. The title itself conjures up visions of colonial Africa. How on earth they came up with a title like that for a national children's riding organisation I cannot comprehend. However, it does give you another insight into the people who were running equestrianism in the fifties and sixties. The Quorn Pony Club had Mrs Wheldon as their DC. She was a short grey-haired lady, always dressed in a tweed suit. She would appear without warning at rallies, putting the fear of God into both the instructors and the riders alike. All the children attending the rally would be formed into lines for inspection. Then, with hands clasped behind her back, she would start her inspection, closely followed two steps behind by the relevant troop instructor. All very military! Every unpolished shoe, unbuttoned shirt or not straight tie was pointed out harshly making the recipient feel totally inadequate. Your nervousness increased as she made her way relentlessly down the line towards you. I cannot understand why anyone joined the Pony Club of their own free will and I think most of us were put there by our parents, who saw it as a social must, a bit like being sent to a good boarding school.

The saving grace to all this purgatory was pony club camp. I attended my first camp when I was eleven. The Quorn pony club camp was always held at Stapleford Park, the family home of Lord Gretton. Our accommodation was in large marquees, one for the boys and two for the girls, plus several bell tents for the members in their later teens.

For mum and dad, sending me to camp was a big strain on the family budget. Not only was there the cost of attending, but there was a huge list of obligatory items that had to be taken, including a folding camp bed, a torch, a wash bag and so on, the list stretched to two pages. There was a similar list for your pony too! One mandatory item on the pony list was that the pony must be freshly shod. As dad did all his own shoeing in those days, it was another unwelcome job for not only dad but for me as I had to wind the handle that powered the fan to turn the coke fire into a furnace for making the horseshoes.

Lord Gretton not only gave us the use of his estate for the week but also the use of his magnificent stable yard. There were endless loose boxes and standings for our ponies all set around a square gravelled courtyard that was accessed through a grand gateway. The horse accommodation was as grand as everything else on the estate. The loose boxes were massive! The lower part of the box was varnished mahogany with the upper part being cast iron railings surmounted with brass globes. The floors were just as grand made from special blue bricks that had a chequered non-slip surface. There were also matching blue-brick gullies to drain away the urine.

The standings were of matching style but only had three sides. The open end was onto the main internal passageway that ran around the whole complex. Standings have all but died out in the horsey nanny state environment that we find ourselves living in today, but they were exceptionally efficient. The horse is tied to the front of the standing in a good leather head-collar with a long rope that passes through a ring about four feet from the ground above the built-in manger that was also at the front. The rope is tied to a special round wooden ball with a hole in it to pass the rope through and secure it with a quick-release knot. The wood ball was often referred to as a noggin and they were often quite ornate. This allowed the horse some movement including lying down. The noggin kept a light tension on the rope so that the horse could not get tangled up. The other great advantage was that all the droppings were in one place at the back of the box right on the edge of the of the service passageway making mucking out very quick and easy. The standings also had a slight slope from front to back so that any urine drained into the gully that ran along the back keeping the straw dry and saving waste. Most of the children at camp schemed to get a big loose box but I always volunteered to have a standing as we had them at home, and I knew how much quicker they were to muck-out.

The tack room was also beautiful, boarded completely in varnished mahogany, including the ceiling. The bridle and saddle racks were also very decorative. There was a large table in the centre of the room for tack cleaning and a long mahogany saddle horse. It was what every serious horse owner dreamt of having.

The downside of these beautiful stables was that they had to be kept in immaculate condition during our stay so there was endless sweeping up and polishing of the brassware. We had two inspections per day, one after morning stables before riding and another after evening stables. Nobody was allowed to go for their evening meal until everything had passed inspection. The large gravel yard in the centre of the stable courtyard also had to be raked every day and then we all lined up shoulder to shoulder and handpicked every bit of hay and straw up right down to pieces the size of chaff that the rakes had missed.

Our days were filled with mucking and skipping out, tack cleaning, grooming and riding our ponies, plus the manicuring of the stable yard. None of this really appealed to me but it was a necessary evil that I had to suffer to get to the fun bit. After our evening meal, we were left to our own devices. We explored the woods and the rest of the estate, raided tents, and tried to ward off raids from other tents. The latter of these activities went on well into the early hours. I became a bit of a legend making my way to other tents avoiding the sweeping torch beams of our elders who patrolled late into the night trying to keep us in order. I soon discovered, whilst hiding in bushes to avoid the adult patrols, that it was not only the children that were up to mischief! Patrolling the grounds at night was a good excuse for meeting up with a secret lover. By my second year at camp I had worked out that most of the adults in charge of us were having a secret affair with another member of staff. Many of the junior staff where in their late teens or early twenties and often aided some of our mischief, such as providing transportation so that we could raid the Belvoir pony club camp that was being held a few miles up the road at the Garthorpe racecourse. This of course brought about retaliatory attacks from the Belvoir camp. It was all good "Swallows and Amazons" style fifties fun and I loved it!

It was at camp that I started to find something else that I liked about riding other than Gymkhana games. Towards the end of each camp week we would go out and gallop around the estate as a group and jump cross country fences. As we got older, hedges got added into the rides as well and I found I loved jumping hedges. As I progressed into my teens, I also noticed that the ratio of girls to boys riding was massively in the girl's favour but for a male teenager starting to take an interest in the opposite sex, riding was starting to have some very positive advantages!

My last year at camp was when I was fourteen. My previous three years of adventurous behaviour had not gone unnoticed and my parents were contacted by the powers that be to inform them that I would not be allowed to go to camp unless I mended my ways. After strong words from my parents and the fact that I loved my time at camp, I agreed to mend my ways. As with a lot of things in my life, once I commit to a project I do it with almost manic dedication. In this case I changed so much, that I was awarded the camp belt for best boy during the camp. It was a very prestigious prize, a bit like the belts you win in boxing and showed me that if I channelled my energy, I could achieve things that I had always thought were beyond me. Dad was always trying to motivate me by telling me how useless I was, and I had started to believe that I was truly totally useless and would never achieve anything. Looking back, I now see that this was the catalyst that made me change and it triggered a remarkable improvement in my schoolwork shortly afterwards.

Winning the belt was not easy and it was never my goal, I just wanted to prove to the powers that be that I would not let them down. An example of this was that after a lecture on 'Haute turnout of horse and rider' I polished my pony's clenches twice every day before inspection with Brasso. Now that is dedication!

That year I was fourteen and found that I had become a senior member of the camp and was allocated one of the prized bell tents which I shared with Kenneth Clawson, who would later become the senior show jumping coach for British Eventing. I was always trying to get him to come out at night to meet up with some of the girls, but he always refused. I just thought that he was being a goody-goody. However, many years later, after the legalisation of homosexuality, all became clear. In the early sixties, it was something I had never heard of and I now realise how blissfully naïve I was on certain matters.

Although I didn't know it then, this was to be my last camp. Winning the belt had given me status and a lot more friends. I left camp that year excited by the prospect of returning next year to defend my belt. As was the norm after camp, I promptly fell asleep in the horse box on the way home and slept all that day and night after unloading my pony, catching up on six days of very little sleep. I always smile when parents tell me that their children have slept all day on returning from Pony Club Camp but refrain from explaining why they are so exhausted.

I was all booked in for camp the next year but then dad was asked by a friend if he could do some welding for him at Pedigree Pet foods in Melton Mowbray. Dad's friend had secured a contract to erect a new steel structure in the plant during the summer shutdown period. What started out as a two-day job expanded to six weeks. It was the management who were so impressed with the quality of the work that they kept asking my father's friend if he could do extra projects. Unfortunately, he didn't have the staff available for the extended period and he also didn't want to upset his new and very large customer. The money was excellent, and dad was put in charge of finding enough people to form a team to carry out the new jobs. Although I had just turned fifteen, I suddenly became a sixteen-year-old and a new apprentice for the duration of the summer holidays. Working at Pet Foods was like entering a new world. It was a Dutch company and was part of the Mars Group. I had been in several factories before but never anything like this.

For the first two weeks during the shutdown period, we worked as outside contractors but when production restarted, we became temporary staff with all the staff benefits, such as the use of the staff canteen, which was out of this world. Something that was really strange and that I had never heard of in England at that time was that workers and management sat down together and even shared tables together for their meals. It was in this canteen that I tried a food that I had never heard of but seemed to be very popular: it was called yogurt! When I tasted it, I thought it had gone off so tried another, which tasted just the same. It was not until ten years later that I discovered that all-natural yogurt actually tasted like that. Other innovative things were changing rooms, fresh overalls every day and individual hot showers. If you got very dirty you could even have a shower and fresh overalls at any time during the day. Becoming official did have its problems and I had to take a year off my date of birth when signing a whole load of forms to become temporary staff. I had a wonderful time working all my summer holidays there and saved up enough money to buy a motorbike later in the year.

This was the reason I missed my last Pony Club Camp, but I came up with a crazy idea to meet up with my old camp mates. On the Friday night of the camp I came home from work and had an early tea. I then set out on my old bike to cycle over to Stapleford Park. My bike had no gears as they had broken the previous year. I had no puncture repair kit or repair tools as this was a last-minute decision. I had no idea how far it was but estimated that it would take about one and a half hours. What I had seriously underestimated was the number of hills and long steady upward gradients that sapped the energy out of you, especially on an old one geared bike. I set off at 6pm and didn't arrive until nearly nine. Being mid-summer, it was still light. I hid my bike and made my way towards the campsite down the back-lane but to my surprise there was security on the gate. I quickly beat a hasty retreat and went into the woods and made my way to the campsite that way. Secreted at the edge of the wood, I studied the campsite, but it seemed devoid of life except for two adults patrolling around the tents. I waited for about thirty minutes but there was still no sign of life except for the two adults the campers were obviously off doing organised activities. It was then that I noticed the light starting to fade. It was at that moment I realised that I had no lights on my bike, so I decided to abandon my fruitless adventure and headed for home.

It was dark by the time I reached Melton Mowbray, but the streetlights were good, and I had no problems in Melton as the road was fairly well lit right through to the far side of Ashfordby. By the time I got that far it was pitch black. I could see alright as I was used to roaming the woods at night and using my peripheral vision to see where I was going. But having no lights, I had to constantly look over my shoulders for cars. Every time I saw car headlights approaching, I would jump off my bike and wheel it onto the grass verge. I was particularly worried about the police, as in those days you got regularly fined for riding a bike without lights. My progress home was considerably slower than going and my legs were exhausted. I ground to a wobbly halt about a quarter of the way up Saxelbye hill. I dismounted and started to push my bike, but my legs had completely gone. I made it to halfway up but could go no further. I knew I had to rest, so I hid my bike under the hedge and climbed over a gate into a cornfield. I walked about ten yards into the field and then lay down and fell fast asleep almost instantly. Some hours later, I woke up much revived and restarted my journey. It must have been the early hours of the morning by then and there was no traffic on the roads, so I made better time and once I reached Saxelbye crossroads, there were some long downhill stretches that helped as well. I reached home a little after dawn and slipped quietly into the house and my bed. I told nobody about my futile journey, and nobody asked what I had been up to that night. Except for a couple of close friends, I have never told anyone about my crazy bike ride until writing this book. It was also the end of my association with the Quorn Pony Club.

During the latter years of my Pony Club days, things were not good within the Quorn Pony Club. Most of the committee members lived in Quorn Friday Country which lies between Melton and Leicester and stretches out to Twyford and consequently most rallies were centred in this area. People living in the north of the area, around Nottingham and Ashby, felt they were being side-lined and campaigned for more rallies in their area. The committee were set in their ways, which was par for the course in those days and this eventually led to the formation of a new Pony Club called the South Trent. Things got very bitter running up to the split, with both sides canvassing parents and children to join one side or the other. I was torn between the two but decided to stay with the Quorn. My two brothers also stayed with the Quorn, as did my daughter in later years.

By a twist of fate, I became the trainer of the South Trent show jumping team in the nineties, which won the pony club national show jumping championship at Hickstead. Since then I have had a long and happy relationship with the South Trent and continue to teach at their rallies to this day, many of which are held at Bunny Hill. Their DC is an old pupil of my father's and much more enlightened than the DC's of old. Life moves on and changes. My granddaughter Katherine is now a member of the South Trent Pony Club.

Chapter 5

Show jumping

In my second year at Rushcliffe Grammar I got an unpaid regular job show jumping in junior pony classes. I am not sure how it came about but it was probably a friend of a friend of my dad's. The man's name was Stan Mellor and he was the father of the then famous champion steeplechase jockey also called Stan Mellor. Before becoming a jump-jockey, Stan was a highly successful junior show jumper, competing at major venues such as White City, Harringay arena and Wembley Pool. His father lived, and breathed show jumping and wanted to return to the glory days that he had had with his son. He lived near Quorn and had a small farm where he kept his horses. The ponies that I was jumping were all 14.2hh and he had quite a few of them. Stan was a dealer, so my string of show jumpers changed constantly. Sometimes I had ponies that had done some jumping but often they were totally green with no jumping experience.

When I started, I was told we were going to be aiming for Wembley and other top class shows but that never happened! Every time one of my ponies started to do well, it was sold on and new ponies appeared for me to train on. This was exactly what had been happening at home with dad, but the enormous difference was that when I was jumping for Stan, I didn't have to look after the ponies, I just had to turn up and jump them. However, I didn't have it as easy as I thought it was going to be, you could say that I served my apprenticeship with Stan Mellor senior. Over the weekend, we would often attend two shows in one day. Stan was very thorough and planned his weekends to the minute. He would contact all the show secretaries and find out what time the 14.2 class was due to start and very often he could he would be able to find a class in the morning and then another class at a different show in the afternoon. We travelled with all the ponies tacked up and ready to go, often travelling several hours between shows. I sometimes had four or even six ponies to jump at two different shows, so I was jumping at least twelve rounds per day and then there were the jump off rounds as well!

More often than not, shows also had two or more suitable classes that I could jump the ponies in, so I was doing an enormous number of show jumping rounds every week. I did manage to keep one pony long enough to compete at the larger shows, such as the Moorgreen and Derby County shows. These larger BSJA shows were so well-run and the courses were a joy to jump.

The world of show jumping in those days was a rough tough world with little regard for the welfare of the horse or rider. Although many will be shocked by what I am about to write, everything I mention was commonplace in the sixties. Firstly, it was the norm to rap a horse both at home training and just before you went into the ring. This was done very openly and shows would provide a rapping pole in the collecting ring for everyone to use. As the horse in front of you jumped their round, two people would hold the pole usually between three and four feet off the ground. You would then jump your horse over the pole. As they jumped it, the pole holders would jerk the pole up higher, so it hit the front legs. You then repeated the exercise but this time it was the hind legs that were rapped and then it was off into the ring to jump your round. Safe rapping took great skill from the pole holders but newcomers to the game often caused the horse and rider to fall when they miss-timed lifting the pole. When schooling at home, it was often a metal scaffolding pole. Another fabled training device was a **pole** with hedge-hog skins nailed to it so that it pricked the horses legs if they brushed the pole. I say fabled because I heard a lot about them but never actually saw one personally.

One day before a big competition, I was being schooled over a solid cross-country style fence. After jumping it a couple of times, Stan nailed some steel fencing wire to the railway sleeper stands six inches above the top pole. He then told me to jump it! Both myself and the horse had a crashing fall. Stan rushed over and picked me up saying, "Well that's a b**ger, didn't think it would fetch you both **down**. **Any** road it'll make him pick his feet up tomorrow." **Then** as an afterthought said, "Not hurt yourself, have **you**? **Big** day tomorrow."

Rather than making it pick it's legs up; the pony showed a distinct reluctance to jump in the big competition the next day. The pony did jump a clear-round, but he hesitated before each fence and I had to kick him every inch of the way. I would say that the training session had, had a profound negative effect on the confidence of both the horse and rider. Shortly after this incident, I was schooling a very hot wayward mount when my rein broke on landing. It had never happened to me before and for a brief moment, that at the time seemed to be an eternity, I could not understand what was happening. I was out of control and galloping very fast, we narrowly missed several large trees and I was beginning to think my time was up! It was only a couple of seconds, but it seemed to be a lifetime before I worked out one of my reins had snapped close to where it attaches to the bit. Pulling on the other rein was pulling the bit-ring into the pony's mouth and causing it to panic, so I forced myself to stop pulling with my good rein and lean forward in order to grab the bit ring on the broken side. After a couple of attempts I managed to grab the bit ring and pull it through the mouth and then get a balanced pull. All these things along with me lying up the neck caused the pony to check briefly but long enough for me to bail out and use my rein like a lunge line to bring him under control. Thankfully both of us were unscathed but after the recent events some of the gloss was starting to fade on this job!

Not long after these events, I started my fourth year at Rushcliffe School and the two years course work that led up to the GCSE exams. I just didn't have the time to carry on show jumping with Stan and do my course work. It was a wonderful experience and I wouldn't have missed it for the world. Although I had a few scary moments, we had some great times together and I learnt a lot about show jumping, I would not have missed it for the world. We parted on good terms, but as everybody was telling me schoolwork must come first.

I continued to show jump until I started to Point-to-Point in the 1970s. In fact, my first point-to-pointer was originally my show jumper but that's another story.

Chapter 6

Late Fifties

L
ife on Bunny Hill was ever changing as dad came up with all sorts of schemes to keep our heads above financial disaster. It was not financial incompetence but just the fact that the country as a whole was desperately short of money after the war. Much of the fruit and vegetables we take for granted today were not available. I remember tangerines being an expensive Christmas treat only available if you bought them as soon as they came onto the shelves because they were gone until the next year. Most of the fruit and veg was grown in the UK and only available when in season. Meat was a Sunday treat with leftovers used in various dishes to stretch the meat out over part of the week. Our little orchard and fruit garden were a vital supply of fruit for the family and also produced a small income as we sold excesses to our clients and neighbours. We in turn bought other fruit and veg from our neighbours in particular tomatoes from the Clements family who lived at the end of the Hill Top who had a greenhouse for growing tomatoes. After tasting picked that day, home grown tomatoes for many years, the supermarket offerings of today are bland, tasteless and most importantly they do not have that wonderful smell.

One of the most exciting side-lines that dad got into was acting as a temporary parking area for army surplus vehicles. Just three miles from Bunny Hill was the old wartime Royal Ordnance Depot. It was built in 1940 and was used for filling and the storage of ordnance. It was situated on the southern edge of Ruddington and was a massive site with its own railway station and during the war over 4,000 people worked there. It was probably sited there as it was close to the Royal Ordnance Factory that was sited on the southern edge of Nottingham. It was decommissioned in 1945 and became a storage facility for ex-military vehicles that were auctioned off on site. I don't know how dad became involved with a man from South Wales, but it was probably through one of his dealer friends that he regularly socialised with down at the Nottingham Cattle Market. The man from Wales was a big buyer at Ruddington but one of the rules of the auction was that all purchases must be removed within twenty-four hours. The buyer couldn't buy as much as he required as he was unable to transport it to South Wales quickly enough. So, we became a holding depot for his purchases until he could get them down to Wales.

For me and my friends it was like a dream come true. Playing war games was the favourite game for boys in the fifties and suddenly I had all the props for a full-scale war film, right in our top field. We had Jeeps, Land Rovers, Austin Champs, canvas covered lorries with holes in the cab roof to mount a machine gun, fire engines and many more odd bits of military hardware. Nothing was locked so we had a free run of the whole collection. I suddenly started to have a lot of new friends!

One of the unexpected by-products of this enterprise was that dad had to build a loading ramp to get the vehicles on and off lorries and this became our first cross- country jump. Unfortunately, while testing it out dad had a crashing fall and broke his collarbone. We kept the bank until the mid-sixties when we lost two of our fields to the new car park, indoor-school and outdoor manage.

During the fifties and well into the sixties there was a huge amount of demolition and re-building due to bomb damage from the war. In fact, even in the early seventies when I visited Nottingham's Lace Market to buy cloth for our jousting costumes there were several car parks that were cleared bomb sites that had not been redeveloped. All this redevelopment produced vast amounts of cheap second-hand building materials. We used these materials to build first pigsties and later to build stables. The timber was often over one hundred years old and of superb quality. Even to this day I occasionally come across bits of this wood still in use when maintaining the stables. I used to spend hours with dad at these yards, that were scattered all over Nottingham, listening to dad haggling with the owners. The people who owned these yards were dealers and real salt of the earth characters. Although I have lost touch with these families, I still remember the family names, and some are now exceedingly rich and very successful businesspeople in Nottingham. Nottingham Cattle Market was where they sold much of their wares. In the fifties Nottingham Cattle Market was still a big livestock market and we bought and sold our pigs there. I loved the vibrancy of the place and it was also a place of information, it was like a library of who had what animals or goods to sell, or what might be coming on the market in the near future. The hub of this information superhighway was the cattle market pub. The downside of my trips to the market was that I always ended up sitting outside the pub for several hours, as in those days under eighteens were not allowed inside a pub. If I was lucky and dad remembered me, I might get a bottle of lemonade, but it was so boring sitting on your own outside a pub for hours. Eventually the monotony outweighed the excitement and I started to find jobs to do at home as an excuse not to go with the dad to the market, although it was still mandatory when we took pigs in. Dad's love of the cattle market would in later years cause a big argument but that was many years later.

One day dad returned from the market with a job for me to make loads of pocket money. One of his Cattle Market pals wanted several hundred bean and pea sticks. I had no idea what a bean pole or a pea stick was and I'm not sure that dad was much better. For several weeks, I wandered through the woods, billhook in hand, chopping down what I perceived to be bean poles and pea sticks. After weeks of arduous work, I still had not fulfilled the order. It was then that I was suddenly told that the man needed them by the weekend. I never managed the several hundred ordered and when dad delivered the ones I had cut, he said they were not at all what he was expecting and rejected them all. Weeks of work all for nothing.

This was just one of the many money earning jobs that dad came up with, to make me rich and financially independent. They all ended up with me getting far less than promised and sometimes nothing at all. Sometimes it was the hourly rate that was drastically slashed or unmentioned costs were deducted leaving muggings me with next to nothing.

By the late fifties all the chickens had gone except for a few free-range ones that supplied us personally with eggs for the house. The pig herd had increased to the point that it was our main source of income. The large deep litter hen hut had been divided into three sections. The top section contained two horse standings and two loose boxes; the middle section had another three loose boxes whilst the bottom section nearest to the house had six pig farrowing units with heat lamps for the newly born pigs. There was also a small area next to the sliding door entrance that was our hard feed store for both the horses and pigs.

Our pig business was now our major source of income. We had approximately 120 pigs including a boar. They were mainly Landrace pigs, but we also had some Large Whites. I also reared some Saddle Back pigs myself which I kept in an old hen hut. They were supposed to make me loads of money, but after dad had deducted the costs of feed and rent of hen hut, I always ended up with just enough to buy another piglet. Do you notice the same old story?

To accommodate our growing herd of pigs we built pig pens down one of the long sides of the old large deep litter hut. These were all constructed with second-hand materials sourced from the demolition yards that I have previously mentioned. It was whilst building these pens that I gained my first knowledge of construction and it has been a vital skill that I have had to employ on a regular basis during my time on Bunny Hill, as no matter what farm animals you keep, they are all very good at breaking things and escaping.

It was during this period that dad had a nasty accident. The accident drilled into me just how dangerous working with animals can be! They do not mean to hurt you most of the time but instinctive reactions by animals can cause terrible and sometimes even tragic injuries to the frail human body.

Dad's injury happened doing something that he did on a regular basis. Our boar had a very placid temperament and dad was moving him a few yards from one pen to another. When moving pigs, you usually use a pig board and stick to control them. The board is lightweight plywood approximately 70cm square and blocks their line of sight on your nearside. It also protects your legs. You tap the pig on the other side with your stick to keep it straight. Dad was only moving the boar into the pen next door, a matter of only two metres. I was holding the door of the new pen which contained a sow ready to be served. The boar knew what he was about to do so we didn't expect any trouble. Dad and I had done it many times before. As dad opened his door, I opened mine about halfway and the boar was into the new pen quick as a flash. On this occasion, I was dressed in my school uniform and about to go and catch the morning bus. It was just a two-minute job! For some reason dad only had his stick that day. As the boar came out, he tossed his head with excitement and dashed into my pen keen to get on with his job. I slammed and bolted the door in a quick fluid motion. When I turned towards dad grinning with the satisfaction of a job neatly completed, I saw him on the ground clutching his leg. I thought he had just slipped but when I got to him, his trouser leg was ripped below the knee and on closer inspection I could see a long deep gash from his ankle to his knee. It was so deep you could see the bone in his leg. Strangely it wasn't bleeding. Dad just said, "help me up, and get me to the car." We hobbled to the car and he climbed in, the leg was by now bleeding profusely. Before he drove off, he said, "tell your mother the boar has gored my leg and I've gone to the doctors, hurry up or you'll miss your bus to school."

When I returned home from school dad was home with eighteen stitches in his leg. It took a long time to heal and mum and I had to shoulder the burden of running the farm for many weeks. It was a long hard slog especially with school and homework to cope with as well.

What had happened that morning was the boar tossed his head in excitement, and as he did so, he had exposed his tusks which were razor sharp. The boar's head had lightly brushed against dad's leg, but the razor-sharp tusk had sliced up his leg like a surgeon's scalpel. It wasn't malicious on the boar's part, just an accident. Like so many accidents it was not one thing that caused the accident but a lot of small errors that contributed to the final dreadful mishap. If we had waited until evening when we had more time, perhaps dad would have delayed the move and gone back for his pig board which was only a few yards away. You can what if for ever! However, it certainly taught me to be very wary and wide awake when dealing with any animal, no matter how friendly they appear.

As we crept into the sixties our equine stock increased very slowly but the income from them rose steadily and brought in welcome funds that improved our standard of living and allowed my parents the luxury of increasing the family size. In 1960 my brother Phil was born, followed by Stuart early in 1963.

The income from our horses and ponies came from many sources. The biggest income was from hacking, followed by dealing in horses and ponies. Many of our hacking clients asked dad to find them a horse or pony that would suit their needs and this in turn started a fledgling livery business. It was the livery business that started us teaching as most of the liveries were not experienced riders and started to ask dad for help in schooling their horses and to improve their riding skills.

By the end of the fifties we had built an oval corral with an ash track for training both horse and rider. It was built entirely of posts and rails that we had chopped out of the wood and was just like the ones that you see on cowboy films. The main difference with our corral was that it had a ditch and jump in its centre. You can still see the raised outline of most of the corral in our top field even to this day, although one of its long sides has been incorporated into our jumping lane.

It was in this corral that I gave my first riding lesson. Dad was supposed to take it, but he had gone off somewhere and totally forgot about the lesson and mum was busy with her young baby, so that just left me. The lesson was for two adults who hadn't ridden before. I think that the lesson must have been alright as I got a generous tip from them after the lesson. I was just ten years old!

It was around this time that we started to do organised hacks through the woods that were on the other side of the main road from the stables. These hacks were just two or three people to start with on Sundays, but quickly grew in numbers as dad bought more horses and ponies with the profits that these hacks made. I was the main person in charge of taking these hacks out through the woods, often doing three or four a day in the summertime. There were no regulations for riding schools in those days and we all rode without riding hats and nobody ever questioned what a ten-year-old was doing taking groups of novice riders out for a hack. The fact that I could ride well was enough.

These days the woods belong to the woodland trust and we are restricted to a fenced off bridle path with safety gates on each end where it joins the road. In those days, we could ride everywhere in the woods and there were umpteen trails that you could follow so you never got bored. We built log jumps in the woods and even constructed a jump in the boundary hedge, so we could jump in and out of the woods from the fields that we had on the other side of the A60. The only benefit we gained when the wood was sold to woodland trust was that they erected bridle gates at each end. This was a great safety feature as until then if anyone from the stables fell off in the woods the horses would always gallop home straight across the main A60. Thankfully the traffic was much lighter in those days and although it happened on a fairly regular basis there were thankfully no traffic incidents, although there were a few near misses.

The entrance to the wood was an overgrown track, wide enough for a car to get down for about twenty yards. It was an extremely popular place for courting couples, and we would often have to squeeze past cars with steamed up windows to get our clients into the woods. This caused mixed reactions from shock horror to great amusement. Saturday and Sunday afternoons were our most popular times and I would often take out three hacks on each of those days at 2pm, 3pm and 4pm. On one occasion at 2pm we passed a car at the entrance to the woods. The windows were steamed up, but the two naked bodies were clearly visible. Usually when we disturbed a couple like this they hastily moved on, but on this occasion the car was still there when I returned with the ride an hour later, still rocking away! All the clients were talking about it when they returned and soon a small posse of liveries left the yard to take a shufftie. Nothing seemed to bother this amorous couple and they were still there when I returned home with the last ride of the day at 5pm. You could say we learned the facts of life at an early age "on the hoof" you might say.

Whilst on this subject, I was out hunting with the Quorn hunt one day in a large tract of forestry, when we suddenly came to an abrupt halt in a small clearing when the hounds checked. Parked in this secluded clearing, miles from anywhere, was a car again with steamed up windows. There were about fifty horses packed around this unfortunate car. Everyone was keeping a stiff upper lip until a child's voice rang out saying, "Mummy, Mummy, what are that man and woman doing in the back seat of the car?" The mother's reply was "I think they have lost something dear and they are looking for it." All talking had stopped amongst the hunt followers. You could have heard a pin drop. The mother took a deep breath and smiled broadly at the fifty odd onlookers with the smug satisfaction of "didn't I handle that well!" Then the child's voice rang out again. "But Mommy why have they taken off all their clothes just to look for something?" A look of horror quickly deflated the smug mother. She was saved from the embarrassment of making a public explanation by the hounds, who suddenly picked up the scent again and we all charged off leaving the poor couple to their nuptials.

Another amusing story in the same vein happened some years later. It happened down Bunny Lane. The Lane runs from the tee junction of Wysall lane at the back of Bunny Park and follows the Fairham Brook into Bunny, joining the A60 at the southern edge on the village. Shortly after Lou and I married in 1973, we rented the farmhouse that is situated at the junction, so our route to work was back and forth along this lane. It's a lovely old lane that twists and turns following the course of the brook. The brook was notorious for flooding and the lane plus large parts of Bunny were under water several times most years. It was sometimes so bad that the council had to close the main road. Some years before our marriage there was a controversial flood prevention scheme carried out to straighten the brook and lowered its bed by about ten feet. This turned the brook from a picturesque meandering waterway into a steep sided canal. When not in flood the sides of the brook were twelve to fourteen feet high and extremely steep rising at about 60 degrees. There was much concern about safety, especially about children who would stand little chance of getting out if they fell in. However, kids being kids, and although they could no longer fish or play in the water, they could amuse themselves with a rope swing across the brook. Although it was regularly removed by safety conscious goody goodies, it miraculously re-appeared again and again! It was used so much that the grass from the roadside to the edge of the brook was worn away to flat bare soil making it look like the entrance to a field. The gateways along this narrow, overgrown lane were very popular with courting couples and it was not unusual to see several cars parked in gateways along this lane as Lou and I travelled home late at night, after closing up the bar at the stables. One morning as I approached the rope swing over the brook, I noticed a pair of red rear lights protruding skyward just below the top of the bank. Someone had most likely seen the flat bare earth in their headlights and swung into what they thought was a nice secluded gateway and gone headfirst into the brook. What a passion killer! Lou and I pondered with great amusement as to what story was told the recovery crane as to how the car managed to be in the brook and better still, if it was someone having an affair, how they explained this mishap away to their partner!

I have mentioned how short money was in the fifties and I remember a very sad day for dad when he tried to expand the thriving pig business. Dad had been offered some breeding sows with piglets at foot. We now had a contract with a company called Gamston Produce that took all our weaned pigs at eight weeks old. This simplified the selling process and saved us all the hassle of transporting them to market which was a long drawn out affair and which sometimes ended up with you having to bring them back home again if they didn't sell. Dad was sure that with his contract with Gamston Produce he would be able to get a loan. I was about ten years old and travelled with him to The National Provincial Bank at Trent Bridge Nottingham. In those days, there was a traffic island opposite the bank for the busy intersection of the A60 that went over the bridge into Nottingham and the A52 Radcliffe/Grantham Road and also West Bridgford Rd. We did the unheard-of thing of today, by parking on the inside curb of the island which was widespread practice in those days. I was left sitting in the car for nearly an hour while cars whizzed around me. For me this was the norm, I was used to being left in cars and lorries for long times while dad conducted his business.

I knew things had not gone well as dad trudged back to the car with shoulders sagging and his head down, something rarely seen with dad. The loan of £200 pounds had been rejected! Today it seems an insignificant amount for a business loan, but my research tells me that in the late fifties £200 computes to about £4500 in today's money! The final twist to the story was a typical fifties solution to the cash short economy: dad raised enough money for a deposit and agreed to pay off the balance as soon as he could. A shake of hands and the deal was done! No paperwork just 'my word is my bond', which sadly is something that you see very little of in our modern society where contracts and litigation are the norm.

We lived with a huge amount of personal debt in those days but without the trust people showed in each other, the war devastated economy would never have transformed itself into the booming swinging sixties. I remember years later when dad took on a partner in the business, our feed merchant, Mr Frank Bradwell to whom we had owed money to on a rolling basis for some twenty years, being quite shocked and upset when we paid off what we owed him. He asked, "have I done something wrong, are you changing feed merchants, there is no need to pay it off all at once you know!?"

This lovely man had quietly supported our business from its inception and never once mentioned our debt other than showing it on our monthly statement. We always made a monthly payment with what cash we had available and like so many small businesses of that era he visited every week to take our order personally. He collected his money personally and shared in our triumphs and failures. He knew exactly how credit worthy we were and we in turn were loyal to him trading with his company until it closed down. It was the same with so many small family businesses that we traded with and in many cases, we became close friends with these families.

This friendship ethos has stuck with me and the one thing that I am most proud of is when I bump into old customers, is that they all say, that their fondest memory is that it was like a big family at Bunny. That same ethos is something that my son Mark and his wife Vicky have continued, and it gives me immense joy to see clients staying long after they have finished riding, chatting away enjoying a sociable drink as only good friends can do.

As the fifties came to an end and life became a little easier, people started to think about ethics and we started to have rules and regulations for everything. Even the world of horse shows started to print lists of rules in their schedules. Two of the most hated rules for competitors that appeared were making it mandatory to wear riding hats for both show jumping and even gymkhana games, the other was the banning of spurs in games events. This didn't happen overnight, and it was well into the sixties before these rules became the norm.

As competitors, we hated these rules tooth and nail. In place of spurs we used round headed wood screws, screwed into the inside part of our jodhpur boot heels but after a few years they amended the wording of the rules to "no spurs or screws allowed". Wearing hard hats was not only disliked by competitors but it was a large unnecessary expense as hardly anyone owned one at the time. The hats of that period didn't have a chinstrap, you just crammed them on your head. Later, especially if the hat became a bit loose, some people would sew a piece of elastic onto the sides of the hat to make a chinstrap, although this was deemed to be very wussy! Competitors got together to try and fight these new rules and we would peruse forthcoming schedules and agree to boycott shows with rules on mass, in favour of the, no rule shows. However, the march of rules continued to grow. We did continue to fight the wearing of hats by simply flicking them off our heads at the start of a race or as we took off over the first fence show jumping. I remember a huge cheer going up as six of us all flicked off our hats at the start of a bending race heat. Again, slowly but surely, they amended the rules to "anyone deliberately throwing off their hat will be disqualified!" So much for freedom. This was also strengthened by a law being passed that made it mandatory for children under the age of fourteen to wear a riding hat when riding on the highway. That still remains the only law regarding wearing hats to this day. It is the insurance companies that have made it mandatory, for everyone competing or riding at a riding school to wear a current safety standard riding hat. It makes my heart sing to see photos of the Queen riding in Windsor Park with only a headscarf on her head. I still like to ride out in my fields occasionally without a hat but having known people who died or ended up with brain damage from falls on the road I would never consider riding out on roads without a safety hat. A hat is not always the answer in these situations, two of my friends that were injured, one fatally, were wearing hats. The early hats protected you from a brushing hit from a horse's hoof or low branch, but they were useless falling on tarmac. It was much later when I started racing and I had to wear a skullcap that I started to realise how woefully inadequate the velvet riding hats were for protecting your head. Several concussive incidents later from jousting and racing, caused me to take head protection very seriously. I was the first man to wear a jockey skullcap out hunting with the Quorn which caused a bit of a stir but a couple of years later large numbers of men including the top hat brigade had made the change. Technology continues to improve hat safety and I regularly change my hat as new safer ones come onto the market.

Sam Humphrey

Chapter 7

1963 A Close-Run Thing

T hings were looking bright as we approached the Christmas holidays of 1962. The small amount of snow that had fallen at the beginning of December had quickly melted and cleared, which was normal for that time of year in those days. We were finally getting our heads above water financially although we still had a mountain of business debt. Dad had stopped working full time as a welder but still topped up the farm income by doing part time welding jobs. Our fledgling riding school business had transformed mine and Dawn's Christmas, from just a few presents that still included an orange as one of the major presents, to a feast of boxed chocolates given to us by our wealthy new clients. Before the riding school we were lucky to see maybe one box of chocolates a year on mum's birthday, when they were rationed out to last at least a month. Suddenly we were now getting two or three boxes each! Mum of course confiscated most of them for rationing out over the coming months, but we were allowed one box each to gorge ourselves over the Christmas holidays. In those days, New Year's Day was still a normal working day not a public holiday as it is today, so the Christmas holidays amounted to Christmas Day and Boxing Day and that was it! I do think it was much more enjoyable that way rather than the long drawn out pig out we have today, starting with Christmas Eve and going on until January the second. Christmas was much more intense back then. If you were lucky some employers would let you finish half an hour or even an hour early on Christmas Eve.

Dad would save as much money as he could in December and then set off to settle as many of his smaller debts as possible on Christmas Eve. This was the country way of doing things, sitting in a warm kitchen paying your friend what you owed him face to face before the year was out and sharing a glass of sherry or whiskey. Dad paid off a lot of debts on Christmas Eve and would always return home happy and inebriated. He always planned his trip so that his last few calls were close to home, so he didn't have too far to drive after an afternoon of festive socialising - no drink and drive laws in those days. The usual crack of dawn, overexcited, Christmas Morning, followed with pillowcases containing presents magically appearing at the end of our beds after Santa had somehow got down the chimney, even though the fire had been banked up with coal slack to burn all night. As is the same routine even to this day, animals were fed watered and mucked out first thing, followed by a late brunch of cold meats and then back out to do essential jobs before feeding the animals a little earlier than usual for their evening feed. Then about four thirty we went in and got cleaned up for our Christmas dinner.

The weather changed on Boxing Day. The temperature plummeted, storm force gales and heavy snow lashed the whole country. Normally the River Trent with its string of power stations along its banks kept the Trent valley warmer than other parts of the county. We sat on the southern edge of the valley and although we got more snow than Nottingham, it was substantially less than Rempstone that was only two and a half miles further south, but out of the Trent Valley. This time we got a lot of snow. The radio reported twenty-foot snow drifts in Wales and up to eighteen inches of snow in the south of England.

It was bitterly cold and as usual whenever we had any snow, we lost our electric supply. This usually only lasted a few hours or a day at the most, so we were not worried and settled down to boiling the kettle on the fire and living on soup heated in the same manner. Paraffin heaters were bought out to replace the single bar electric fires that were now useless. The smell of burning paraffin pervaded through the whole house. The electric did not come back on and the radio told us it would be several days before power would be restored in rural parts as the gales and heavy snow had brought down countless power lines all over the country. We hunkered down to sit out the cold snap. Bunny Hill was blocked by snow and we were cut off but that was not unusual in winter and mum always kept a good supply of tinned food to see us through these inconvenient times.

In those days local farmers were given snowploughs and it was their job to keep the roads clear. The County Council would telephone them and authorise them to start clearing the roads. Unfortunately, being the Christmas holidays, the authorisation was very slow which made the road clearing much harder. There were no four-wheel drive tractors in those days so many of them couldn't even get out of their farm drives onto the roads. We weren't worried - the snow never lasted more than a few days! The expected thaw never came and instead we had more snowstorms throughout the last few days of December and into January, and as we got into January the temperature started to fall dropping down to lows of minus twenty-two degrees Celsius in Scotland and the teens all over England. When it was not snowing, we had lovely sunny days but bitterly cold. It stayed that way until the beginning of March when finally, a thaw set in.

The U.K. lay under a thick blanket of snow for over eight weeks. All our water outside of the house froze, so we had to fill and carry a constant stream of buckets from our kitchen out to the animals. Any water that was not drunk immediately froze in the bucket. If carrying endlessly buckets of water wasn't bad enough, breaking out the ice from the buckets before refilling them was another horrible job. Water that spilt from the buckets froze instantly creating a treacherous icy pathway from the house to the stables and pigsties. We could not afford salt and any gravel that we had was frozen solid, so we resorted to sprinkling the ash from the kitchen fire onto the polished ice pathway to give us some safe traction. Falls were a regular occurrence and spilt water froze on our clothing. It was a torrid endless grind, frozen hands and feet followed by excruciatingly painful hot-aches and chill-blains.

The diesel fuel in lorries and tractors turned to wax causing endless breakdowns and disruptions to the movement of essential supplies and it was commonplace to see lorry drivers lighting fires under the fuel tanks of their vehicles. In those days, anti-freeze was not very common and what supplies there were in the country soon ran out. For us we had to drain all the water from our vehicles' engines as soon as we had finished using them or else the freezing water would crack the engine block due to the water expanding as it froze. The cold also caused the engine oil to thicken making it impossible for the starter motor to turn the engine over fast enough to start it. Again, it was forward planning. We used to cut the top off a five-gallon oil drum and fill it with diesel-soaked rags to make a brazier which we positioned close to the side of the engine. It took approximately thirty minutes to warm the engine enough to start it. It was a high-risk strategy lighting fires in a garage next to a lorry or tractor, but it had to be done to survive. I got the warm but risky job of watching the fire and dragging the flaming pan around the vehicle so that it cooked nice and evenly, quite a responsibility for an eleven-year-old. We mixed paraffin with the diesel to thin it and prevent the wax forming. You had to get the mix absolutely just right or else you ruined the engine. The fumes were very smokey and smelt of paraffin. It was illegal to do this with road vehicles, but the police overlooked it as it was the only way to keep essential supplies moving.

Although it was now a major job just to keep the animals fed and watered, once that was done there was nothing else to do. Even schools had to shut down on a regular basis when the electricity failed, or we had more heavy snow closing the roads yet again. I loved to find the tracks of animals left in the snow and dad taught me how to identify the different animals from their tracks. One day I followed the tracks that a fox had left in the new overnight snow. It was new snow on top of old snow that had frozen into a hard crust. I tracked the fox from close to stables into the woods and then out the other side onto Proudman's land. I was so intent on following the fox's trail that I didn't notice the hump in the corner of the field, too late the snow under my feet gave way and my body dropped into the deep snowdrift. It was so deep that I went down until just my head was sticking out and my arms were forced straight up in the air as if I was surrendering. In those days, cold weather clothing was not what it is today for an eleven-year-old. I was dressed for my Arctic tracking mission, in wellingtons, long wool socks to over my knees, short trousers, a knee length woollen overcoat, scarf and a balaclava. I was terrified, I was on my own, stuck up to my armpits in a huge snowdrift, for as far as I could see which was for several miles, there was no sign of life and to make matters worse it was starting to snow again. I tried to wriggle my way out but to no avail, so I started to move snow with my elbows until I could get my arms lower enough to use my hands and then enlarged the hole around me. My legs and hands were numb with cold, but my torso was sweating with exertion. It took a lot of digging before I could move my legs and then gradually extricate myself from my snow hole. At first it was hard to walk because my legs were so numb, and I was exhausted from digging myself out, but I knew I had to get home as quickly as possible.

As the circulation returned, I got hot aches and the pain was excruciating but I kept stumbling my way home through the woods tripped constantly by snow covered branches. By the time I reached home my wellies were full of snow and snow clung to my rough woollen clothes making me look like the Abominable Snowman, much to the amusement of my family.

Mum stripped off my frozen clothes, wrapped me in a warm dressing gown at sat me in front of the fire with my feet in a bucket of hot water and left me to thaw out with a mug of hot chocolate. I never told the true story of what happened that day as I was convinced that I would be banned from wandering in the woods ever again!

The cold and blanket of snow caused an eerie silence throughout the countryside even the birds didn't sing. The horses and ponies in the fields had frost on their coats and had icicles dangling from their bellies. Dad carried a bale of hay out to them every day carrying the bale on a pitchfork over his shoulder, no mean feat in deep snow, but it had to be done! The horses would come galloping towards us as soon as we entered the field, what a sight, I will never forget it. The whole herd galloping towards us throwing clods of snow from their hooves high into the air like a large wave about to break over the rocks on the shore line, steam pumping out of their nostrils like an old steam train, the whole herd whinnying to us with joy at us bringing the food that would keep them warm through another bitterly cold night. I am saddened by people's lack of knowledge these days, panicking to put rugs on their horse when a slight overnight frost is forecast in late September. Sometimes I think that we have lost more equine knowledge than we have gained in these modern times!

Although these were desperately tough times, we did have a lot of free time between tending to the stock and so we had fun. We had lots of visitors who came to help us in return for snow fun. We would drag sledges through the woods onto Proudman's fields that were on the Bunny side of the hill and were very steep, ideal for sledging but exhausting to pull your sledge back up to the top again. These were not the cheap plastic sledges that you can buy today, but sturdy home-built contraptions that were very heavy to pull and they could do a person considerable damage if hit by one. Some of our wealthier clients joined us with very expensive shop bought Nordic style sledges that were much lighter to pull but there was much more satisfaction hurtling down the hill on something that you had designed and built yourself!

Mum was an excellent ice skater and had taken part in several ice dance shows held at the Nottingham Ice Rink. The ice rink was hugely popular in the fifties and sixties, mum and dad were regular visitors even before they were married and taught me to skate at an early age. Many of our friends and clients were also good skaters and we all owned our own skates. When we heard that the lake in Bunny Hall Park had frozen deep enough to withstand people walking on it, we all headed down there to try skating on it. To our disappointment the lake was covered in snow but when we scraped down, the ice was lovely and smooth. A short trip back to the stables to collect brushes and shovels and we returned to clear the snow away. An hour later we were skating on our own private ice rink. At first, we were happy just to skate around but after about a week we started to play ice hockey with a stone for a puck and dead branches from by the lake as our hockey sticks. Everyone had a whale of a time. The next day we cut several pucks from a straight three-inch diameter branch and then coated them with wax polish. They sped across the ice like lightning. For our hockey sticks, we scoured the local woods for branches with the right-angled off-shoots. We played ice hockey with increasing ferocity until the thaw finally came and put an end to it. Even as the thaw started, we still played, ignoring the tell-tale groaning of the ice, until one day there was a loud crack and water started to bubble up onto the ice and we realised that we had pushed our luck far enough.

Dad and the local farmers also did a lot of shooting but not for sport but out of dire necessity to protect their winter crops such as kale and cabbage. Hungry wood pigeons had formed into gigantic flocks and they descended on anything green poking through the snow like a swarm of locusts. The problem was so serious that the Ministry of Agriculture were issuing free cartridges to farmers to help them defend their crops. Dad was asked to go and help along with any other locals that owned a gun. He told me that the pigeons were coming in such numbers that he had to stop shooting because his gun barrels became too hot to hold, such was the rapidity of his shooting. The added bonus was an endless supply of free pigeon which was very welcome as we were desperately short of money due to the fact that our riding school side of the business had ceased to exist, and delayed shipments of our pigs meant they munched away our profits until the lorries could get through.

As the big freeze continued, my family faced bankruptcy! Our small stock of hay was rapidly disappearing as we now had to feed the horses that were out at grass hay and hard feed on a daily basis, just to keep them alive in the bitter cold. We tried to sell some of the horses and ponies, but nobody wanted to buy, as everyone in the horse or farming business was in the same desperate boat. To make matters worse the price of hay and straw had rocketed because of the increased demand. Another problem for us was that horse people had a bad name for not paying their bills and farmers just would not trade with us. Luckily the local farmers who knew us tried to help us, but they were also short of fodder and loathed to part with any more than a few bales as nobody could see an end to this terrible weather. The radio reported that the sea was frozen around the south coast for up to a mile out to sea and four miles out from the port of Dunkirk. There was talk that the English Channel might freeze over completely closing all the channel ports. It was horrible to listen to my parents trying to come up with solutions to the desperate state we found ourselves in, we just had to find another source of income!

The gales and heavy snow had not only brought down power lines but also countless trees which had to be cleared. One of dad's pals had a contract with the council to clear fallen trees and was under intense pressure to clear trees from council owned sites that had trees brought down in the storms. He offered dad the job of removing a huge cedar tree that had come down in the garden of an old peoples' home in Gedling. Like many deals that Dad got himself into in those days, it wasn't straight forward. He didn't get paid for cutting up the tree and removing it, but he could keep all the wood. He would also need to buy a large chainsaw which was a rare and expensive commodity in the early sixties. The chainsaw that he needed to buy was £100 which equates to £1500 in today's money. You could by a good horse for £50 and a pony was about £20, and dad was destitute! I don't know where he got the money from, probably my grandfather, but he did, and bought the saw. You may think it was a stupid act to spend such a vast amount of money and only get the wood from a tree in return but there was a reason to his madness. The severe weather had produced a much higher demand on coal and electricity and both industries were struggling to meet demand. There were power cuts on a regular basis and domestic coal supplies were virtually non-existent. People were chopping up anything that would burn just to try and keep warm. The Clean Air act had been passed in 1956 and had been implemented on a rolling basis starting with the large conurbations so Nottingham was still allowed to burn coal or wood on domestic open fires and as coal was in very short supply people were turning to wood for heating.

Armed with a new Stihl chainsaw, dad and I started to cut up the huge cedar tree and turn it into logs. The tree was magnificent and it seemed such a shame to use it for logs. However, cedar is a good burning wood and easy to split with an axe. We bought empty paper feed sacks off a neighbouring farmer and filled them with logs. An advert in the Nottingham Evening Post caused the telephone to never stop ringing, we had no idea just how desperate people were for fuel. We filled our horsebox with the bags of logs and delivered them all over Nottingham. I soon knew my way around the whole of Nottingham. Wherever we delivered we were mobbed by people wanting to buy logs. When we told them, they were all ordered they begged us to sell us just one until we could return with a full order. Their stories were harrowing, frozen water pipes and absolutely no heating in the house if they relied on coal.

We worked seven days a week and many friends and clients lent a hand to help the riding stables survive. The money was not a fortune and the work arduous, but it put food on our table and paid for hay and straw to keep our animals alive. On many nights it would be nine or even ten o'clock at night by the time we had finished our deliveries. The ecstatic greetings and thanks we received from our clients gave us renewed energy to keep going. We delivered to The Meadows, St Anne's and Broxtowe areas of Nottingham which now have a very bad reputation for crime and violence but in those days, we only met polite, kind, hardworking people. Again, I have to ask myself, have we really built a better world today!

As the country learned to cope with the big freeze, many of our riding school clients started to visit us to see how the horses were coping with the dreadful weather. They often stayed several hours and helped us with the daily chores. We in turn invited them into the kitchen for hot drinks and biscuits. I think that this was the start of the Bunny Hill riding community that is so special and still exists to this day. The numbers grew week on week and our clients along with their friends joined us on our sledging and ice-skating expeditions. We became known as the Bunny Hill Mob!

One of the problems we had during the long freeze, was exercising the stabled horses. At first, we cut a track in the snow and led the horses out in hand, but the track soon became icy and dangerous, so we had to make endless new tracks. We had to oil the bottoms of the horses' hooves to stop the snow compacting and balling in the hoof. As the temperature dropped, we noticed that the snow didn't ball in the foot, so we started to ride the horses in the field. This could only be done when there was sustained, very low temperatures but it started the hardcore riding enthusiasts asking if they could ride in the snow. The thought of actually earning some money from the horses again was just too appealing to refuse. Nobody gave a hoot about safety they just wanted to ride! So, we started our snow rides around our fields and later our neighbour allowed us to ride around his fields as the ground was frozen so deep the horses would not damage the land. My wife remembers me taking her on a ride in the snow through the farm where we now live on a Shetland pony called Clem.

The big freeze ended on March 6th when the temperature finally rose above freezing and shortly after rose to the dizzying height of 17 degrees causing a rapid thaw and with that came some flooding, but nothing too serious. We had survived and like so many businesses only just. Again, the Country had pulled to-gether and we had come through. The debt of gratitude that we owed to the people who trusted us and gave us the credit we needed to survive was immense. I still remember them to this day.

I also remember every one of those people who would not trade with us or sort to profit from our misfortunes.

The rest of 1963 was constant hard work to try and pay off the debts which we had incurred during the long winter. It took some time for coal supplies to be replenished so we continued delivering logs until early April when we finally finished our tree clearing business, that had grown to clearing several other trees that had come down in the vicinity of the old peoples' home. Many of our log customers had regular deliveries and we got to know them well. People in those days were very generous and even if they were short of money, they would offer you a cup of tea and a scone or something similar after you had made their delivery. It was while having a chat with people over a cup of tea that they found out we had horses and that many of them were keen gardeners. As soon as they found out we had horses they wanted to know if we could sell them some old well-rotted horse manure.

We had a massive heap of manure and until that moment, no way of getting rid of it and so started our new side-line of selling bags of horse manure. The manure business was very seasonal spring and autumn were the times when the demand for manure in the garden was at its highest. It was harder work than the log business and the rewards were not quite so good, but the raw material was free, and we did need to get rid of it. My job was to bag it up and then dad and I would deliver the bags in the horsebox. The problem was that well-rotted muck was wet and if you left the paper sacks filled with muck overnight the moisture seeped into the paper and the bottoms fell out when you picked them up. This meant I had to fill as many as I could before lunch and then deliver them in the afternoon before the bags disintegrated. I usually managed to bag about fifty in a morning. We sold them eight bags for a pound or half a crown a bag (12.5 new pence) so a day's work netted us just over £6 which seems a paltry sum these days but in 1963 the average wage was only £18 per week with many people earning a lot less, so a weekend selling manure brought us in nearly a week's wage, which was a welcome boost to the family income and to my pocket money. I turned twelve in May 1963 and was not such a soft touch when it came to be getting paid as I had been in my younger days. It was cash in hand at the end of the day or I refused to bag up for the next day.

Through this work I became relatively wealthy for a twelve-year-old. I bought a car which I drove around the fields and several motor bikes which were usually non-runners. My plan was to restore them and either sell them or drive them around the fields. That first year of having some money of my own made me a bit cocky and it caused me to learn a hard lesson that my grandfather had taught me but that I had never really understood at the time. At some time in my twelfth-year dad allowed a gypsy to camp in our field for about two weeks. He was a kindly sort and did jobs for dad as payment for letting him camp. I often worked with him and he told me lots of stories about nature, life and how he travelled around the country living off the land. One day he told me he needed to collect some money that he was owed and asked me if I could lend him five pounds to buy petrol for his lorry (yes, many lorries still ran on petrol in those days) so that he could go and collect the money. He said he would pay me back five pounds two shillings the next day. Money without work I liked that idea, so I lent him five pounds which was all my savings. He went off to collect the money he was owed. He told me he would be gone a couple of days and so I waited for his return and the returns on my first investment.

He never returned! I never told anyone about my loss, I was too embarrassed, but I had learned a hard, expensive lesson. I had lost my life savings. The words of my grandfather came back to me and now made complete sense, "Never be a borrower or a lender because it will always end badly".

I was to suffer many costlier painful lessons on my way to manhood. Members of my family have accused me of being over cautious and being unwilling to trust people in business, but it has been the many times when I did trust people and then got ripped off by them that made me this way!

Chapter 8

Indoor School

The harsh winter of sixty-three, our close shave with bankruptcy and nearly losing the farm focused dad's mind on creating a more sustainable business model. He and mum realised, that a lot of Lady Luck helped us survive, not the strength of our business. When you have lived through weather like that winter you believe that it will happen again. Dad had lived and worked on a farm during the winter of 1947 when the snow drifts were much higher, and food, coal and electricity shortages were even more severe. Dad told me that in Ravensthorpe, the snow drifts were so high, only the tops of the telegraph poles protruded a few feet out of the snow. I was also told by the building inspector for Rushcliffe Council that the embankment part of the A60 outside our house which is over twenty feet deep, totally filled with snow and that dynamite had to be used to clear it. With first-hand knowledge of two severe winters in sixteen years, dad totally believed that there were more to come and in 1963 there was no knowledge of climate change, in fact the majority view was that we might be heading for another ice age. However, as if to balance things out, the summer of 1963 was a lovely long hot one. Dad's plan didn't happen overnight, but the long sizzling summer was good for the riding school side of the business.

It's a small world and Lynn Benson, who edited my previous book, recalled moving down from Liverpool to study at Nottingham University. She rode before moving to Nottingham, and a boyfriend at the time drove her out to Bunny Hill in the summer of sixty-three and she remembers leaning over a gate looking at the horses blissfully grazing in the field. She never rode with us at that time and it would be another thirty odd years before we would actually meet when she married my great friend Dick Benson.

By the end of the summer, we had recovered enough financially to buy some lorry loads of clinker ash: the ash was a by-product of Wilford Power station and was very cheap! It was used extensively for farm roads and had great drainage qualities. This was used to make our first (nearly) all weather riding surface. It was only about one third of the size of our manège today but in those days, it was something really special!

It was building this manège that was the real start of Dad teaching riding, rather than hacking out and teaching people as they rode through the woods, or around the fields. Before the manège, we had beginners' hacks, intermediate hacks and advanced hacks and that was it, except for our little corral for first-timers and very nervous riders.

During the harsh winter, an unofficial sort of club had been formed by the people who came to visit and help us during our challenging times. They cared about the riding school and wanted to see it succeed and develop.

Things were changing in the country as a whole in so many ways. There was talk of leisure time, people finally had some money to spend and anything and everything seemed to be possible! The unofficial club mainly rode on Sunday morning and then retired to the Rancliffe Arms in Bunny for the all, too short, Sunday lunchtime with permitted drinking hours of 12-2pm. Because it was a short opening period, people tended to drink a lot very quickly. It was so popular that the small locals bar that separated the lounge and the large bar soon became known as the riders' bar. Although very popular with our riders, it was not so popular with mum who always cooked a traditional roast for Sunday lunch and although he promised, and I'm sure genuinely intended to be home for 2pm, Dad never made it home before 3pm. I hated Sunday lunch, mum was always upset as her special lunch was not so special after an hour or more delay and Dad was easily riled when he had been drinking. Thankfully Sunday lunch was eventually moved to an evening meal and life became much more bearable.

It was in late 1963 that Dad heard about a possible indoor riding school. It was the pre-war gymnasium at RAF Cranwell which was, and still is, the pilot officer training college where cadets are first taught to fly. I clearly remember going with Dad to visit the airbase to view the building, or should I say the piles of large lengths of timber and piles of corrugated metal sheets. The visit to view the prospective indoor school held no interest for me, but oh! the excitement of seeing the planes taking off and landing at close quarters was amazing.

The demolished building lay at the edge of an area where the planes were parked. There was a mixture of propeller and jet aircraft and on a windswept rainy day, there seemed to be nobody around to stop me having a closeup peak at these magnificent machines.

I wandered around for about five minutes before a man in uniform captured me. He was absolutely astounded to find a young boy wandering around the parked planes and only a hundred yards or so from taxiing planes. I calmly told him we were there to inspect the demolished building. The man in uniform was not so calm and marched me double quick time back to Dad who hadn't even noticed that I had gone missing. Dad got a severe dressing down and shouted at me to show that it was all my own doing. When the man in uniform had gone, he sighed and said, "Can't you ever behave your bloody self?" I didn't get to go back to Cranwell again although Dad made several trips to organise the transport of this vast structure back to Bunny.

The building was 60 feet wide and 90 feet long, perfect for indoor riding. I think it was one of his demolition friends that had the contract to demolish it and he virtually gave dad the building if he would pay for removing it. The demolition contractor also knew someone who had extra-large lorries to transport the large wooden components.

All the many thousand components finally arrived at Bunny and were stacked haphazardly in our home paddock, where they lay for over a year. Dad had not thought about planning permission or any of the practicalities of erecting such a large structure let alone the costs. However, somehow the ground got levelled and the concrete base pads were put in for the large wooden uprights that would support the huge roof structure. Most of this was done by people who worked for our riding clients. Many of our clients had successful businesses covering all kinds of things and they would send workers with various skills up to the stables if they had a quiet time between projects. Hardcore came free of charge from dad's various demolition friends and even the sand that topped out the hardcore came from an old iron foundry which was being demolished. The sand had been used for making castings and we had to constantly remove chunks of cast iron which had been part of the casting process from the sand as we levelled it by hand. The chunks of cast iron were saved and sold to the scrap yard as every penny counted on this project.

The uprights were erected using a very basic hydraulic muck fork on an old Fordson Major Tractor, and lots of manpower. It often took a whole weekend to raise just one upright. How we got them levelled with each other remains a mystery to me even to this day. Erecting the uprights was the easy part, rebuilding the huge wooden roof trusses was a much more complicated project.

Although the uprights had been numbered and labelled left and right, only part of the main beams had been marked to link up with a corresponding pair of uprights. The problem was that each truss consisted of seven components, of which six were unmarked and all had individual handmade joints. It was like a huge jigsaw puzzle but with no picture to guide us. We could spend an entire day trying to find which of the huge timbers had joints that perfectly matched one of the cross-members. A further complication was that laying in a field for a year exposed to the elements had caused the joints to swell and distort. Thankfully the wood was top quality pitch pine otherwise I think we could have ended up with a pile of rotten wood. For many months the uprights stood alone like Neolithic standing stones. We were constantly asked when the next phase was going to happen. There were three major problems, the first was finding which bit fitted which truss, the second was when we finally reconstructed a truss it filled a massive area, after building two trusses we had filled our home paddock and had no room to build another. Finally, the third problem was that no amount of manpower was going to lift the trusses onto the tops of the uprights.

We needed a proper mobile crane and their hourly rate was a small fortune. There was no credit for a crane; it was cash up front or nothing! It took a long time to save up for one day's crane hire and if we were lucky, we might just get two up in a day. The plan was to erect two and then reconstruct another two to erect at a later date and finally the last two of the six even later when enough funds for the crane to come back again had been raised. The first set back came when it took two days not one to raise the first two trusses. This severely drained our resources, delaying the erection of the next pair of trusses by several months. However, we learned a lot from erecting the first trusses and the subsequent pairs went up in a day for each pair. Having the first pair up however gave us plenty of manual work to be getting on with, such as joining the two trusses together with purlins that not only gave the two trusses some stability but also gave us a base to nail the roof sheets onto.

The corrugated roof sheets were not like the modern ones we

use today, which are thin and lightweight. The roof sheets for this building were Ministry of Defence standard and at least five times thicker than its modern-day equivalent. At thirteen years old I could just carry a six-foot sheet but the ten and twelve-foot sheets were much too heavy for me and even the adults struggled with these monsters. I tried to help with the fitting of the purlins and the roof sheets but soon discovered that walking up a nine-inch beam forty feet up was definitely not for me. Unfortunately, all our enthusiastic free labour also felt the same way. Again, work had to stop while we saved up to employ professionals to join the trusses together. By the end of 1964 we had just four of the trusses up and only a few sheets nailed on. There were many anxious moments during the winter as the usual winter gales lashed our fledgling structure.

It was late spring before we could start work again and the last two of the trusses were assembled and lifted in place. The cost of the crane cleaned us out financially but the lads who had put the other purlins on, were short of work and agreed to fit the rest and get paid when we could afford it. With another year under my belt and some of the roof already in place, I found I could contain some of my fear of heights, so with dad and my uncle Ron we started to nail the roofing sheets on. It was very slow going as it was a major job just to get a sheet off the ground and up onto the roof. Also, none of the holes in the sheets matched where the purlins were so we had to make new ones by hammering an extra big centre punch that dad had forged specially for the job. Each hole took several minutes of constant hammering to pierce the sheet. There were a lot of sore knuckles and each sheet needed twelve to fourteen holes painfully punched into it.

It would take nearly two years to complete the sheeting of the roof. I was set the task of nailing on two to three sheets every night when I came home from school. To achieve this, I needed a way of getting the heavy sheets from the ground up onto the roof. We came up with a simple pulley system that was counterweighted by a large bucket filled with bricks and sand. I clipped the sheet onto one end of the rope with special clips that dad had made in the forge and the heavy bucket was released lifting the sheet easily up to the eves where I could slide it onto the roof and into place. I was extremely proud of our pulley system and many of the clients would come over and marvel at the ingenuity of it. I also got some pleasing comments about doing such a dangerous job on my own at such a youthful age, which was just what a young teenager craved to hear on the long road to manhood. One day, eager to show off to some of the teenage girls in the yard, I decided to make a spectacular exit from the indoor school roof by leaping off and using the counterweighted pulley to glide effortlessly down to earth. I think I had seen a similar stunt by an action hero on television. I leapt off the roof, rope in hand, and started to glide down to the floor. All was going swimmingly well, I could see the girls were impressed, then I met the bucket of bricks and sand coming up to meet me at a rapid rate. Too late I realised that I hadn't thought my stunt through. The bucket crashed into my shins and I let go of the rope! I crashed the last seven feet down to earth, quickly followed by the bucketful of bricks. Thankfully the bucket missed me as it could have killed me but the bricks that spewed out hit me from every direction. I had certainly made an impression on the watching girls, who told me, that it was the most stupid, idiotic thing that they had ever witnessed in in their lives.

That winter, 1965, we had an enough roof on to keep most of the rain off and had somewhere dry enough to work horses all year around. However, the sides and ends were open and un-sheeted. The indoor facilities caused a lot of excitement within the local riding community and demand for livery and people wanting to ride grew rapidly. Our clients had fingers in many pies and were keen to help us develop facilities that would enhance their leisure time. I don't know how it came about but the Manor Club in West Bridgford was being redeveloped and their clubhouse which was a sectional wooden building, was about to be demolished. Again, through the old pals act we managed to acquire this building, dismantle it and rebuild it at the stables, all for the princely sum of ten pounds and a lot of hard work from willing friends.

This was the beginning of Bunny Hill Riding Club and the old Manor Clubhouse became the Riding Clubhouse. The informal club became formalised with subscriptions and a committee. The club organised parties and dances, which along with raffles and tombolas, brought in large profits for the club that were used for the development of the Riding School facilities. The committee was made up of mainly wealthy riders or parents of children who kept horses or ponies with us along with some not so wealthy people who were prepared to put lots of hard work in setting up competitions and making all sorts of things. The Riding Club horse shows became immensely popular and very profitable.

An example of the power of our committee to provide things for free was a man called Bill Bilham who was in charge of the Redifusion company in Nottingham. He provided a full public-address system with massive horn speakers that covered all the competition rings and warmup areas complete with music playing facilities such as was only seen at large county agricultural shows. Another committee member owned a pub and applied for outside bar licences for all our shows. The shows grew to such a size that we even had a policeman on duty at the entrance to direct traffic.

As in the whole of Great Britain, things started to change at home at an alarming rate. In the early days children were dropped off by parents in a car sometimes and very rarely, a very wealthy customer would arrive in a car and park it on the hilltop road outside our house, but the majority of our customers arrived by bus. Even our two farriers used to come by bus and carry all their tools, including an anvil with them. Thinking about it nowadays, it's a wonder that they had any energy to shoe any horses after carrying an anvil weighing over a hundredweight from the bus stop to the stables, which must be almost a quarter of a mile. Dad actually had a forge and an anvil in the workshop, but they still insisted that they brought their own. Dad did much of his own shoeing in those days, as there were no regulations about being qualified to shoe your own horses. From my early gymkhana days, dad taught me how to remove nails from horses' shoes and replace them with wedge shaped frost nails. The special nails gave my ponies better grip when turning at high speed. He also taught me how to remove a shoe, something I wish I had never learnt as I was often required to perform that service for clients and friends. It always killed my back and I usually managed to cut myself during the process. I have the upmost respect for Farriers who do this, and much more, on a daily basis.

As the riding business grew, two things became top of the list of things we desperately needed. The first was a car park, as cars were now blocking the service road and upsetting our neighbours. We lost our fruit garden at the front of the house along with part of our orchard and we gained parking for about ten cars. We also erected a sign saying Bunny Hill Riding School. It was erected on the top of long poles about fifteen feet in the air so that it could be seen by traffic using the A60 road. The second urgent requirement was to build an outside toilet as the only toilet on the premises was in our bathroom and poor mum had to now put up with an endless stream of people wanting to come into our house. It was an annoyance, when we first started the riding side of the business but eight years on, with trade more than quadrupling, mum had a meltdown and told dad she couldn't stand it a day longer. Very quickly after that meltdown, we had an outside toilet for clients built onto the side of our bungalow! This was just the beginning!

Chapter 9

Cars and Motorbikes

I learned to drive a tractor at an early age but then a law was passed making it illegal for anyone under the age of thirteen to drive a tractor even on your own land. To me this was the most wicked and evil law ever passed. I was about eleven when the law came in and I was a competent tractor driver as were many of my farming friends. We just couldn't believe anyone could be so cruel. Our entire world shattered by people that had never set foot on a farm in their lives. Even worse was that the penalties for anyone allowing this to happen were very severe, so the farming community just had to accept it. The government even sent inspectors around to do unannounced checks. It was a disaster for small farms like ours. I did a lot of jobs with the tractor which helped dad immensely. Now he was going to have to do all those jobs himself.

It was the beginning of the dreaded farm safety officer, who was hated by farmers even more than the taxman. This was the beginning of the Health and Safety Law which is something I have been at odds with all my life. I was always taught to look out for and to anticipate danger. The farmyard has always been a dangerous environment and always will be. For me, working with animals has brought many more injuries than working with machinery. The sad thing today is that people don't see danger and walk around assuming that there is no danger around. To make a point, I wrote this section whilst on holiday in Turkey and watched an English guy jump into a boat tied up in the harbour to have his photo taken by his girlfriend. Quick as a flash, a Jandama (military police) appeared pointing a sub-machine gun at him and told him to get out of the boat. Rather than comply he argued with the officer. He seemed oblivious of the fact that he was in danger of being shot. I think this is the weakness of Health and safety. The current generation assume that there is no danger and we live in a safe environment, whereas my generation expect danger everywhere. If I had been in that boat, I would have been out of there like someone who had just stuck an electric cable up my backside and would have expected to be shot at any moment.

I moaned to everyone about the injustice of not being allowed to drive the tractor and a kindly client donated an unroadworthy car to me to drive around the fields. With a cushion on the seat and some blocks of wood strapped to the pedals so that my little legs could reach them, I was up and away flying around the fields at breakneck speed. Unfortunately, when the tank of fuel ran out, I discovered the true cost of motoring. It took a lot of pocket money to buy a gallon of petrol and driving around the fields in first and second gear quickly guzzled fuel. It was then that one of my uncles told me about syphoning fuel from a car or lorry fuel tank during the war when fuel was rationed. He taught me how to do it with a length of rubber pipe and a milk bottle. He said they did it all the time during the war but only ever took a small amount from each vehicle, hence the milk bottle. If you took more than a pint from one tank, an observant driver might notice the fuel gauge had gone down. I kept saving up and buying the odd gallon, so nobody ever suspected anything. I never really thought of it as stealing, just a clever trick my uncle taught me. However, it must have been a widespread problem as I soon started to encounter new cars that had locking fuel caps. End of the free fuel era!

The solution to the fuel problem was solved by changing from cars to motor bikes or to be more precise, mopeds. In reality, they were a push bike with a tiny engine that would power you on the flat or down hill but would conk out as soon as you hit the slightest gradient due to lack of power. Dad acquired several of these useless machines that were non-runners. It was about this time I became friends with Brian Hinksman who became a lifelong friend. I don't recall how he first came to the stables; I think it was through someone who used to help, they just brought him along for a day and somehow, he drifted into the workshop where I was busy dismantling a moped. He had a great mechanical mind and we spent the day dismantling various parts of the engine to find out why it wouldn't run. There seemed to be no obvious problem, so we put it all back together again. It ran sporadically but required twice the pedal power of an ordinary bike just to keep it running, and with the benefit of hindsight and bad experiences with many more tiny petrol engines. I think it was just worn out and lacked enough compression to have any guts. The next weekend Brian returned, and we fiddled with engines every weekend for many years to come. I was about fourteen at this time and spent nearly every lunch break at school in the library reading about the workings of the internal combustion engine and soon felt confident to start doing major repairs on larger engines.

With the benefit of very long hindsight, I made two very regrettable motor related decisions. I was given a BSA twin cylinder 650cc A65 that had failed its MOT. As fourteen/fifteen-year olds we had great trouble kickstarting it but when we did start it the power was awesome. Unfortunately, one day I opened the throttle a bit too far whilst riding it around the manège and crashed it head on into the back of the barn. I put a huge dint in the back of the barn which stayed there as a reminder of my foolhardiness for thirty years. Unfortunately, the front forks were damaged beyond repair, so it was sold for scrap. Just recently I bumped into an old motorbike pal Mick Smeeton, who is now into vintage bikes. Whilst reminiscing, he delighted in telling me that today that bike would be worth a small fortune as it is a very rare bike.

The second motor blunder I made was that I was given an old Sunbeam Talbot Coupe in my grandfather's will; it was a model from the late forties or early fifties. Thinking back, it was a beautiful car but to me and my parents it was just an old car without a mot. It had lovely leather seats, sweeping wings that ended as running boards, huge chrome headlights and doors that opened the opposite way that modern cars do today. I think they are known as suicide doors in the trade. I drove it around the fields for some time and then I burned the clutch out trying to tow start a tractor. The spares were hard to come by and removing the gearbox to change a clutch was beyond my technical skills at the time, so like the motor bike we cut it up for scrap.

Dad taught me to gas weld and to use an oxyacetylene cutting torch by the age of ten. When I started secondary school, I fell out of favour with the metal work teacher when he was teaching us to braze. I simply asked the question why not weld the two pieces together. His answer was because you had to be an adult before you could learn to weld. I told him, that was not true as I could weld. The metalwork master called me a liar and then told me to get out of the class for the day. After that he had it in for me all of the time always calling me a "Cocky little Bastard".

In our workshop at the stables, we made our own acetylene with a carbide generator. It was a strange contraption into which you added carbide granules to water and stirred it all together in a sealed metal vessel, which then produced acetylene gas. Every now and then we had to empty the waste by-product which was a bluey white paste that smelt horrible of the gas and always made me vomit. I used to impress my friends and girls at the stables by taking a small amount of the carbide granules pouring water over them and then throwing a lighted match on the bubbling sludge causing it to burst into flames with a loud "whoomph" making everyone jump backwards with surprise!

I've always had a vivid imagination that is also creative. I grew up around some very clever people who were always making things or altering things to make them better. The instant fire trick with the carbide gave me an idea for lighting the forge.

It was always my job to light the forge for dad. It was a slow and smokey job. First you had to chop some very small kindling sticks, dig a hole in the coke, fill it with screwed up newspaper and the kindling sticks. When lit, it would burn very slowly creating enormous amounts of smoke that filled the workshop. Once the kindling was burning well, you slowly added coke and a little air from the fan, this created even more smoke that was very acrid, causing you to cough and choke. Finally, after about ten minutes you had a clean burning coke fire.

I came up with an ingenious invention to have a smokeless instant fire. My plan was to make a hole as usual, put some carbide and water in the hole and then cover it coke and light it. The carbide would provide enough gas to light the coke without any smoke and hopefully a lot quicker. I waited a minute or so for the gas to get going and then I threw a lighted match onto the coke. Instantly, there was a big flash of flame followed almost simultaneously by a very strong "Whoomph". My elation quickly turned to terror as I was bombarded with flaming pieces of coke. Luckily, I had jumped back quickly as I threw the match, so much of the energy of the mild explosion had dissipated by the time the coals hit me and once the absorbed gas had burnt out of the coke it stopped burning. However, for a brief moment all I could see was a workshop covered in burning pieces of coke. I truly believed that the workshop was going to burn down and what Dad was going to do to me didn't even bear thinking about! I finally recovered and was relatively unscathed but when I looked at the forge it was completely devoid of any coke. It took me over an hour to pick up all the coke and cover up my experimental tracks. Like so many events in the book they have remained a secret for over fifty years and I only feel comfortable mentioning them now that my parents have passed away.

One event I could not hide from my parents was an accident that could have been easily so much worse. I had to own up to it as there were several witnesses and they probably saved me from being injured a lot more seriously. I was using an oxyacetylene cutting torch to cut up an old lorry for our neighbour, who was building a house in Bunny New Wood adjacent to our property. I was busy cutting off the rear axle and was trying to cut off the shock absorbers. Suddenly a sheet of flame spurted out of the shock absorber like a flame thrower and set my clothes on fire. Unbeknown to me, the shock absorbers were filled with oil which the cutting torch had heated to boiling point. I had then accidentally melted a pin hole in the casing, creating a nozzle for the super-heated oil to spurt out of. Luckily, it was a bitterly cold day and I was wearing a thick coat, gloves and a cutting mask. I let out a terrifying scream and John Hibbitt who was a neighbour and was working only a few yards away from me ran over to help. He was a big powerful man, he grabbed me and hurled me into a deep tractor rut that had filled with icy water. He proceeded to roll me back and forwards in the water until all the fire was put out.

I was hardly burnt at all; it was mainly singed hair and minor burns on the wrists. My only problem now, was not the burning but hypothermia as I was soaked to the skin with icy water on a bitterly cold afternoon, nearly a quarter of a mile from home. Poor Mum was very upset when I staggered into the room, clothes all charred, dripping wet and shaking from a mixture of shock and cold. Mum never seemed to be fazed by whatever injuries the male members of the family presented to her. She calmly dispensed basic first aid and TLC and arranged for us to be taken to Casualty if our injuries were beyond her capabilities. That day was another powerful health and safety training day.

Gas welding and cutting always carry risks and both Dad and I had some narrow escapes when welding up rotten chassis on old cars. Some of the older cars were a mixture of wood and steel and it was very easy for these to catch fire. Even when stringent precautions had been taken, things could go wrong. One day, Dad decided to try and repair a leaking petrol tank by welding it. He had removed it from the car, drained the tank and washed it out with water several times. He also made everyone go away from the area where he was going to start welding the tank. Not long after we had retreated there was a huge bang! We ran to see what had happened. Dad was lying flat on his back semi-conscious and the petrol tank was nowhere to be seen!

Remarkably dad had no serious injuries but was extremely shaken! We finally found the petrol tank on the other side of the workshop 20 yards away. Before dad started to work on it, it resembled a closed suitcase, now it looked like a fully opened suitcase. Dad remembered it flying over the top of the workshop roof as he was thrown onto his back. How he escaped more significant injury I will never know. However, it taught me to be very careful with petrol and petrol vapours. Another on the job health and safety lesson. After this incident, it used to frighten me to death seeing people filling up at a petrol station with a lighted cigarette hanging out of their mouth. A commonplace practice in the 1950s and early 60s!

In my fifteenth year I bought a BSA C15 motorcycle, which was powered by a 250cc engine. It was cheap and in pretty poor condition. Over the next year, up to my sixteenth birthday when I was legally allowed to ride it on the road, I stripped it all down, had the frame repainted, rebored the engine and fitted new bearings to all the major components. By the time I got my driving licence, it was like a new bike and I was extremely proud of it.

On my sixteenth birthday, I excitedly got ready to go to school riding my motorbike. I left ten minutes later but soon caught the bus up and started to pip my horn to attract the attention of my mates who always occupied the upstairs back seat of the bus. I was so busy waving and grinning like a Cheshire cat that I failed to notice that the bus had suddenly braked and slowed down dramatically. When I realised what was happening, I braked as hard as I could in panic, causing the bike to skid and swerve all over the road. All my dramatic, all too late actions, were not enough as I slid ever closer to the back of the bus. I was already cursing myself for being so cocky and careless on my first, and probably my last day riding my cherished motorcycle. I mentally prepared for the impact with the back of the bus, now only a few feet away. At that moment the bus started to pick up speed again allowing me those extra vital seconds to slowdown. I was so relieved, embarrassed, and annoyed with myself, but most of all, thankful!

I had dreamed of arriving at school and being surrounded by my classmates admiring my gleaming C15 for weeks prior to my sixteenth birthday. A couple of other lads had scooters, but none had anything as powerful or meaty as my bike. These were the days of Mods and Rockers and I was definitely a Rocker. A very embarrassed Rocker who was now surrounded by laughing classmates as the tale of my near miss with the bus had spread like a wildfire throughout the school.

I wasn't allowed to park my motorbike in the school grounds, so I had to park in one of the quiet suburban roads nearby. I also had to park far enough away from the school so as not to be seen wearing my leather jacket as the school had a very strict uniform rule. I once got a detention for not wearing my school cap when I got off the bus at Bunny Hill just as a member of staff drove past. Where I parked was a very quiet respectable area, so I would leave my helmet clipped to the handlebars and tightly roll my leather jacket up and secrete it in my ex-army haversack which was the "IN" schoolbag of the day so that I could stroll into school perfectly dressed.

Having a motorcycle gave me a new freedom to expand my

wanderlust and explore more places further away from home. My favourite place was Matlock in Derbyshire which was and still is a Mecca for motorcyclists. They still gather there to this day in their hundreds to enjoy the testing winding roads of the Derbyshire Dales and the magnificent scenery. More about my trips to Matlock later. Most of all having a motorcycle allowed me to socialise with a much wider range people. The bus service to Bunny Hill after 6pm was non-existent, so unless it was in walking distance or pushbike distance, I couldn't go to meet people socially.

The great downside to using a pushbike was that you had to negotiate Bunny Hill and unfortunately you needed working gears on your bike for that and my bike lacked any working gears due to the fact that the gear change cable had broken, and I couldn't afford to buy a new one. I did try to change gear by bending down and pulling the small chain that came out of the rear wheel hub whilst speeding down Bunny Hill. Unfortunately, I wobbled during the manoeuvre clipped the grass verge, somersaulted the bike into a very deep ditch full of nettles and brambles. Worst still the bike seat struck me between the shoulder blades severely winding me. I can still remember lying in the ditch on a sunny summer morning at 6am, cut all over, staring up at the blue sky desperately trying to breathe. It seemed like forever before I started to breathe again, I really thought I was going to die and never be found as I was laying in an eight-foot-deep ditch, completely covered by brambles. It was extremely painful extracting myself from the ditch and my bike was a write off! I can't remember where I was going to at the crack of dawn in such a hurry, but I never got there and that was the end of my push biking era as my sixteenth birthday was only a few weeks away.

For the last year and a bit of my push biking era, my friend Brian came up with a way of extending my travel range on a pushbike by giving me a tow on his Francis Barnet motor bike. Brian was slightly older than me and like me had a motor bike ready and waiting to go as soon as he turned sixteen. Brian's Francis Barnet was a 125cc two stroke engine that produced a very distinctive high-pitched sound and all his mates including me called it a Frantic Barnet, much to his annoyance. The one wonderful thing this little motorcycle did have was a luggage rack fitted over the rear mudguard. After some painful failures, we developed a technique that enabled Brian to tow me and other push-bike members of our group at speeds of up to 40mph. It was a bit precarious as you had to ride your bike one handed and hold onto the luggage rack with the other hand. This worked great until one day, unbeknown to us, we were followed by a police car whilst Brian was giving me a tow. The policemen were not amused, and we received a very severe warning that if we did it again Brian would lose his driving licence.

The only problem with my motorbike was that I was not allowed to carry a passenger on the seat behind me as I had not passed my motorcycle diving test and learner drivers could only ride alone. By the time I was sixteen, I had discovered girls and not being able to pick them up and take them out was severely cramping my style. I had heard a rumour that you could drive a three-wheeled vehicle on learner plates and still carry passengers, could this be true? A trip to the vehicle licensing office at County Hall Trent Bridge confirmed all my hopes (no internet in those days, you had to travel, queue, and then ask your questions). At first, the only three wheeled vehicles I could think of were Reliant Robins and Morgan's. The Reliant Robin had a bad reputation of rolling over when negotiating tight bends, even at slow speeds, but more importantly, had absolutely zilch street credibility. The Morgan on the other hand had the reverse wheel configuration with two wheels at the front and one at the back. It was powered by a large twin cylinder motorbike engine that was completely exposed at the front of the vehicle. It was quick, stable, noisy and came with heap loads of street credibility. Unfortunately, it came with a massive price tag, way, way, out of my budget! After more research,

I found out that motorcycles with a side car attached also came under the same rules and that there were no restrictions on engine size, even for learner drivers. The other wonderful thing about motorcycles with a sidecar was that they had been very popular but had now fallen out of favour and they could now be bought very cheaply!

I never told anyone what I was planning, as I thought that it would be a great surprise. However, I think that the word horror, better described the reactions that I got when I turned up riding a 600cc Norton with a huge fully enclosed sidecar attached. The sidecar was so big that you could lay down flat in it. I bought it early in 1968 and the sidecar soon became my travelling bed, although in the depths of winter you could easily freeze to death, even using a good sleeping bag. As the weather warmed, I came home less and less. It was a marvellous freedom and allowed me to party and not have to drive home drunk as a Lord.

I drove the Norton and sidecar until just before my seventeenth birthday. I was coming home from West Bridgford about midnight on a Friday night in early May. I was due to go on my first overseas holiday with my Uncle Ron the next day. We were taking a ferry to Gothenburg in Sweden from Hull and then taking a round train trip to Stockholm and then back to Gothenburg. It was the time of the £50 travel limit. The British Economy was in a dreadful mess and the Labour Government had imposed a £50 maximum for the amount of money that could be taken out of the country per trip. However, you could get around this to some extent as travel paid for in the UK prior to leaving was not included. Ron had discovered a camping holiday in Sweden where the ferry and the train ticket for Sweden that gave you unlimited travel for five days, was not included in the £50 limit. I was very excited to be leaving the homeland shores for the first time in my life.

As I drove through Ruddington on the main A60, I started to

overtake a minivan. I was alongside it when his right indicator came on. I was not concerned as the Flawforth Lane crossroads were still several hundred yards away. As I went to open up the power to quickly finish overtaking him, he turned immediately into a driveway. He hadn't seen me alongside him, and I had wrongly assumed he was turning into Ruddington at the crossroads. I slammed into the front wing of the van and woke-up wrapped around a lamp post about 50 yards down the road on the opposite side, relatively unscathed, although I did hurt my neck which has plagued me ever since. I can't remember a thing after that, but I did make it onto the ferry the next day although moving was very painful. My leather jacket saved me from more serious injuries as did my helmet. Both were severely ground away from me sliding down the road. When I see people riding motorcycles on a hot summers day riding their bikes in jeans and a short-sleeved shirt, I always think back to my accident and how my flesh would have been ground down to the bone if I had not been wearing proper motorcyclist clothes.

The police took my bike to check it over for any faults and I somehow got home, and the next day I caught the ferry to Sweden. My first foreign adventure!

Sweden had received a lot of publicity in the UK about its stunning tall blond women and its liberal attitudes to sex, in particular free love. Everyone talks about the sixties being a wild time in Britain with drugs and free love but in truth there was a battle going on between the Establishment who were backed by a very powerful church lobby and the younger generation who were demanding change to the whole stuffy regulated life that dated back to the thirties. The Establishment were backed up by a very reactionary and often brutal Police Force. It was not until the very late 60s that things slowly started to change and well into to seventies before there was any notable difference. Travelling over to Sweden, we just could not wait to experience this supposed enlightened utopia!

As we sailed up the North Sea, I felt dreadful. My body had received a lot more damage than I thought. I have discovered that my body is always more painful on the second day after a fall, but my bike accident was the first time I had received a serious battering (little did I realise how many more were to come in the future) so when I awoke after my first night on the ferry, I could not lift my head off the pillow. After several failed attempts to sit up, I grabbed hold of my hair with one hand to support my neck and used my other hand to pull myself into a sitting position. Once upright, as long as I moved very carefully and slowly, my neck seemed to be able to support my head, although being on a rolling ship in the North Sea didn't help matters.

When we docked in Gothenburg, we were surprised to find that most people spoke fluent English and we had little difficulty finding the railway station and our train. Our train ticket allowed us to get on and off the train as many times as we liked and so armed with a free map and some recommended campsites from the helpful tourist office, we set off on our adventure. The train chugged its way through deep forests until we reached our first recommended stop, a small town of wooden buildings on the shore of a large lake. The town was called Jönköping. It was when we looked for a pub that we realised we were well out of our depth. The food and drink on the ferry had been fabulous, my first experience of the famous smorgasbord! And it was relatively cheap. In Jönköping, there was only one café. They sold pastries and coffee. The food and coffee tasted fabulous, but the bill frightened us to death. We immediately realised that at our £50 worth of Swedish krona was not going to go very far. As for beer, that was definitely off the menu. In England a pint of bitter was one shilling and eleven pence or approximately 9p in today's decimal money. In Sweden it was over £3, luckily our holiday was only for five days. Just to put the icing on the cake we were eaten alive by midges at the campsite.

The next morning, we had to do some serious budget recalcu-

lating. If we were very careful with what we ordered, we calcu-
lated that we could afford one very basic meal a day, two cups
of coffee and maybe a small snack per day. We travelled on
towards Stockholm through wild forests and past many beautiful lakes. Wherever we stopped, everyone spoke good English
but with an American accent. They referred to a pavement as a
sidewalk and used many other American words which we don't
use in England and this sometimes, caused minor confusions.
Everywhere was very parochial, extremely polite, and the odd
thing was that all the young men smoked pipes. It turned out
that Sweden had some strange ideas on taxation. Instead of
taxing tobacco like most other countries, they believed that
smoking cigarettes was bad for you, but smoking a pipe was
the healthy option, so they taxed cigarette papers, and pipe tobacco was tax free. Another strange thing was that smoking was
banned on all public transport, something that was unbelievable to us and was thirty years ahead of the U.K. Although Ron
and me both smoked, our tight budget didn't run to such luxuries, so we never contravened the smoking regulations.

On the third day we reached Stockholm. The weather had
changed, and it was cold, wet, and windy. We had packed fru-
gally for our expedition and had omitted to pack any warm wet
weather gear. Stockholm looked drab and foreboding, built on
a series of islands. It was not easy to get about on foot and public transport was out of our budget. In fact, everything was out
of our budget! We walked around a public park full of drunks
sleeping rough and after a couple of hours wandering around in
the cold and rain, we left Stockholm and caught a train to start
our homeward journey. On our journey back to Gothenburg we
stopped and camped at two more little towns in the forest and
were again well bitten by mosquitoes. We arrived at the port
with barely a krona to our name and very hungry. Thankfully
we still had some sterling that we could spend on the boat. Once
aboard, we immediately ordered large steaks, washed down
with copious amounts of English beer. Our holiday had been an

adventure that was so nearly a disaster.

My overriding memory of Sweden was how clean it was everywhere and how friendly everyone was to us; also, how good their coffee was! This was reinforced to us when we docked in Hull. It was raining, cold and the place was filthy. We went into a café for a coffee; it was instant, the tablecloths were plastic and the floor filthy. Welcome to the not so Great Britain. What I did learn, was to do your homework before travelling and not to believe what you read in the newspapers. We never saw any promiscuity at all in Sweden not even a mini skirt. Where they dreamt up all these wild stories from was beyond me!

Chapter 10

Brian Hinksman

B rian was my best friend from the age of about twelve after our chance encounter at the stables, which I recounted in the last chapter.

It was mechanical things that brought us together but, in many ways, we were exact opposites. We had and also developed many shared interests. Brian lived for the moment and never gave a thought about the consequences of his actions. He hardly ever discussed the future with me unless it was a short-term project like rebuilding an engine. He lived in the past only to recant about diabolical things that he had got up to. He seemed to be blessed with no conscience, and in the 55 years that I knew him I can count on my fingers the number of times that he told me that he regretted doing something.

I, on the other hand, lived way in the future, planning my life for years to come most of the time and agonising over every set back, however small. Brian's favourite saying to me was, "For f**k sake stop thinking about it and let's just f**king do it." He got me to do so many things that I would never have got around to doing.

We progressed from messing about with mopeds to going shooting in the woods and exploring much further afield as we heard tales of interesting things to discover for ourselves. We were at that transition age where part of us still wanted to be kids and play but we also wanted to be seen as more serious teenagers. The word teenage angst comes to mind.

One day Brian announced that he had heard of a network of underground dens in Rancliffe Wood. The woods stretch from the crossroads of the Bunny-Keyworth lane and the Bradmore-Wysall Lane all the way up to Keyworth village. It is a very large tract of woodland to search and a long trek to get there. What made it even more exciting was that there were signs saying, "Private Keep Out." The main entrance to the woods was at the crossroads but this was always busy with traffic and dog walkers, so we secreted our bikes in a field and proceeded on foot towards Keyworth, when the coast was clear we scrambled under the fence into the woods, adrenalin pumping. We lay still, listening for any sounds of movement or voices before moving deeper into the woods to search for the fabled underground den system. It took several days to locate them and when we did, they were only about thirty yards from the main gate by the crossroads, unfortunately we had started our search at the wrong end of the woods. The dens were quite impressive. Ditches with square sides had been dug about three feet deep and three wide. The open top had then been covered with corrugated roofing sheets and the soil from the excavations had then been spread over the sheets making it blend into the woodland floor. We spent several hours exploring the network, always on edge in case the builders of this labyrinth came back and caught us. We were disappointed that they seemed to have been abandoned for some considerable time and that there was no loot to plunder. The tunnels were so impressive I still wonder if they were built by Army Cadets or something as a training exercise or may be even the Army during the war.

We returned home determined to build our own underground den. We selected a site not too deep into the wood next to our farm and took a spade and pickaxe from dad's workshop. We immediately hit two problems - firstly the trees were much closer together in our wood and we were constantly hampered by roots. The second problem was the soil, unlike the loamy free draining soil of Rancliffe Wood, the soil on Bunny Hill was heavy clay and retained water. We slogged on until we had a hole about four feet long and three feet wide, then it rained, and our hole filled with water. Instead of a den we had created a very small pond. Bunny Hill was just not suitable for building underground dens. Our little pond remained for over twenty years to remind us of our folly until it was covered over when a new owner used the wood as an illegal tip.

Not to be defeated we then set about building a secret base much deeper in the wood. It took a lot of creeping around in dense undergrowth until we found the right site and much planning to make the route to our base invisible. We used numerous routes that converged on the hidden start of our path to our base so that an outsider could not see a worn path. The main path started at the back of a willow tree whose branches touched the ground but could be lifted up a bit like a tent flap. Under the tree was bare earth so you could not see a worn path. We also made false paths that led away from the site.

The site itself was under a dense leafy canopy causing the undergrowth to die off through lack of sunlight. This made it relatively easy to clear a bare patch for our tent and fire. The brash that we cleared made a fence around the perimeter. A hole was dug for our campfire and surrounded by large stones. We scrounged old camping cooking vessels and actually went into Nottingham and bought some extra bits ourselves. We acquired a tent from somewhere, but I can't recall exactly where. After weeks of hard work our secret campsite was ready and we disappeared for a weekend of living off the land. We took several tins of baked beans, a loaf of bread, bottle of milk, tea and our guns. We shot, cooked and ate wood pigeons, made tea from water boiled over our fire and cooked baked beans. We told nobody where we were going and only told mum that we would be back Sunday night. We vanished for a whole weekend and not even dad could find us, it was magic!

During the summer holidays we vanished for a whole week returning unwashed and smelling of wood smoke. Dad was furious as he had lost his free labour. Once he came up the main path shouting for us, but he never found our camp. Brian was also in hot water when he returned home as he had told his parents that he was only going to stay with us for a couple of days. The days in the woods living off the land were magical days and I would not have missed them for the world. We were still children in some ways, but we were laying down our first markers of independence.

Another adventure concerned a plot of land at the end of Old Bunny Wood at a place known as Windmill Hill. The land was adjoined to Bunny Wood at the far end of the wood where it terminates at Wysall Lane and was on the Wysall side of the wood. Local scuttle-bug had it down as a place of satanic worship. This theory was based on the strange planting of trees in the overgrown paddock that was attached to a ramshackle wooden house with a veranda similar to the ones I described on Ash Lane. The trees had been planted in a big circle then another circle had been planted inside that circle. There were several circles getting ever smaller. Each circle was a different species of tree.

Having heard all the stories, we decided to go and reconnoitre this evil place. It took us about thirty minutes to walk through the woods and get to the property. It was a blisteringly hot day with a stillness that gave one a feeling of foreboding. Witches and Satanic rituals scared us shitless and the heavy stillness had us trembling with a mixture of excitement and fear as we threaded ourselves under the barbed wire boundary fence and entered the property. The grass was very long and came up to our shoulders, strands of brambles wove their way through the grass and constantly tripped us up, making our stealthy approach a joke. The trees set in concentric circles loomed up in front of us just as we had been told, we became more and more nervous. We circumnavigated the trees in case an evil curse was waiting to grasp us. Our hearts and pulses were racing, and we decided to leave the demonic circles alone and examine the ramshackle house, where perhaps the witch lived. After nearly an hour of creeping up to the house we threw stones at the house to see if anyone was inside. No witch appeared so we crept onto the veranda only to find a large padlock on the front door. Embolden by the padlock we peered through the window to try and see if we could see any Satanical objects but were surprised to see a sparsely furnished holiday cabin. By now our nerve was burnt out and we decided that we had achieved all our objectives and it was time for a rapid tactical withdrawal before our luck ran out. We returned like commandos returning from a successful raid. Although it was the early sixties, the events of the Second World War were still very present in our minds and much of our play centred around the exploits of The Commandos, The Long-Range Desert Group and the SAS.

Recently I joined the local shoot who now have their pheasant rearing pens on that site. I was asked to mow the grass in the field with our tractor and had time to study the site. Fifty-five years later the trees have grown so big that the smaller varieties have been swamped or just died off. The circles are not there anymore it's just a clump of trees surrounded by brambles. The original cabin burnt down in the seventies but has been replaced by another cabin of similar design. It was just a lovely peaceful place, nothing at all sinister. During the late sixties and early seventies, we used to ride around the field, and it was called the racetrack as we rode in a big circle around the edge of the field. Nobody had permission to ride in the field, but whoever owned it was never there, so we just did.

Although we didn't realise it at the time, all our fantastical thinking and gameplay was preparing us for something much bigger in the future. The main idea of mischievous behaviour was to either impress or frighten the girls who helped, or had ponies at the stables, who were of a similar age to us. And looking back we were really quite good, considering the technology that was available in those days.

The feed house was always a scary place to go in the dark due to the infestation of rats. If the girls had to enter after dark they always went in pairs or as a group. To make matters worse someone had spread a rumour of a ghost in the feed house as well. Brian and I decided we would add a little zest to the story and came up with a plan. At the time I was in possession of a Grundig reel to reel tape recorder that was about the size of today's onboard cabin luggage and decided to record some ghostly sounds to give a bit more substance to the rumours. We recorded heavy breathing, sighing and finally we did a spine-chilling scream. The tape recorder was set up in the workshop which was only about ten yards away from the feed house and then ran a speaker wire along the overhead power line that fed electricity from the workshop to the feed house and connected it to a large loud speaker in the loft of the feed house. We could now hide in the workshop and wait for the girls to open the feed house door and play our ghostly sounds before they had time to switch on the lights. To make it more plausible we played the heavy breathing and sighs when people were in the vicinity at a low level for about a week before. Lots of people started saying they had heard strange noises at the bottom of the yard near the feed house. After a week everyone was in a nervous frenzy and were hearing voices even when we were not playing the tape. The icing on the cake was that me or Brian would offer to chaperone them if they wanted to use the feed house or go up the yard in the dark while the other one played the sounds. When they heard the sounds, they would say "Did you hear that!" and grab hold of us. We would nonchalantly say, "I'm not sure, perhaps it was just the wind." By then end of the week the whole yard was like a ticking time bomb. The night we sprang the trap we played some low-level sighs before they tugged at the feed house sliding door that had a habit of sticking, and then as it flew back, we upped the volume and played an ear spitting scream! Their screams quickly drowned out our recording. One girl stated later the it caused her to wet her knickers, but then it backfired on us as they all ran screaming to the house and disturbed dad having his evening meal. Once more we were in hot water and got given hard labour for the next week!

At this point you may wonder about the large amount of time Brian spent at the stables and did he ever go home? The answer was that over weekends and school holidays he often stayed at the stables as did other drifting souls before and after him. The classic was Harvey Broadhead who came to stay one weekend with my brothers and stayed long after my brothers left home, not leaving until he was in his mid-thirties. I considered him to be another brother as he was just part of the family. Mum would always welcome visitors, even if there wasn't a bed, the settee was always available and even during the hard times, she always fed everyone exceedingly well. One of her secret weapons was a wartime cookbook with recipes that gave you tasty meals even on the very severe food rations that were available during the Second World War. It also had great ways to stretch food and feed more people with less. One of mum's favourite stretches was lots of mashed potatoes with plenty of gravy.

Brian's mum was much like my mum and as we grew older, venturing into West Bridgford and Nottingham at night, I often stayed over at Brian's, always welcomed, fed and watered.

Another stunt we created to shock people was a gun fight using our 4.10 shotguns. Unbeknown to anyone at the stables we had carefully dismantled a number of cartridges and removed all the shot so that they were blank, all except one. We had already carefully worked out our movements; I think today you would say that we choreographed our movements. Anyway, we started a fake argument and did some pushing and shoving then one of us ran off and the other one fired a live round supposedly at the other. However, we had done some secret test shots to check the spread of the shot so that we were well out of range and completely safe when the live round was fired. The reason for the live round was that it kicked up dust from the ground and convinced onlookers that we were using live rounds. People are easily deceived by what they see. We proceeded to fire blanks at each other whilst the ever-growing audience screamed at us to stop before we killed one another. When we owned up to the prank nobody seemed to be amused except us. Too close to reality? Worst of all dad took our guns off us for a couple of weeks when he heard about our stunt. Hopefully, you can now understand why we took to jousting and stunt arranging. It was in our blood.

Brian was always a heavy sleeper and could fall asleep anywhere. If he had been drinking alcohol he would just pass out and it would be impossible to wake him. Once at a party at his house he passed out and his sister Sonia and some other girls made his face up with foundation, lipstick and eyeliner. It was the full works! Everyone was up and had eaten breakfast by the time Brian arose from his slumbers. He always looked rough in the mornings after a heavy nights drinking and took no notice of people bursting into laughter when he confronted them. He wandered around the house looking like a transvestite for more than half an hour before he caught sight of himself in a mirror causing him to leap back and utter the word "Shit." After studying himself in the mirror for several minutes he turned towards his giggling audience gave a deep chuckle smiled and said, "You f***ing b***ards when did you do that, brilliant just f***ing brilliant. Now how the hell do I get it off!"

Brian never took offence at someone having a joke on him as long as it made people laugh and would laugh along with everyone else, usually slapping the perpetrator on the back and congratulating them on their ingenuity. Brian even saw the brighter side of something that could have killed him and did some considerable damage to his motorbike. We had gathered outside the White Lion pub at Rempstone one summer evening and were having a competition to see who could ride their motorbike the fastest around the famous sharp right-hand bend just past the pub. In those days the main road literally passed the front door of the pub with only the pavement separating the pub from the road. The road was moved at the end of the sixties as the bend was so tight that modern lorries could not get around it, even today with its modification it is considered a very tight bend. One by one we drove our bikes as fast as we dared from the Melton Mowbray end of the village, rapidly changing down through the gears as we approached the evil bend before dropping our bikes so far over that the footrests scraped the ground and sent a shower of sparks flying from the bike. As the evening wore on, the pub emptied to watch our exploits and cheer the riders on. The onlookers also included several teenage girls who lived in the village and as Brian did his run, he couldn't resist turning his head to flash a smile at the girls. It only took a split second, but it was enough for him to totally misjudge the bend. His bike lost traction and slid away from him, both bike and rider disappeared sliding along the road around the corner and out of sight. There was a loud crash and we all ran around the corner with trepidation! The wooden bus shelter just around the corner was full of smoke and noise from the motorbike engine that was still running and being a two-stroke engine, it was very smokey. The scene was like an action hero movie as Brian appeared through the smoke from the wreckage of the wooden bus shelter. His first words were, "What a stupid f**king place to put a bus shelter." He then, despite being battered, gave one of his famous chuckles and said "F**ked that up good and proper didn't I. Think I need a stiff drink!"

Surprisingly both bike and rider lived to fight another day, but the bus shelter was a complete right-off. The council chased Brian for reparations, but he never replied to their letters and they eventually gave up.

Brian's heavy sleeping was usually aided and abetted by a night of heavy drinking which became legendary and provided many amusing incidents.

He would often return home from the pub and decide to have a cup of tea or coffee before going to bed. The kitchen had a gas stove and he would light the largest gas ring and put the kettle on to boil and promptly fall into a deep sleep. Next morning his mum would find him still sound asleep, the gas ring still burning and an aluminium kettle that was now just a blob of melted down metal. After about six melted kettles his mum put her foot down and declared no more late-night hot drinks or else, he would have to find alternative accommodation. Not long after the ban we returned back to his house one night and Brian immediately started to make a hot drink. I reminded him about the ban and with a wicked smirk said, "Ah yes! But she didn't say anything out having a bowl of soup." Giggling away he opened a tin of tomato soup and heated it up still giggling at circumnavigating the ban. By the time he had heated the soup I was starting to nod off but was forcing myself to stay awake until I was sure the gas had been safely switched off. With the gas safely off I must have relaxed and nodded off. I awoke suddenly to a strange sound and to my horror saw Brian face down in his bowl of soup fast asleep!

At first, I thought he had drowned in the bowl of soup but as I jumped up to pull his head out of the soup a reassuring bubble of air plopped up. It must have just happened and the noise of his face flopping into the bowl must have woken me Luckily, I am a light sleeper, even after a skin-full of ale. Sadly, this was well before the days of mobile phones with instant access to a camera as the sight of Brian's face covered in tomato soup would have gone viral on social media.

In the mid-seventies we owned a large twin wheeled transit van which we used to transport some of the jousting equipment including a huge dragon that was operated by a person inside it's body. Brian often borrowed the van and would use it to go out sometimes. On one occasion the jousting troupe was all assembled at the stables ready to set off in convoy down to High Wycombe, all except Brian who had also borrowed the kit van to take a girl out the previous evening. After waiting patiently until it was past our leaving time, I decided to go in search of him and more importantly our kit van. Brian lived in Ruddington, so it was only a ten-minute drive to his house which was going to be my first port of call. Hopefully he had made it home and had just overslept.

As I arrived at his parents' house, I was relieved to see the van parked in a parking area near the house. As I pulled into park next to the van, I noticed a dim glow coming from the headlights and then saw Brian slumped over the steering wheel, hopefully just sound asleep. After much shaking, I manage to wake him; he was blissfully unaware of the time or why I was so agitated. When I reminded him, we were supposed to be on our way to High Wycombe, he gave me his usual reply of calm down don't get wound up we will still get there on time, never an apology. Still angry with him, although I knew it was a waste of time, I shouted at him saying, "Well get the bloody van started and let's get going." He turned the key and all we got was an ominous clicking from the starter. The headlights had been on all night and drained the battery. I ranted and raved at him, but it was water off a ducks back. Luckily, I had a set of a jump leads in my car and we set about trying to re-energise the battery by revving my car to the max. This was something that didn't go down well with the neighbours as it was still only 6.30am on Sunday morning and bedroom curtains were starting to be opened by angry neighbours. I mentioned to Brian that we might soon be attacked by his neighbours to which he calmly replied, "I have just remembered that I didn't get home until 5.30 so the battery shouldn't be too flat". He turned the key and the engine turned over, I didn't think it was fast enough to start it, but the engine must have still been a little warm and to my relief it cracked up into life. We disconnected the jump leads in double quick time and sped off just as angry men wearing pyjamas or vests appeared from several back doors around the housing close. By the time we arrived at the stables Brian was fully awake and when we got out of respective vehicles he was grinning and said, "I think I'd best stay at yours for a few nights if that's ok, until things settle down with the neighbours." So annoying but it was impossible to remain angry with him for long!

Chapter 11

The Riding Club

During the sixties, our riding club developed and thrived. It started life as the Bunny Hill Riding Club but in 1967 changed its name to Rushcliffe Riding Club. Rushcliffe is the parliamentary area for south Nottinghamshire, and it was thought that this name more accurately described the catchment area of the club. The other reason for the change was that the new clubhouse was nearing completion and we intended to apply for a liquor license, and it was the general opinion that Rushcliffe would go down better with the Licensing Magistrates than Bunny Hill. Getting a liquor license was a long drawn out process in those days. Going up before the licensing magistrates made you feel like a licensed drug dealer and they questioned you harshly about your ability to refrain from serving drunk people, preventing the access of minors onto the premises and keeping an orderly house. The Licensing Justices were typical of the Magistrates characterised in in the TV series The Darling Buds of May starring David Jason and the young Katherine Zeta Jones, haughty and evangelical.

The Bunny Hill Riding Club spawned after the terrible winter of 1963 and had, at its heart, the people that came to work and play at bunny during those tough times. They helped us survive and had enjoyed doing it. Now they wanted to help us grow, and grow we did!

First came the gymkhanas, which were just games for children, but they soon became a much more all-round horse show with the dreaded show classes and show jumping. The show jumping grew to the level of running The British Show Jumping Association affiliated classes.

To digress briefly, one of my clients, Louise, is a schoolteacher and has kindly offered to read through and edit my work. During the course of editing my work she often marks up words as wrong or misspelled when they are actually correct because she has never heard of them. I now realise that many words that I use regarding riding or the countryside are no longer widely used in mainstream dialogue. I will try and add a glossary of those I can remember. Gymkhana is probably one of these words and also jodhpurs and jodhpur boots. These are all Anglo-Indian words that came back to Britain with the Army during the British Raj. Gymkhana was a gathering place for games of equestrian skills and jodhpurs were loose baggy riding trousers designed to give ease of movement and keep you cool. Another commonly used Anglo-Indian word is bungalow.

Back to the riding club! The riding club also raised money through social events. Most of these were dances that were held in the clubhouse that I mentioned earlier and always had a lavish buffet. In the early sixties the music was from a simple gramophone and the music was mainly strict tempo ballroom dance music with a little bit of rock and roll such as Bill Hayley's Rock Around the Clock. The nights would always finish with some chaotic country dancing such as the Gay Gordons which usually ended up with drunken couples crashing into one another and ending up in heaps on the floor. Alcohol was always a big part of both the gymkhanas and the dances. People of that period did not have the money to drink every day of the week but Friday and Saturday nights they would really go for it. Sunday lunchtimes in the pubs were also a very hectic time. The licensing laws at the time only allowed a strict two-hour drinking period on Sunday lunchtimes and it was not uncommon to see a large queue outside pubs waiting for the pubs to open their doors. As we passed through Nottingham one Sunday on the way to a horse show in Ripley, there was a queue of over fifty people snaking down the road outside the large pub situated on the ring road opposite the now defunct Raleigh Cycles Factory.

I mention this way of almost binge drinking because the revenues from the bar often exceeded the profits of running a horse show. Obtaining a special bar license for the whole of Sunday was a license to print money. When we held our horse shows on the fields on the opposite side of the A60, we used the old barn as the bar, it was very dark inside with a mud floor, but nobody seemed to care as long as the booze flowed.

All this drinking provided some memorable moments for us children to witness. There was much rivalry between the riding school proprietors and one day an argument broke out about who owned the fastest games pony. Some clever person suggested that they settle the argument by all riding their best pony in the veteran's race which was usually the last race of the day. By the time it came around to the veterans race, the competitors had been in the bar a full five hours. Four of them staggered out of the bar wearing what were their Sunday best suits at the start of the day. Their mounts awaited them at the starting line. Word had got around the whole show about the challenge and the edge of the arena was packed five deep all the way around. After much help from the younger competitors all were loaded onto their crack games ponies.

Now these ponies were highly tuned racing machines; the drag racers of the horse world. When the starter shouted go. They could explode from halt to gallop in half a horse's stride. The competitors all lined up with some help from the younger competitors. The starter came forward. The race was the bending race, a true test of speed and agility. The starting procedure began, "are you ready", the ponies knew all the words and started to tremble in anticipation, "steady", the ponies started to fidget and spin around, "Go!" They exploded forward at the gallop.

Three of the four riders promptly did a backward somersault off the back of their mounts, all three were knocked senseless on the start line. The other one had the sense to hold onto the pommel of the saddle and just managed to stay onboard. Spooked by the flaying body on his back, his pony veered across the arena straight for the audience. In those days, a single rope held up by metal stakes marked the boundary of the arena. The audience started to scramble out of the way causing the pony to spook and flip the last man in the saddle sideways. He landed astride the boundary rope at speed and slid along the rope at great speed superheating his private parts. There were cheers and whoops of laughter from the onlookers, only the relatively sober organisers realised the gravity of what had just happened. Miraculously there were no serious injuries and the battered competitors were carried back to the bar for medicinal whiskey on the house.

On another occasion, during a very wet summer, the last hour of the show was washed out by torrential rain. The only way off the field was a farm track past the front of the barn where the bar was situated. As the cars and lorries left the field, the track gradually turned to a quagmire and we had to fetch the tractor to tow vehicles off. In those days, cars and lorries had very strong bumper bars both front and back. Usually you could hook a tow-chain over the bumper where it was bolted to the chassis and that was a strong enough anchor point for the tow. Towards the end of the day a horse box floundered in the now bottomless black stinking mud. We hooked the chain to the bumper as usual and started the tow. With a loud crack, the bumper broke off the lorry enraging the owner.

This brought an immediate audience from the bar. We all knew what to do next, but that involved crawling underneath the lorry to fix the chain hook onto the front axle and nobody was keen to do that. We wandered around the lorry trying to find a suitable strong point that didn't involve wriggling through the black stinking mud. All of a sudden, a loud voice boomed. "Get out of the bloody way you load of Nancy's I'll do it." A huge man burst through the crowd of onlookers, obviously the worse for wear from drinking, taking off his jacket and tie. After handing them to one of the onlookers he took hold of the chain and dived into the black mud and slowly wriggled under the lorry. When he reappeared, his white shirt and light grey trousers were unrecognisable, as was his face and hair. A loud drunken cheer erupted from the bar, he drew himself to attention, glared at us and said, "Bloody load of wusses!" and walked back into the bar casually putting his jacket and tie on over his muddy clothes.

At another show one of the horsebox owners was refusing to leave the bar, despite pleading from the children that he had brought. They had loaded their ponies onto the horsebox themselves and desperately wanted to go home as theirs was the only solitary horsebox left on the field. After much pestering, it was decided that he was incapable of walking, so his pals carried him across the field to the horsebox and with great difficulty stuffed him into the driver's seat. After a few missed gear changes, he proceeded on his way home. Thankfully they all got home safely.

Another story that was recounted to me by a pal from those gymkhana days was that when they got back to their stables, after one of our shows and well inebriated, they discovered that the horsebox ramp had fallen down and that they were missing two ponies. Retracing their route, they eventually found the two ponies happily grazing on a traffic island in the middle of Nottingham. They managed to reload them and get back to their stable yard without attracting the unwanted attention from the police.

The membership of the Riding Club grew steadily through the sixties and in 1967 the new clubhouse opened. It was built onto the end of the indoor school with windows that allowed you to watch the riding lessons and competitions from the bar. It had a fully licensed bar and its own toilet block with separate Ladies and Gents toilets.

We had a grand opening on a Sunday afternoon that included show jumping competitions in the indoor school. We were the first riding school to have an indoor school in an area that covered Nottinghamshire, Leicestershire, Derbyshire, Lincolnshire and probably a few more adjoining counties. We were mobbed with customers and we had managed to get an all Sunday afternoon bar license. The party continued on well into the evening until the customers had drank every drop of alcohol on the premises.

We took a fortune in bar takings: the amount that we took on that day was six times higher than we have ever achieved since, even considering inflation. It was late autumn when we first opened the clubhouse. It was the first indoor show jumping competition to be held for at least a fifty-mile radius, and probably even a one-hundred-mile radius. This was because at that time there were hardly any indoor riding schools in the whole of the U.K. However, that would change rapidly over the next ten years but for now we were swamped by people wanting to continue show jumping throughout the winter months. Demand was so great, that not long after we opened the Clubroom, we were holding competitions every Sunday afternoon. Unfortunately, after a few months the Licensing Magistrates decided that our show jumping competitions were not a special occasion anymore as we were having them with such regularity and refused to give us any more special licenses for Sunday afternoons. Things got very nasty when we announced that the bar was closing at 2pm and we had a near riot on our hands. Although the competitions continued to be a success, there was a noticeable decrease in competitors after we lost our special Sunday license.

In the sixties, there was a tough unsavoury element of people involved in show jumping that has left me with an uncomfortable feeling about the sport. One day I witnessed a child being dragged out of the saddle after knocking several poles down during their jumping round and being severely thrashed by their father with their riding whip. The worst thing was that was done in front of dozens of onlookers and nobody said a word. I was just sixteen at the time and of no age to rebuke a parent for disciplining their child.

Cheating in unaffiliated show jumping was very common. Children lied about their age to continue jumping in an age group that they had grown out of on a regular basis. However, the biggest problem was riding oversized ponies in classes. In the sixties, the class and rider age groups were as follows: - 12.2hh and under, twelve years old and under, 13.2hh and under, fourteen years and under, and finally 14.2hh and under and 16 years and under. The hh stands for hands high which is the way horses are measured: a hand is four inches and the two stands for two inches extra. These days show jumping ponies are measured in centimetres, which always confuses me.

It was possible to get a height certificate from a vet, but these were open to corruption and also manipulation. The most common manipulation was to pare the horse's hooves down more than they should have been to the point of cruelty and then fit worn-out wafer-thin shoes. The measuring rules allowed half an inch for shoes. Another unsavoury trick was to hang sandbags on the pony's withers overnight before the measurement and this would compress the joints so that the pony measured less.

However, the most common way to cheat on pony size was to brazenly enter your oversized horse in the wrong class. Horses were rarely measured at shows and you had to be a very brave man to object to the height of a pony owned by some of these characters.

The situation got so bad and so blatant in the seventies that our riding club decided to measure all ponies at the start of the season. Over fifty percent of the ponies were oversize for their classes. The worst case was five inches too high for the class it competed in. I had the unenviable task of conducting the measuring and suffered great verbal abuse, including threats to my life and having teeth knocked down my throat. It was the right thing to do but it halved our entries and was one of the reasons that we stopped having the shows shortly after this new rule was introduced.

The lead rein pony games were always another flashpoint. The idea of lead rein classes was to introduce very young children to the fun of gymkhana games but unfortunately the fathers were more interested in showing off their running prowess. They would often have several metres of lead rein which they would extend as they raced for the finish line like a top athlete running the 100 metres. They just didn't seem to understand that it was when the pony and rider crossed the line that mattered! On one occasion, two very competitive fathers crossed the line in a true photo finish. When I didn't call either of them forward as the winner, they rounded on me saying that I must have been blind if I could not have noticed that they had crossed the line way ahead of the person I had announced as the winner. It was only when I pointed out that neither of ponies had a rider onboard when they crossed the line that they accepted defeat. Both had spun their ponies around the turning post at the far end of the arena so vigorously that they had ejected their poor children out of the side door leaving them crying in a heap while they dashed the final 30 metres to the finish line. The argument was swiftly settled by the two mothers who arrived screaming at their husbands for not taking care of the children and being stupid chauvinistic fools. Oh, the joy of judging the Gymkhana games.

Nearly all Gymkhanas had a special licensed bar and it was not only the spectators that used the facilities. Underage drinking was extremely common and most of us were drinking alcohol at shows, aided and abetted by the adults, from the age of thirteen and it wasn't the weaker stuff. The boys drank mainly bottles of IPA at around 5% alcohol and the girls drank whiskey and orange or vodka and lime. A classic day was when one of two very successful brothers had jumped a faultless clear round show jumping in the main competition of the day and then had to wait for over an hour before the jump off. The talented rider had spent the time waiting in the bar. It took several tannoy announcements to get him out of the bar and loaded into the saddle. He galloped into the ring and promptly fell off at the first corner without jumping a fence dead drunk. He managed to stagger to his feet, take his hat off and bow to the audience before staggering off back to the bar to a standing ovation.

The pinnacle of the riding club year was the annual dinner dance. We outgrew several venues through the sixties until we finally moved to the Sherwood Rooms in the centre of Nottingham, where we sat down a record number of 360 people. Other notable venues were the Reform Club in Nottingham and County Hall at Trent Bridge West Bridgford.

As the riding club grew more and more, people wanted to serve on the committee, and this led to inevitable power struggles as the committee expanded. Many of the hard-working members were replaced by wealthy businesspeople who gave generous prizes both at the shows and the dances. We lost the people that used to set up and clear up after the shows and more and more of that fell to me and dad. We were starting to work for the club unpaid rather than the other way around. Although the bar had a proprietary club license, which meant it was owned and run by our family as a facility that the members could use, the shows and dances were still run by a committee still called Bunny Hill Riding Club. Certain members wanted the profits from the bar the go into the club funds so that they could control all the money.

The tables were being turned so that instead of the club raising money to help offer more facilities for the riders using the riding school, it now proposed that we should work for the riding club. There was even talk of moving the shows away from Bunny Hill to a larger show ground. It all ended with a lot of bad blood and the closing down of the Bunny Hill Riding Club and so the Rushcliffe Riding Club was born owned and run by the Humphrey Family.

Things were going well, the indoor school was up and running and our new club house with its bar, function room and toilets was also running smoothly. In the four years since the big freeze, the number of horses and riders grew steadily.

Then in October 1967 there was an outbreak of foot and mouth disease. It started in Shropshire but quickly spread. We had never heard of the disease and never imagined that it would affect us.

Although horses can't get foot and mouth disease, an order to ban the movement of all animals swiftly came into force across the whole country. This immediately shut down all our competitions and a large source of income. We were also banned from taking horses off the premises, so all hacking stopped as well.

However, our biggest concern was our pig herd, which like the riding school business had continued to grow steadily alongside the riding school. Our pig business was breeding and growing porkers and selling them on between 6 to 8 weeks old to a specialist firm that grew them on until they were the correct size for slaughter. As in the big freeze, we were again stuck with an ever-growing population of pigs that had to be fed without any income coming in.

Horses do not get foot and mouth, but pigs do, so we had to have mats of straw soaked in strong disinfectant at all our gateways to sanitise car and lorry tyres. We also had to have a foot bath of disinfectant for all visitors to sanitise their boots or shoes. This was not a pleasant experience for people with leather footwear. as the chemicals ruined the leather. Not a good way to encourage clients to visit your establishment.

With hacking prohibited, our riding income fell whilst our costs rose. Our bank balance, which had just started to creep into the black, plunged steadily back into to the red. Bankruptcy raised its ugly head once again! Worst of all, this crisis didn't last just a couple of months like the big freeze but went on until the middle of June 1968 eight long months later. The pressure of not knowing if tomorrow may be the day that the Ministry of Agriculture would turn up to cull your pig herd even if it was healthy, really weighed on Dad and it went on day after day, week after week, month after month. I clearly remember Dad saying to me that if we survived the outbreak, he was going to sell all the pigs, because he could not stand the stress of losing everything he had worked for, at the stroke of a pen.

In the end, we were amongst the lucky ones: our pig herd survived, and our business survived! However, things would never be the same again. We sold all the pigs, something that greatly saddened me as I loved having them, and although we never had any more pigs at the Riding School one of the first things I did when I bought Bunny Hill Farm was to buy some pigs but that was nearly fifty years later. We also had to change the way that we ran our Riding School business.

Because we could not hack out, we had to attract customers solely on our teaching of riding. Thankfully the indoor school was now fully functional and combined with the clubhouse facilities we were still a very desirable place for people to come to ride and relax. We started to hold regular group lessons and because the indoor school was a more confined space, we adopted the army drill ride way of teaching large groups of riders. This proved amazingly popular and a very successful way of training all levels of riders. We started to become a proper school of riding with classes graded to the ability of the rider.

When all the pigs were sold in the autumn of 1968, we converted the buildings used for pigs into more stables. By the latter half of the sixties, people were becoming more prosperous and people started to be able to own their own horse or pony and so our livery business started to develop.

It was at this time that Dad started to take a real interest in High School Dressage and the teaching of Equitation. It was not an overnight revelation, his interest in dressage started in the early sixties and I remember being dragged along with a large contingent of riding club members, to watch a demonstration by Robert Young in the finer arts of dressage somewhere in the Dukeries, I think it could have been Clumber Park. I was just thirteen years old; it was really boring and very drawn out. Some of the club members kept buying me bottles of cider and when it was finally time to go my legs had lost all feeling and I could not walk. From that day to the present I have never been able to stomach cider ever again. My feelings about dressage are not dissimilar. Although these days I do coach people in the discipline but it's never been something I wanted to do myself.

Throughout the sixties, Dad trained with many top equestrian trainers, including some polish equestrians who had settled in the UK after being refugees during the Second World War. They were all world class trainers, famous in their time but now mostly forgotten in the mists of time. I will mention a few but they will probably mean nothing to most readers. Dorothy Popov, Dick Stilwell, Charles Harris, Geoffrey Hatton, John Lasseter, Nuno Olivera, and Molly Sivewright.

So, as we put foot and mouth behind us in 1968, we became a standalone Riding School and Livery Yard with a Club house and a licensed bar. This made us unique as to my knowledge there was no other like it anywhere in the country. We also had accumulated massive debts riding out the foot and mouth outbreak. I got a job away from the stables, fell out with Dad and not long after left home.

Chapter 12

Cannon, Bombs, and Rockets.

It all started after Bonfire night, 1964. There had been a big bonfire party at the stables and Brian Hinksman, and I were tidying up around where the bonfire had been gathering up unburnt logs, old firework casings and general combustible litter into a new fire to clear the site. We soon discovered that there were many fireworks that had failed to go off. We decided that there must be some genuine fun to be had if we harvested all the gunpowder and other chemical goodies that resided in the unexploded fireworks.

Our original plan was to find some used rocket casings and refill them to make our own rockets. Although it seemed a promising idea at the time, it soon became clear that you needed an awful lot of gunpowder to refill a rocket and our stock of reclaimed powder was not that great. Also, near the end of our gunpowder harvesting I had a bit of an accident. As true recyclers we were trying to separate out the different components of the fireworks so that we could then re-blend them to make our own special fireworks. Many of the pretty fireworks had different compartments for different effects. We would pour the powders into our hands, inspect them and put them in separate tubs. As I poured the contents of a firework into my hand, there must have been a spark still inside the firework. There was a blinding flash and a searing pain in the palm of my hand. The palm of my hand was severely burnt and like the electrical burn I suffered many years before, I still bear the scars to this day! I never told anyone what we were really up to and made up a story that the firework exploded when I picked it up.

My injury took several weeks to heal, and it gave us a breathing space to consider all our options. We eventually came up with the idea of building a cannon. We found some old steel steam pipe in the workshop, which had an internal diameter of half an inch and then searched around to find some suitable sized ball bearings that were to become our cannon balls. Luckily Dad was a great hoarder and we soon found a box full of bearings of assorted sizes. Getting the ball bearings out of their steel casings proved quite a challenge but after much hacksawing and chiselling, we finally managed to release the ball bearings. The ball bearings were slightly smaller than the bore of the pipe, but we considered that to be better than a tight fit. We had done much research on cannons during my convalescence and were well aware of the dangers of the cannon itself exploding.

To make our cannon, we first flattened one end of the pipe with the help of a blacksmiths vice and much hammering on the anvil, then folded the flattened the section back on itself and finally sealed it by arc welding it. We then drilled a small hole near the sealed end for the touch hole, this allowed us to ignite the gunpowder inside the tube.

We were unsure as to whether the steam pipe was strong enough to withstand force of the gunpowder exploding inside the tube. So being very safety conscious, we opted to use a fuse instead of igniting a small pile of the gunpowder over the top of the touch-hole as they did in the olden days. Again, after a little research we discovered that you could buy what was called "JetX fuse" from model maker's shops. It was used to ignite the propellant in model jet planes and was an ultra-thin wire coated with something like the flammable part of a sparkler. After timing the speed at which the JetX fuse burnt, we were able to set a length of fuse that gave us enough time to run a safe distance from the cannon before it fired or exploded!

We were now ready to fire our cannon! It was only eighteen inches long and the ball bearing was the size of a marble. We lit the fuse and ran like hell. We had aimed the cannon at an old scrap car. There was a loud bang and a puff of white smoke. We let out a cheer and danced up and down with joy before going to inspect our cannon.

To our amazement the cannon was still intact and even more amazing was that the ball had made a neat hole through the outside and severely dinted inside panel of the driver's door. We were ecstatic! We just could not get over the fact that two young teenagers had made a working cannon entirely by ourselves.

Unfortunately, after several more firings we ran out of gunpowder. We did however manage to fire a ball bearing through both of the driver's door by slowly upping our powder charge. This was no mean feat as the car had been made in the early fifties when the body panels were made of much thicker steel than in later years. It was far too exciting to stop making cannons and we were already designing larger models. What we needed was an alternative propellant.

We had of course boasted to all our mates about our cannon success and it was through one of them that we heard about a possible, alternative propellant. Apparently, if you mixed sodium chlorate weed killer with an equal amount of sugar it burnt furiously, not unlike gunpowder. The weed killer could be bought from any hardware shop and it was very cheap. Mum did become a bit suspicious that something strange was going on when she suddenly started to unexpectedly run out of sugar.

We mixed up a small batch of the weed killer and sugar and tried to light it with a match, but nothing happened, it would not ignite. However, when we stuffed a match whose head was still burning into the mixture, it erupted into a fierce burn not unlike a newly struck match head. It was slower than gunpowder but we both agreed it might well work. We charged our cannon with our new mixture and as we had run out of JetX fuse opted for the traditional way of firing the cannon by lighting a small pile of the mixture that had been placed over the top of the touch hole.

There was a hissing sound and much more smoke than with the gunpowder. It seemed to go on for ages. Just when we thought that it was a failure, there was a huge bang! We ran to the car to examine the new hole in the door but couldn't find one. As we turned towards the cannon, we saw smoke coming from out of the ground. When we reached the cannon the sealed end of the cannon looked like an opened flower, the metal was all splayed out. There was also a hole in the ground about the size of a kitchen mixing bowl. Our first reaction was despondency, our beloved cannon was no more, but then it dawned on us that we had inadvertently made a bomb. Perhaps a similar accident hundreds of years ago led someone to make the first bomb or grenade. It was like walking back in history and very exciting....

Being the inquisitive pair that we were, we wanted to know why the cannon had turned into a bomb instead of firing the ball bearing. At first, we thought it might be metal fatigue so we built another cannon out of heavier gauge pipe but the same thing happened, only this time it was an even louder bang. We were intrigued, so we collected all the fragments of the cannon that we could find, put them into an old biscuit tin and took them back to the workshop for analysis. On examination we discovered that the internal parts of the firing chamber were covered with a glass like substance. This required some scientific analysis, so we made up a new mixture of weed killer plus sugar and set fire to it in the open. As it burnt there was intense heat and much smoke, the mixture turned into a gluey state much like magma from a volcano, which eventually enveloped the fire, but the interesting thing was that the fire kept burning underneath. Every now and then a bubble would form and explode spraying the molten lava type material everywhere.

We now understood what had happen inside the cannon. The molten "lava" had sealed both the touch hole and the barrel, pressure had built up and an explosion occurred. We were very pleased with our analytical discovery and for once could understand why we were being taught these things in chemistry at school. A by-product of our accidental bomb and making a cannon was that my grades in chemistry at school shot up and it became one of my best subjects.

Readers of this who were born in the seventies or later, might find it almost unbelievable that we were making bombs and cannons as children, but we were not alone. It was a major craze of the time. I discovered that there were several bomb making groups at my school and that it was a common subject at break times. It became such a problem nationally that the government ordered that a fire suppressant should be added to the weed killer so that it couldn't be used as a constituent in making explosives. Two other developments brought a swift end to this craze. First, there were some serious injuries to bomb makers and the other was the renewal of IRA activities and their use of bombs. This caused the police to take a lot more notice of random loud bangs. I never heard of any bombs made by children used to do harm to others, although several bomb makers did harm to themselves. We were all just budding scientists or engineers who wanted to experiment with readily available materials. Some years later, Brian would become an engineer working in research at Boots and I went to work in Research and Development at BPB Industries. So, our childhood experiments did have a positive outcome a few years later.

I can imagine that many readers will be shocked at what children got up to in the fifties and early sixties, but the parental attitude of the time was out of sight, out of mind. During school holidays it was quite normal for children to go off early in the morning and not return until teatime.

I was talking to my brother-in-law at a christening party for my grandchildren and he asked how the book was coming on, which sparked some childhood reminiscing. Bert is a few years older than me and grew up near Wymeswold. Wymeswold was the site of a World War Two air base. To reduce the damage inflicted by enemy air raids barrack huts and storage facilities were dispersed over a wide area of several miles around the air base. During the fifties although the base remained active it was much reduced in size with many huts on local farmland being just left abandoned. Bert told me how the local children used to go and play in them and regularly find clips of live ammunition and boxes of cordite left forgotten in these ramshackle huts.

Apparently, they collected empty shotgun cartridges tied a willow wand to a cartridge, so that it looked like a firework rocket. They then popped some cordite into the spent cartridge and used litmus paper from the school chemistry lab as fuse paper to ignite the cordite, which worked much better than any bought firework rockets.

There were apparently over eight hundred wartime airfields in the UK, so it seems logical that many other children had access to abandoned wartime ordinance. Imagine the outcry today if even one abandoned hut was found to have live ammunition left in it accessible to children let alone many hundred.

If the children of the day were a little feral then the Establishment of the day were also guilty of gross negligence that would have provoked a public enquiry and massive court cases if it had occurred today. But this was another time with different values.

Chapter 13

Motorcycle Days

From about the age of fourteen, I started to widen my circle of friends. Becoming friends with Brian Hinksman took me to Ruddington. Also, several of my classmates lived in Ruddington and they caught the same bus as me to and from school. There was also a group of girls who attended our sister school, Rushcliffe Grammar School for girls who resided in Ruddington. It was about this time that I started to go to Ruddington youth club or that's what I told my mother. I think it was every Thursday night and I would cycle there with strict instructions of what time I had to be home by. We didn't actually go to the youth club because that cost money, so we just hung about outside admiring the motorbikes of the older lads. It was outside the youth club that I met Mick Smeeton, another motorbike addict who became another lifelong friend. Again, the friendship was built around motorbikes and all things mechanical. Mick's older brother built and raced motorbikes which was just about the coolest thing in the world for a would-be motorcyclist. Mick would later introduce me to other unsung mechanical geniuses.

Steve Amos, my childhood friend had left Costock School and went to Harry Carlton Secondary School in East Leake. I was banned from setting foot in East Leake because my mother thought it to be a dangerous place after someone was stabbed there in the early days of us living on Bunny Hill. I think the main reason was that she never went to East Leake until my brothers went to secondary school there many years later. Mum did all her shopping in Ruddington, all our animal feed came from Bradwell's and our bread was delivered daily by Horspool's Bakery, all based in Ruddington. Mum liked Ruddington, so it was an ok place for me to go, mum didn't know East Leake, so it was not an ok place to go, end of story.

I desperately wanted to go to East Leake just because I was told not to. However, it was not an easy place to get to and still isn't even today from Bunny Hill if you have to use public transport, as there is no direct bus route. Although it is barely three miles from Bunny Hill, you have to catch a bus to Loughborough and then a bus back to East Leake a round trip of about 28 miles. Steve had two likeminded petrol head friends in East Leake who needed to escape from the watchful eye of their strict mother so by a twist of fate we all started to meet up in Costock, although nobody lived in that village. There was another reason we were attracted to Costock and that was the Generous Britton Pub. The landlord was a black man of African descent. It was a real novelty as we had never seen, let alone met a black person ever in our lives. We called him the "Choco" but never to his face. He was a nice affable guy and very easy-going when it came to underage drinking hence the attraction. It became our meeting place, inside if the bar was empty, or in the car park if there were customers. We renamed the pub the "Choco's" it was always "see you at the Chocó's tomorrow". It sounds so racist these days but, in the sixties, it was quite normal.

When I was about fifteen, we acquired a new friend, John Stevenson, who was a friend of Mick Smeeton, and John had a Ford 15cwt van big enough to transport us all to exotic destinations, such as Skegness, Matlock and Santa Pod Raceway, the home of Drag Racing.

I believe that Santa Pod Raceway is still going strong even to this day. For mechanical minded teenagers it was a Mecca, massive gleaming chromium plated engines supercharged and running on nitro fuel. Engines belched flames from their exhausts and reached speeds in excess of 200mph in a quarter of a mile from a standing start. So fast that they needed to deploy a parachute to stop. Sometimes, these highly tuned engines would explode in a ball flames as they tore down the track following a catastrophic mechanical failure. All thrilling stuff for budding mechanical engineers.

One Christmas, a small group of us decided we needed to get away from our families, so we decided to drive to Mablethorpe for Christmas Day in John's van. Armed with sleeping bags, we set off on Christmas Eve with the plan of waking up on the beach Christmas morning. Just outside Lincoln we stopped for a drink at a local pub. It was supposed to be a quick one, but we stayed to well after closing time as there was a good party atmosphere. We joyfully set off into the night full of excitement about our adventure. Not long after we left the pub, John announced we needed petrol. We drove several more miles but no sign of an open petrol station. It was then that we realised we were on a very unpopulated road. After much discussion we decided to pullover and kip down for the night and then ask at a local house in the morning where on earth we might find a petrol station open on Christmas Day. Next day we got our answer, nothing at all nearby, our best bet was to turn back and try Lincoln. They also had to ask what on earth we were doing driving on a lonely road on Christmas Day with an empty fuel tank, surely, we must have known all the petrol stations closed early on Christmas Eve and nearly all were closed all Christmas Day. Yes, we realised that now, but we were so focused on our adventure that none of us gave it a thought.

We drove very slowly back to Lincoln and after making several more enquiries we finally found our saviour petrol station. It was touch and go as we had been running in the red for far too many miles. Filling up took up most of our spending money and the coast seemed to have lost its appeal, so we slunk home and tried to avoid our friends because we had bragged incessantly about our great Christmas adventure over the preceding weeks driving them all mad. Oh well! We all learned a few lessons in life for the future.

My First Drive up to Matlock on my BSA C15 was one of the most exhilarating things that I had done so far in my life. First, I had to negotiate the outskirts of Nottingham, a rather frightening experience after my normal country roads but then I hit a new section of dual carriageway that allowed me to fully open my throttle and keep it open for a sustained length of time. My speed slowly increased to the dizzying heights of over 60mph. As it crept passed 65mph the noise became deafening and the bike started to shake and vibrate violently. I thought the engine was about to disintegrate so I abandoned my attempt at the world speed record and throttled back to a safer 45mph. The engine seemed to be running fine, although when I glanced down at it, I could see oil leaking out of several more places than usual. The closer I got to Matlock, the more I understood why bikers loved to drive up there. The scenery just got better and better and the continuous sweeping bends were motorcycling heaven.

To my surprise, I discovered that the main place of pilgrimage for bikers was not Matlock town itself but Matlock Bath, an old Victorian spa resort that had reinvented itself as a mini Skegness in the Dales with amusement arcades and ice cream parlours. The Heights of Abraham loomed high above the resort giving it a spectacular back drop whilst at the foot of the Heights flowed the beautiful river Derwent. The roadside parking was full of hundreds of gleaming proper motorcycles, their owners clad in black leather jackets decorated with silver studs. They looked very intimidating but the fact that many were enjoying an ice cream made me think, perhaps they were not as fierce as they looked. I definitely felt at the very bottom of the pecking order as I chugged into town on my 250cc BSA C15 complete with L plates.

Motorcyclists had a bad name in the sixties mainly because of the running battles that took place at the south coast London resorts, such as Southend, Margate and Brighton, between the Rockers and the Mods. However, as I spent time with motorcyclists around my area, I found them far more interested in things mechanical than fighting, although there was no denying, that there were a few hell raisers around as well.

When motorbiking in the Peak District, if you broke down, which was a common occurrence in those days, it wouldn't be long before a fellow biker would pullover and offer help either lending tools or their knowledge.

After several trips to Matlock and the surrounding areas, we started to hear tales of underground cave systems and disused mine tunnels from Fluorspar mining. The mining tunnels were easy to find and at that time you could happily explore them without asking any permission. Looking back, two or three teenage lads, disappearing into old mine workings without telling anyone about what they were up to, and only kitted out with a dodgy pushbike lamp was not the safest thing to do, but to us it was very exciting, and we thought it was very a very cool thing to do.

During our exploration of these mines, we met likeminded fellows who were happy to share knowledge with fellow explorers. One piece of information led us to the location of an entrance to a cave system. It was on private land and if caught you would be in trouble. To locate the access to the caves you took a left turn off the A6 just before the bridge over the Derwent River in Matlock itself and then climbed steeply up the narrow lane until you could look down over the whole of Matlock. I can't recall the exact location of the entrance to the cave system, but it was on rough ground that had been spoil heaps from the Fluorspar workings. The entrance was a hole in the ground a bit smaller than a well shaft. It was covered over with some rusty corrugated roof sheets. To access the cave system, you required a long rope. Luckily at that time, we had many long ropes that we used for sheeting down the hay and straw stacks and nobody noticed if one went missing.

As we entered the cave system, I was surprised how warm it was. I had expected it to be cold and damp, but the air felt dry and the temperature was warm and even. We made several trips into this system gradually pushing deeper and deeper into the myriad of caves. We soon met up with other caving enthusiasts in pubs and around the mining area. These guys were keen to share their knowledge with other enthusiasts and this gave us the confidence to explore even further. They also gave us wise safety tips, such as taking several backup torches plus food and water. They also recommended wearing boiler suits to keep us clean and prevent our clothes from snagging in tight situations. During one of these meetings with other cavers, we were told that you could access a new cave system if you were prepared to get wet. We knew exactly the place the guy was talking about. There was a large stream that came up from the ground at the end of a cave. It appeared to be a dead end but apparently if you climbed into the stream and went underwater for a few seconds you came up into a new cave system. This new knowledge both exited and terrified me. It terrified me for two reasons firstly I hated putting my head under water and secondly, I could not swim.

We all gathered around the pool where the stream disappeared into the rock. Nobody wanted to go first. We had been promised it was no more than a yard under the water before you gained access to the next chamber. Looking back, it was a bit like a scene from an Indiana Jones Film. Finally, I think it was John Stevenson who reluctantly volunteered to give it a try. He ducked down into the water and disappeared. We all stared into the pool for what seemed an age becoming more and more concerned. Finally, a flash of orange light appeared quickly followed by what at the time seemed to be an explosion as Johns' head burst upwards breaking the surface of the pool. The story was true, it was just a couple of feet under water and you were into the next cave system. John had been a long time because he was overawed by the new chamber. One by one we submerged ourselves and scrabbled under the rock. I went in the middle order so that someone could rescue me from either end if I had a panic attack. I had to have a bit of a sharp talk to myself before going under, but I eventually did it. The new chamber was wondrous, and we all agreed it was worth getting soaked for.

We explored the cave with our torches for about five minutes before taking the plunge again to retrace our steps. We had been warned not to linger in new chamber because if there was a storm above ground the water level could rise very quickly making difficult to get back out and possibly drown. We made it back to the surface as quickly as possible as we were getting extremely cold in our wet boiler suits. Thankfully, it was still warm and sunny when we came out, so we stripped down to our underpants and lay on the hillside sunbathing until we had warmed up and dried our clothes. We all felt a great feeling of elation, we had done something dangerous and seen something few others had seen, and we had survived. In short it had been a great adventure.

My caving period ended abruptly some months later. We were exploring some disused fluorspar mine workings near to Matlock. The tunnel got smaller and smaller the deeper we penetrated the mine. In the end we were crawling along on our bellies. We wriggled along on for a brief time, but it was not very exciting so after many contortions we all managed to turn around and start to make our way back to the surface. Not long after our change of direction, there was a terrible rumbling noise and the walls of the tunnel started to vibrate. I panicked and in seconds had squeezed over the top of the lead explorer and made for the surface at the speed of a bolted rabbit. I honestly thought we were going to die, and that part of the tunnel had collapsed. The roof and the walls appeared to be moving. When I reached the surface, I instantly realised what had caused all the panic. There was a huge thunderstorm directly above the entrance to the tunnel. It was a clap of thunder we heard, not a rock fall and the powerful sound wave must have shaken our bodies giving the illusion of the walls moving. I now know this for a fact because later in my life I worked in the research department for British Gypsum and several times I experienced the moving walls illusion when they blasted the rock face during visits to various Gypsum Mines. Now I think about it, they were always just about to blast every time I had to visit a mine, perhaps the miners found it funny to scare the shit out of wimpy office whallahs.

So that was the end of my caving career, I was deeply embarrassed about my panic attack and very shaken for several days afterwards. Writing about this today it seems crazy what we did, not telling anyone where we were going and having no safety equipment but that was the norm in those days health and safety just didn't exist at all. You never thought "what if", you just did it!...

My first six months of motorcycling were very pleasant but as winter came, I started to see the downside of this mode of transport. The winter of 1967/68 was cold and very snowy although it was nowhere near as bad as the 1963/64 winter.

When I left school, I had started to help the builders that were building the new clubhouse at the stables and this turned into an offer of a full-time job when they had completed it. Albert Thorpe (Bert) and his Uncle John were jobbing builders working mainly for the farming community in the villages close to their base at Six Hills near Wymeswold. That summer was a wonderful time for me, it was a long hot summer, I had my motorbike to get around and I was earning very good money.

Having money allowed me to branch out and explore different experiences. On one occasion Bert asked me if I fancied a trip to Margate. I had never heard of Margate, but he told me it was a seaside town near London and a friend who was holidaying down there had invited him to come down for the weekend, he wondered if I fancied a weekend away as he was driving down on his own. Up for anything at that period in my life I said yes. We spent most the evening in the Hammer and Pinchers at Wymeswold before setting off to drive through the night down to Margate. Bert's car was quite old, and he was not the fastest of drivers also the roads down to Margate were all very windy single carriageway A and B roads, so the trip took most of the night.

It was an eventful trip. We had planned to find a pub on the way down and stop for a drink just before closing time however, at the vital time roadside pubs seem to have vanished into thin air so we continued into the night with an ever-increasing thirst. At about one o' clock in the morning we rounded a sharp bend and came to a screeching halt as a policeman stepped out into the road and signalled us to stop. The road ahead was lit up by car headlights and blue flashing lights, the policeman told us to stop and wait, as there had been an accident up ahead. Bert looked across and said "Good job we didn't stop and have that late drink" a few minutes passed and then we were waved on. As we passed the accident, it was not what we expected to see. We were expecting to see two cars that had crashed into each other, but there was just one car with its back end sticking out of a gaping hole in the side of a house. Steam and dust could be seen rising into the cool night air and accentuated by a pool of bright light from a searchlight mounted on the attending fire engine. An elderly couple in dressing gowns shuffled about in what had been their garden. We moved slowly past aghast at what we saw, with the bright lights it resembled a film set. We drove on into the night not speaking and slightly shocked.

About an hour later just as the first streaks of dawn were appearing in the night sky, I awoke from a fitful doze with a mouth so dry that it felt like my mouth had been filled with plaster. As I rubbed my face and neck muscles back to life, I asked Bert if he had anything to drink in the car hoping for lemonade or orangeade. After about half a mile of deep thought he suggested that I have a furtle about under my seat, if I was lucky, I might find a pint bottle of Guinness, he thought it was there a few weeks ago but he might have drunk it already. As luck would have it was still there and with the aid of a screwdriver, I flipped off the crown top. The bottle was warm and well shuck up, so it foamed up like champagne, I quickly stuck the bottle into my mouth so as not to waste any. I had never tasted Guinness before, and bottled Guinness was a very different drink to the draught that we drink today. My first taste was like strong black coffee with some rust added and if I had not been so thirsty, I would have spat it out. "God this is awful, I think it has gone off" I said as I choked. Bert beckoned for me to pass the bottle over and took a good swig. "Nothing wrong with that but it is an acquired taste he declared. As a sixteen-year-old I could not lose face, so I asked for another swig. It tasted just as awful and I almost gagged, but I told Bert it tasted better, and that I might be getting a taste for it.

After a few wrong turns we eventually arrived in Margate and joined Bert's pal and his young family for breakfast. It was another glorious day, so we all went straight to the beach. Having two much younger brothers myself I was happy to help out entertaining our guests children. I played games with the kids until Bert shouted that the pubs were open. When I returned the kids to their mother who had been taking a well-earned rest in her deck chair, she burst out laughing. When I asked what was so funny, she explained that Bert, myself and her husband who also worked in the building trade stood out like sore thumbs on the beach. When I asked why? She replied "Have you not noticed that you are the only ones on the beach who have heavily tanned upper bodies and lily-white legs" when I looked at my two pals, I had to admit we did look very strange!

In the pub I ordered a pint of Guinness to prove my manhood and cover up my young age of only sixteen. This Guinness was the draught variety, cold and much more palatable but I still could not say that it tasted nice. Later in the afternoon I was enticed into trying to drink a yard of ale, which is not a good idea after several hours drinking. I nearly managed it until I just tilted the glass a bit too much and large wave of beer rolled down the yard and hit me in the face causing me to gag, run outside, and be sick, to the accompaniment of loud cheers and much laughter.

When we returned home, I continued my quest to get to like Guinness and become a man! It seems strange logic now but when you are sixteen and just joining adult society you do have strange ideas. I got gradually used to the bitter/coffee taste and started to enjoy it. Working in the building industry we drank a lot of beer both at lunchtimes and in the evenings, after my change to drinking Guinness I started to get nosebleeds. The nosebleeds gradually became longer and more frequent. My worst lasted a whole day, and I used a whole toilet roll try to stem the blood flow. I started to stuff my pockets with toilet roll before I went out just in case, I got another nosebleed and I was seen regularly with bits of tissue struck up my nose.

This of course caused much hilarity amongst my friends who started to say that I was having a period and probably turning into a woman. My friends were so kind they even bought me a box of Tampax! It was my mother who suggested that my nosebleeds might be connected to drinking Guinness as it was often prescribed to people after operations to build up their blood. I stopped drinking the Irish nectar and the nosebleeds stopped. I still love a pint of Guinness especially when visiting Ireland but if I overindulge the nosebleeds return and I know it's time to stop.

I was self-employed and we shared out the money we made from each job. On big jobs we got staged payments every week, so I often had a regular wage but on smaller jobs we would get paid on completion. However, farmers are notoriously slow payers and it could be several months before we got paid for a job. Being a teenager, I spent all my money and was broke by the end of the week. We had two big jobs to start with wages every week. I lived like a king I was earning £20 per week; my friends were earning about £3 and ten shillings (50p). I partied every night and went to all the expensive clubs in Nottingham. It came as a sharp shock when the money stopped rolling in on a regular basis, friends expected drinks and girlfriends expected to be taken to nice places and I was skint. I even had to borrow money for petrol so that I could get to work. Luckily mum never pressed me for my board.

This was my first really tough time financially and it taught me a lesson that has stayed with me all my life. Never assume that the money will keep rolling in and always save for rainy days! As so often happens, the long sweltering summer gave way to a long cold winter. I had no idea how snow and frost affected the building industry. John had wisely kept some indoor jobs back for the winter but by Christmas these had all dried up. The new year started with my savings dwindling and threatening letters from the Department for National Insurance demanding that I pay my overdue stamps or be taken to court. In those days, if you were self- employed you had to buy a national insurance stamp from the Post Office every week and stick it into a card and I was months behind.

One day I got a call from Bert (Albert) to say we had an emergency inside job for the next day and if I wanted the work to meet him at Uncle Jonny's farm at 7.30am. I was desperate for the work and even though it had snowed overnight, I set out on my motorbike to drive to the farm at Six Hills. I travelled at a snail's pace as the roads all had a healthy covering of snow on them and it was bitterly cold. When I finally arrived at the farm gate, I discovered I couldn't move my body. I was so cold nothing on my body worked and when I came to a halt the bike fell over on top of me. As I lay in the snow, I gradually managed to start to work some blood back into my arms and legs. It was excruciatingly painful but eventually I managed to wriggle out from under the bike. I didn't have any strength in my arms or legs to pick the bike up, so I left it laying in the gateway and set out on foot to the farmhouse. Unfortunately, Johnny's house was very remote, two whole fields away from the road. My legs were not working properly, and I had frequent falls into the snow that was about six inches deep. I finally made it to the house. They were extremely surprised to see me as they had abandoned any thought of work after the overnight snow because they couldn't get the van off the farm. They sat me down in front of a roaring fire and fed me several cups of steaming hot sweet tea until I thawed out. All I could think about, was roll on the day when I would be old enough to drive a van with a heater!

The lane was the same lonely lane that I mentioned earlier when Dad abandoned me out hunting and I rode home on my own. This meant that my motorbike was fairly safe dumped in the farm gateway. In fact, when Bert and I went back to retrieve it, I was still the only idiot to have driven up the lane. I drove home with my feet sliding along the ground like two stabilising skis. I returned home in much the same condition as I had arrived at the farm. My love of motorbiking was rapidly diminishing.

It was during the first few months of 1968 when I had no income and I was stony broke, that the clutch cable broke on my motorbike and I could not afford to buy a replacement. In fact, I could not even afford the petrol to go to the shop in Carlton to buy one. I was surviving on odd job money and a very kind mother who didn't charge me my board and lodging. If my father had found out he would have gone ballistic, but I kept it a close secret just between mum and me. Determined not to be stranded on Bunny Hill, I developed a way of riding my C15 without a clutch.

I would push my bike as fast as I could and then vault onto to it and knock it into first gear with my foot. The bike would fire-up and we were off in first gear. Changing up through the gears was fairly easy by just accelerating hard and cutting the throttle for a split second whilst I changed up. Changing down through the gears was somewhat more difficult as you had to match you revs with the road speed. This led to a few interesting experiences in the early days, but my gearbox survived, and I was soon going up and down through the gears as if I had a working clutch. Traffic lights and junctions however were a real challenge in that I had to cut my engine and flick the bike into neutral and then coast to a halt just using my brakes. This took time to master and a lot of careful forward thinking. When the lights changed, I had to repeat the running and vaulting to get going again. I got some strange looks from my fellow road users but was never challenged. My cover story was that I had a flat battery so need to bump start my bike. I left the broken cable in place so that I could claim it had just broken if stopped by the Police.

Somehow during those winter months, I managed to scrape enough money to change my 250cc C15 for the 600cc Norton sidecar combination. My C15 was a desirable bike and the Norton very unfashionable so the price difference was not too great. This meant I didn't have to find hardly any extra money to make the change. This bike ended my motorbiking days in a terrifying way as I described earlier.

Both my Mother and Father were keen for me to pass my car driving test for different reasons. Mum hated me riding a motorbike and was worried about my safety as several of my friends had been killed or seriously injured riding motorbikes in the brief time that I had been riding one. After my crash I had to agree she had a point. Dad's reasons were purely mercenary, as always Dad saw me as a source of cheap labour. If I passed my test, then I could do lots more jobs for him. Whatever their reasons, they paid for me to have driving lessons and I passed my driving test about six weeks after my seventeenth birthday and thus ending my motorcycling days.

Sam Humphrey

Chapter 14

Guns and Shooting

I seem to recall that we had guns around the house from the moment we arrived at Bunny Hill. In those days there was no requirement to keep shotguns locked in a cabinet. In fact, there was no licensing of shotguns until 1967. We always had a shotgun behind the kitchen door and at least another six in a cupboard in the conservatory all of varying calibres. The most common calibres were 12 bore, 16 bore and 20 bore. All of them were hammer guns, barrels side by side and most with damasked barrels and a trigger to fire each barrel. The damasked barrels were beautiful to look at and much thinner than modern shotgun barrels making the weapons much lighter.

These days, modern shot guns are hammer-less and most having one trigger which fires the first and then the second barrel, you can even select which barrel is fired first. The other significant difference is that most shotguns nowadays have their barrel placed on top of each other. This configuration is called over and under, whereas the older guns were side by side guns.

Dad also owned a BSA point 22 calibre rifle. It was a bolt action model with a clip in magazine that held five bullets. If you chambered a bullet into the barrel and then clipped in a full magazine it gave you six shots. We used to call chambering a bullet as having "one up the spout". It's a taboo practice today with health and safety, but in the fifties, it was common practice. Again, the rifle also resided behind the kitchen door ready for instant use on any crow or magpie that dared to land on our property. Dad did remove the magazine full of live rounds and put it on the mantelpiece in the kitchen for safety.

One day my sister Dawn, who was about four years old at the time, toddled into the kitchen. She was just big enough to reach the top of the mantelpiece if she stood on tiptoes. My mum saw it happen from across the kitchen. Dawn had grabbed the magazine full of bullets. Mum rushed towards her saying "Give that to me darling". Dawn, as toddlers often do, instantly tossed the magazine away. Straight into the burning coal fire! Mum quick as a flash grabbed hold of us both and thrust us through the door that led to the lounge and the bedrooms slamming the door behind us. She bustled us into the bedroom and sat us on the bed and then said to me, "Now think very carefully Mervyn" (she still insisted on using my real name long after everyone else had started to call me Sam), "how many bullets does the magazine hold". It was a question I could easily answer as Dad let me refill the magazine on a regular basis, so I told her five. I expected five loud cracks but all we got were a sort of "Pffutt" five times. After waiting a couple of minutes after the fifth "Pffutt" we returned to find several burning coals scattered around the hearth and kitchen floor. Mum quickly scooped them up into a metal dustpan and returned them to the fire. Remarkably, there was hardly any damage to the kitchen or the fireplace just a few scorch marks on the kitchen floorboards.

The biggest scorching, however, was left for Dad, but he just turned it around claiming that it was Mum's fault for not keeping a better eye on what the children were up to.

Dad got into more hot water with Mum over guns when someone lent Dad a 3 bore pistol. A three bore doesn't relate to size of the barrel bore like other shotguns. If it did it would be more like a miniature canon than a shotgun. The 3 bore, was actually somewhat smaller than a 410 and was known as a garden gun. It was in reality a miniature shot gun. The pistol version was used as a ratting gun. It was a strange weapon with a single barrel about 12 inches long and a curved handle. To fire it you pulled the hammer back to cock it (pulled it back until it locked back ready to fire) and then pulled the trigger. The short barrel meant that lead shot spread out very quickly giving it an effective killing range of only five yards, but it was great for fast moving rats inside our feed house. At the time, we were infested with rats and if you went into the feed house at night and switched on the light the floor and walls appeared to be alive and moving because of the vast number of rats!

The pistol was rusty when Dad got it, so he decided he would clean it up and oil it. Mum was reminding Dad that she had said over and over again that she would not have guns in the kitchen and Dad was saying that it was his kitchen as much as hers and that he would bloody well do as he pleased in his own house. Dad had used some wire wool to clean off the rust and then lavished plenty of oil all over all the metal parts. He was waiting for the oil to penetrate into the moving parts before wiping off the excess when he saw a rat on the bird table just outside the kitchen door. Dad was still ranting and raving at Mum as he loaded the pistol. He knew he only had a split second when he opened the kitchen door to get a shot off at the rat so started to cock the gun as he moved towards the door. He hadn't reached the middle of the kitchen before a loud bang frightened us all to death. Mum screamed and staggered back stumbling over a chair. At first, I thought Dad had shot Mum but thankfully it was just the bang that made her jump back into to chair, but it was a very close thing.

What had happened was that Dad's thumb had slipped off the oil covered firing hammer whilst cocking it. Although nobody was hurt, we were all very shaken and to make matters worse, Dad had blasted Mum's silver-plated tea caddy clean off the work surface. The tea caddy had belonged to my grandmother and had great sentimental value. It now lay on the kitchen floor, tea spilling out of it and peppered with deep dints. I decided it was time for a sharp exit as a mighty row was about to explode!

The shot blasted tea caddy remained in use for over forty years and Mum took great delight in retelling the story every time anyone asked what on earth happened to her tea caddy.

Guns are dangerous things and anyone using a gun must always put safety first. Dad drilled gun safety into me from an early age. Never walk with your gun cocked and only cock it when you are about to fire. Always break your gun and remove the cartridges before climbing over a fence or opening and shutting a gate. Never ever point a gun at someone whether it's loaded or not. And finally, always think about what is behind your target before you pull the trigger and think about the range of your weapon. This last piece of advice was particularly important when firing the .22 rifle as it had a potential killing range of one mile. Although I mention cocking shot guns, it is very rare to see this type of gun anymore, as all the modern guns are now made with what is called a hammerless action which means that the firing mechanism is now hidden inside the gun. The firing pins are armed by opening and shutting the gun. You then have a safety catch to stop the gun being fired accidentally which is pushed forward just before firing.

I have sadly witnessed two people being shot. They were not seriously injured but the outcome could have been much worse. The first time I saw someone shot was when I was about nine years old. A group of us were out shooting, armed with air rifles and we had drifted onto an area of rough ground covered with gorse bushes and brambles at the end of Bunny New Wood. The area was known locally as the Bumpy grounds. There were deep round hollows covering the whole of this area which we were convinced had been caused by German bombs during WW2. It was only fifteen years since the end of the war and machine gun posts were a common site on the hills around Bunny, laid out to defend the Ransom and Marles factory. The factory still stands to this day on the East Leake to Bunny Lane and is now called the Appliance Warehouse. Much later in life, I discovered the true cause of the hollows. They were caused by the quarrying of the local grey stone that lies just a few feet under the surface.

As we stalked rabbits, a sudden argument broke out, as happens with groups of children. It started to peter out until there were just two shouting at each other. They were the eldest and youngest, the eldest was remorselessly belittling the other to the point that the youngest threatened to shoot the eldest if he didn't shut up. The rest of us were horrified by this ugly turn of events and tried to calm things down, but the eldest just sneered and kept saying he would not dare over and over again. His opponent pulled the trigger! It was at about five yards range and the older boy let out a scream and doubled up onto his knees holding his side. We dived over and wrenched the gun from the younger lad. He was screaming that he didn't mean to do it while the other lad just kept saying, "He shot me!" over and over again. We had no sympathy with either of them. After removing the shot lad's jacket and shirt, we were surprised to find nothing more than small red area about the size of a sixpence and no broken skin. Luckily the air-rifle was an old small .177 with a worn-out spring. The pellet hadn't even penetrated the clothing. The older shot lad was very embarrassed about his screaming for such a small mark and the younger mortified at what he had done. When things calmed down both were remorseful, they made up and we all agreed to keep silent about the incident as we all realised that our parents would confiscate our air-rifles if the incident became public knowledge.

We were not a group of friends but all friends of friends and looking back I can see it was all about one person wanting to be top dog of this new group. As I trudged back home through the woods, the recent events swirling around in my head, I resolved to do my shooting on my own. I became a lone sniper!

Many years later, I re-joined the world of group shooting when Dad and I took a gun in a shooting syndicate in Lincolnshire, only to witness another shooting. The beaters were beating out a strip of woodland towards the line of guns lined out at the end of the wood. I was the last in in the line, standing about twenty yards out into the field. The next gun stood on the corner of the wood. Several birds had already been pushed over the guns and the beaters were now about fifty yards away. I had a clear view of what happened next standing out on point in the field. A pheasant broke cover from the side of the wood and turned back down the side of the wood away from the line of guns. My neighbouring gun was presented with a classic down the line shot. Only problem was that it was flying quiet low, but there was a clear view all the way down the side of the covert. He took the shot. At that very moment one of the beaters had met with an impenetrable block of thorns and stepped out of the wood and into the field right into the blast of pellets.

The beater fell back into the ditch screaming, the shooter, an elderly gentleman, stood rooted to the ground, transfixed by the horror of what he had done. Luckily none of the pellets struck the beaters' face and at over fifty yards, most of the energy of the shot had started to wane, that combined with the beaters' thick clothing, meant that thankfully it was more shock than bodily injury. His hands however did suffer some minor cuts.

Every time I take part in a formal shoot, that day haunts me. I always double check the position of my shooting colleagues and the position of the pickers up with their dogs behind us. Try to log in as much information as possible because game shooting is split second reaction and you need to have all your no shoot zones pre-programmed into your brain for when things get manic.

As children, we shot at virtually anything that moved, encouraged by my father and my uncles. It was Dad that taught me to shoot ducks on water with the rifle from a high vantage point, on the road bridge over Ravensthorpe Reservoir, telling me to aim at the waterline. We were shooting for much needed family food. In Ravensthorpe my grandparents village, game shooting etiquette was not mentioned, and I grew up believing that it was quite normal to shoot wildfowl whilst they were swimming on the water.

One day, when I was in our bar not long after it had opened, so I would have been 16/17 years old, someone commented he had seen a large number of ducks on some flood water near Bunny. This caused great excitement and plans were quickly put forward as to the best way to maximise our bag. I had just finished reading a book about wild fowling in Norfolk and how they used to use a punt gun to shoot many birds with just one shot. So, my suggestion was that a group of us creep up to the water's edge and on the count of three all fire our guns simultaneously.

A gentleman at the bar quickly scoffed at this suggestion saying very loudly, "You can't shoot ducks on water!" Completely misunderstanding his meaning, I instantly and proudly announced that, "Oh yes you can, you just have to aim a little lower!" The whole bar erupted in laughter, the joke was on me, but I had no idea why, until a kindly friend explained that in the world of game shooting one never shoots at birds unless they were flying it just wasn't sporting. My old friends still remind me of that almighty clanger that I dropped to this day.

All my country friends had air rifles from about the age of six. We shot mainly sparrows, starlings and wood pigeons. They were pests to the farmers, and we were actively encouraged to shoot as many as we could. The only way we could get close enough to shoot Wood Pigeons was to shoot them when they were sitting on the nest during the breeding season. This may seem rather barbaric in the nanny state world that we live in today, but it was actively encouraged by the Ministry of Agriculture in the post war era when home produced food was vitally important because the country had no money to import food. As kids, we were paid by farmers to go around the woods with long poles poking out the pigeons nests to stop them breeding. Another common practice was to climb up the trees to the nests and tie the squabs (unfledged chicks) to the nest and then harvest them for food when they were fully grown. Food rationing continued after the war until 1954 and food was expensive and in short supply until the sixties.

As I got older, I progressed from the smaller .177 to the larger .22 calibre air rifle and was finally allowed a 410 shotgun when I was ten. In later years, I had access to whatever shot guns dad had. Over my teenage years, I shot guns with a range of bores from 12 bore being the largest through 16 bore 20 bore 28 bore and the smallest being the 410, there was also the 3 bore pistol, which was even smaller. We also had an air rifle that was way ahead of its time called a Crossman. It had an under-leaver action but instead of locking back a spring that fired the plunger that compressed the air to fire the pellet, this lever worked a pump to compress air into a small firing chamber. The more you pumped, the more power you got. It was an awesome bit of kit: extremely powerful and deadly accurate because you didn't get the usual air rifle recoil from the spring. It was the fore runner of the modern gas-powered air rifles of today. The Crossman was so powerful that police decided that it was a lethal weapon and classed it along with high powered hunting rifles, so that you needed a police firearms certificate to own one. Sad but great fun while it lasted!

When I was in my twenties, I went to visit my old jousting buddy Clive Broadbent who had emigrated to West Virginia. Knowing my interest in guns, he arranged for me to shoot a Colt 45 that belonged to a friend of his. I stood 15 metres away from a huge metre square target. I thought that this was ridiculously close but after shooting off all six rounds I was mortified to discover that not one of my shots had hit the target let alone the bullseye that I had been aiming at. The owner told me not to be too downhearted as all the shooting in westerns was laughable and that gunfights were fought at distances of feet rather than yards. My love of westerns sadly waned after that day.

People and governments are motivated by the terrible atrocities committed by people with a gun and laws have been passed to restrict to ownership of guns. We now have some of the most stringent gun licensing laws in the world. However, nearly all gun crime is committed with illegal weapons that are unlicensed and smuggled into Britain from Eastern Europe. I found this article on the Internet about our gun laws. It makes frightening reading and I will leave you to make up your mind whether it all makes sense

A Brief History of British Gun Control
(or, How to Disarm the Law-Abiding Populace by Stealth)
by P.A. Luty

www.thehomegunsmith.com

Attribute to *The Libertarian Enterprise*

In 1900 the British government trusted the people with firearms and to be their own guardians. Prime Minister Robert Gascoyne-Cecil, the Marquess of Salisbury said he would "laud the day when there was a rifle in every cottage in England". However, in 1903 Britain passed its first ever "gun control" law, a minor one requiring a permit to carry a handgun and restricting the age of purchasers. It was the first toe over a slippery slope towards *complete firearms prohibition.*

In 1919 the British government, in fear of communist insurgents and domestic and foreign anarchists, passed its first sweeping anti-gun laws (*under the smokescreen of crime control*) even though gun related crime was almost non-existent in the England of the day. British subjects could now only buy a firearm if they could show "*a good reason*" for having one and the firearm certificate system that we have today (implemented and abused by police) was introduced. The 1920-gun control act was the beginning of the end for private firearms ownership in England. So much for Robert Gascoyne-Cecil's remarks of "a rifle in every cottage in England" being a laudable goal.

In 1936 short barrelled shotguns (such as shot pistols used for ratting) and fully automatic firearms were outlawed. Why? Not because such firearms were ever misused but because the government dictated that civilians had *"no legitimate reason"* for owning them. Where have we heard that before! Another slide down the slippery slope. The reasoning has now changed from the government NEEDING TO SHOW REASONS FOR THE RESTRICTIONS to the people NEEDING TO SHOW REASONS TO EXERCISE THEIR RIGHTS, to a government TELLING them that there was NO ACCEPTABLE REASON.

The English Bill of Rights states "That the subjects which are Protestants may have arms for their defence, suitable to their condition and as allowed by law" Sir William Blackstone, commenting on this in his Commentaries on the laws of England said, "The fifth and last auxiliary RIGHT of the subject, that I shall at present mention, is that of having arms for their defence, suitable to their condition, and as allowed by law, which is also declared by the same statute IW & M ft.2c.2 and is indeed a public allowance, under due restrictions, of the *natural right of resistance and self-preservation*, when the sanctions of society and laws are found insufficient to restrain the violence of oppression". I wonder what happened to *"the natural RIGHT of resistance and self-preservation"* (from domestic criminals and out of control governments). Have not the "sanctions of society and laws" been shown "insufficient to restrain the violence of oppression"?

In 1936 the government added a "safe storage" requirement on the owners of handguns and rifles to "prevent the guns falling into the wrong hands". Where have we heard that one before, and how often do the British police use that particular requirement to harass what is left of the British gun owning community?

As a direct consequence of the 1920-gun control act, not only did Britain not have "a rifle in every cottage" but they had to ask American citizens to send them every type of rifle and handgun at the outbreak of WWII, so British people would have some means of defending their homes and islands against the Nazi hordes massing across the English Channel. Americans responded by sending every type of firearm to the unarmed and helpless people of Britain. No surprise, but at the end of the war the British people did not get to keep the guns, the government seized many of them back and dumped them in the sea. Such was the British government's gratitude to the American public and distrust of their own people.

In 1946 "self-defence" was no longer considered a good reason for requiring a police officer issued firearms certificate. The slippery slope got even steeper.

In 1953 carrying any type of weapon for self-defence was made illegal, making the streets even safer for the criminal element and giving great "crime control" soundbites to the police and press.

In 1967 a chap by the name of Harry Roberts blasted three policemen to death in a London street using a 9mm Luger pistol and the British government restricted *shotguns* for the very first time. Try to figure out the logic... handgun used... shotguns licensed for the first time in British history. Opportunistic, or am I just being a cynical bastard?

In 1982 black powder muzzle loader shooters and hand loaders were required to allow police inspection of their security arrangements to ensure "safe storage" of the powder they possessed, meaning that agents of the state could demand entry into an Englishman's home at any time of day or night without a warrant.

In 1988 all semi-automatic rifles were banned, including pump action rifles. The private property of law-abiding people was once again outlawed and seized. All the guns were registered and easy to find, that is to say, *all the legally held ones*.

In 1996 *all handguns* were banned, and they too were all registered with the agents of the state. Well, need I say more? You get the picture. Also, in 1996 carrying any knife with a blade longer than 3 inches was made illegal. Presumably one cannot stab someone to death with a three-inch knife. You now had to show *"good reason"* for carrying a knife, the presumption of innocence, until proven guilty of a crime, was gone.

In England today, you cannot carry any type of weapon for self-defence and you cannot use a firearm to defend your home, family, or property. The gun and weapon laws have made crime safe for criminals and the other violent thugs and miscreants who infest our country today.

In 2006 the government passed the Violent Crime Reduction Act. The VCRA restricted all "realistic" toy/replica guns. Now Britons were not to be trusted with even imitation non-firing replicas. "Violent crime reduction" was once again used as the smokescreen to enact oppressive laws and deprive the law abiding of their property. As part of the VCRA an airgun can no longer be purchased by mail order and the name and address of the purchaser must be registered with the seller. *Is the bigger picture now getting clearer?*

In 2009 talks with the British government were started to devolve airgun laws to the Scottish parliament. If and when the Scottish parliament is given the power over airgun legislation the Parliament has vowed to ban the sale of all airguns in Scotland. In the coming years, England will follow the Scottish example and airgun registration and an eventual licensing system will follow. The slippery slope is now in a vertical freefall.

Am I suggesting that there has been some nefarious plan all along to disarm and subjugate the British people? Yes, partly. I am also suggesting that this is a cycle of government behaviour long recognised, one we should be paying attention to, and breaking. We KNOW what governments do; they acquire power at the expense of the governed. They do it slowly, almost imperceptibly, and usually for nefarious reasons and political expediency.

You can always rely on your *Expedient Homemade Firearms* book though, can't you? They would not dare to ban books, would they? Oh yes, it's already started.

Don't say I didn't warn you

****

Another interesting fact that I discovered when visiting friends in Switzerland was that every adult male in the country had to do military training every year. They are required to keep rifles, pistols, and in some cases machine guns at their home along with extensive amounts of ammunition. Despite having the highest gun home ownership in Europe, they also have I am told the lowest gun crime.

I think our politicians have got it very wrong!!!

Sam Humphrey

Chapter 15

Starting to work for a living

I had been required to do work from an early age. It was entirely unpaid work as I didn't even get pocket money until I was ten. Whenever I brought up the subject of pocket money I was always directed to dad as he held the family purse strings and those strings were always pulled very tightly closed. The reason he always gave me for not getting pocket money or wages was that I had much more than the children that got pocket money. I had a pony and that cost a lot to buy and keep. The fact that I didn't like riding and never asked for a pony was dismissed out of hand. The truth was that I was made to ride and school the ponies so that dad could sell them on at a profit. I was constantly told that this pony was mine only to find out that dad had sold it after a few weeks as soon as it started to go nicely. The only time a got to keep a pony was if it was a bit quirky and nobody wanted to buy it.

I was never given pocket money ever, I always had to earn it and I believe that is correct. I strongly believe that children should be taught basic economics at an early age. If the family is short of money, explain this to your children and they will understand. I always treat children as adults when I talk to them and never lie to them about unsavoury subjects. I was lied to by well-meaning teachers, clergymen and family friends and I have never ever forgiven any of them for thinking that I was so immature that I could not cope with the truth. Did they think that I was so gullible that I would just accept what they told me and not cross reference what they told me? When people lie to me, and that happens most days, I never contradict them, and I let them feel I believe what they say but the more they lie the more it amuses me. The respect for that person just keeps going further and further down.

My first job was collecting eggs. That was at an early age and a joy to do as it involved working with my mother. I also helped her wash the eggs and grade them into trays of small, medium and large ready for the egg man to come and collect them. It was quiet quality time with my mum.

As we moved from hens to pigs, I became involved in the feeding of the pigs. First, I would just feed the dry sow and weaner meal but later on as I got stronger, I would carry the buckets of whey. Whey is the by-product of cheese making and had a strong sour smell that made me wretch at first, but you soon became oblivious of the smell. Pig shit and hen shit also had the same effect on me. Unfortunately, other people didn't become "nose blind". Once I overslept and fed the pigs in my school uniform. When I caught the bus to school, I started to notice people that sat down close to me got up and moved away after a few moments of sitting in close proximity to me. My towny friends at school were more direct saying, "Get lost you stink." Some years later, the local bus company contacted us saying there had been complaints from passengers about the smell of horses and could our staff change out of their work clothes before using the bus. The staff at that time were all girls and were mortified that their smell was offensive to others, again they had just got used to the smell. My wife Louise had to change her clothes in the porch before entering her house because her parents could not stand the smell.

My father was always coming up with money making ideas for me and to avoid giving me pocket money, some of these have already been mentioned. As I got into my early teens, I took over the most lucrative job which was bagging and selling old horse manure. I placed adverts in local papers and hired drivers to help me deliver the bags to allotments and gardens. Dad always wanted his cut but at least I got my hands on the cash first. A couple of years later, when dad bought and an old Thames Trader tipping lorry, I started delivering in bulk. It was great. I loaded the lorry using a tractor with a hydraulic muck fork in about ten minutes, whereas bagging the same amount of muck would take half a day. Also, we didn't have to carry the bags on and off the horsebox. We could get two large loads of manure on the tipping lorry; I always loaded a generous amount of muck and with carful manoeuvring of the tipper we could tip half a load at one address and then the other half at another.

Once, at our second and final delivery of the day, we got a really fussy and demanding client. He wanted us to carefully tip the manure onto his drive but also make sure that none of it spilt onto his precious lawn. He also expected us to then wheelbarrow it up his drive, around the side of the house and then up to the far end of his very long garden. We told him our boss insisted that we were paid before we actually tipped the muck from the lorry. He duly paid us and then we informed him that we didn't carry a wheelbarrow. That was no problem, he had one at the top of the back garden and off he went to get it. As soon as he was out of sight, we quickly tipped the muck in his drive and onto his precious lawn. We then raced off down the road with the tipper still coming down before he had chance to stop us. After that, I always made it clear that we tipped on the road or in the drive and they were responsible for moving it. Several customers were not expecting such a large amount of muck and actually paid us not to tip it all. We delivered all over Nottingham and met some really lovely people, especially at allotments. When delivering to allotments, we often picked up several more orders from other allotment holders when they saw it was genuine well-rotted horse manure.

I looked into buying a bagging plant and a heat sealer for the plastic bags so that I could stockpile bagged manure. Unfortunately, the cost of the equipment and printed bags were way out of my budget. I recently saw bagged horse manure at a nursery, and it made me think that I was 50 years too early and what if....

I learned to drive and mend many different motorised vehicles, and this led me into several short-term jobs. Although at school I hated anything to do with the stage or acting, I realise that in my teenage years I did several things that prepared me for what was to come later I my life.

The first happened when I was sixteen. Dad had just bought a Ford Thames Trader tipping lorry on the strength of a pal saying he had loads of work for a tipping lorry and dad could make some easy money. The first job was at a concrete works in Sileby near Leicester. The job was due to start on Monday but on the Sunday, dad injured his eye and had to stay in hospital for the whole week. Before he went to hospital, he took me to one side and told me that if they kept him in hospital, I would have to do the job. It was all on a private site, so I didn't have to worry about a licence and his pal who had persuaded him to buy the lorry had all the details. He was sure his pal would drive the lorry over to the site and mum would ferry me back and forth for the duration, which was a week's contract. When I contacted dad's pal, he gave me precise instructions of where to go, what job I was doing and who to report to, but unfortunately, he was unable to drive the lorry over to the site as he was already committed to being elsewhere. I tried several other friends, but all declined as it was such short notice. Dad had impressed on me how important this job was, because without it he couldn't pay for the lorry. I decided the only thing I could do was to risk driving the lorry the seven miles to the site myself.

Mum was very against the idea but understood the implications for the family if I didn't do it. So, after much discussion, it was agreed that I would drive over to the site.

With a cushion under my bum to make me look taller and my flat cap perched jollity on the side of my head like a proper lorry driver, I set off to work. I left very early in the morning to avoid any traffic and was waiting at the site gate long before the site opened. The site manager was impressed but commented that I looked a bit young. I told him I was eighteen, but my nickname was Tiny as I looked so young and small. The job was very simple. A building was being demolished and the rubble was loaded onto my lorry and I took it about a quarter of a mile to a tip on the site where defective or damaged concrete products were disposed of. After I had tipped the rubble, another machine pushed it over the edge and levelled it out. Everything went fine and even my story of being called Tiny seemed to be holding up in the canteen as I fended off endless questions about my age. Luckily, I sat with the men I was working with during break time in the canteen and they started to stick up for me, telling the others that I was a good driver and to leave me alone. All went well until the very last day late in the afternoon. The job was all but finished, I was backing up to make my tip when there was a big crash and I came to an abrupt stop. I jumped out of the lorry thinking that I had backed into something, but I was sure that is was clear behind when I had started to reverse.

When I got to the back of the lorry, I got the emotions of relief and horror simultaneously. I had not crashed into anything, relief. However, both back wheels had disappeared into the ground, horror! What had happened was that a large diameter pipe had been dumped at some time in the past and levelled into the tip. I had backed over it many times not knowing that it lurked under the road before it had finally collapsed. Two big machines had to be diverted from other work to get the lorry out of the chasm and it took over an hour before I was pulled and lifted out. Luckily there was no damage to the lorry. Unfortunately, the incident disrupted production and the plant manager became involved. The pipe should never have been buried whole in the first place and he was going to have to explain the loss of production. Everyone was looking for a scapegoat. I was the outsider and it looked like I was going to be that scapegoat.

I knew I was in deep trouble. The manger tried to say that it was my inexperience that had caused the accident, but the other lorry drivers backed me up saying that there was no way I could have known about the pipe. To save face the manager brought up my youthful looks again and demanded to see my driving license. From somewhere I summoned up a confident look and said, "No problem, I don't have it with me, but I will bring it in Monday morning." I didn't have a problem, I finished the job later that afternoon, dad was out of hospital, mum drove him over to collect the lorry and I went home with mum in the car. Job done!

Another job that dad got me was cleaning old bricks. This involved chiselling all the old mortar off lorry loads of bricks that came from demolished old houses so that they could be reused in the restoration of other historic houses. It was a dusty, painful job with sore fingers and knuckles but most of all it was slow and boring. I was paid for every, one thousand bricks sorted to size, cleaned and stacked onto a pallet. The money was good, and I hired several of my friends to help me, but few lasted more than a couple of hours. Brian was my best helper as he would work as long as it took to meet my required quota if it meant it released me to go off and cause mischief with him. The spoil of this enterprise can still be seen in the two banks in the front field across the road from the stables know as Coopers.

Dad was always buying horses and getting me to school them on for re-sale, but like the pig enterprises. when it came to share the profits, nothing came my way due to unexplained expenses.

Although I had attained seven O levels and the school wanted me to stay on into the sixth form, I could not wait to leave. I had always felt an outsider, misunderstood by both students and teachers alike. For them it was A levels, University, get a nine to five job, live in suburbia, get married and have kids. They saw this as freedom, I saw it as being shackled. Dad couldn't wait for me to leave school and actively encouraged me to leave as he saw free labour. However, Mum wanted me to stay on as she still clung onto her civilised suburban roots. Dad's plans backfired immediately when he offered my services to the builders, who were extending our bungalow and building the new clubroom, for free to keep the costs down. After a few weeks, they offered me a place in their group. We shared all the money we earned from each job and I had my first real job. I have already mentioned this in my motorcycle days, and only mention it for the sake of continuity in this chapter.

As the harsh winter closed down all building for several months, I started to understand the downside to the building trade. I still had no ideas about a career, only that I did not want to work for dad as I knew he would not pay me on a regular basis. My girlfriend of the time was also pushing me to get a more respectable job now that the big money days of the summer had come to an end. She lived in West Bridgford and had the suburban mind set of to get a nice respectable, nine to five job, five and a half days a week and two weeks holiday per year etc, etc.

I decided to apply for an apprenticeship as an agricultural engineer at Sutton Bonnington School of Agriculture. In the interview, I proudly told them that I could weld with oxyacetylene and electric welders, could strip down and rebuild a tractor engine and that I was pretty good at spraying cellulose paint onto cars or tractors. I think that the two interviewers thought I was grossly exaggerating my skills and one came very close to calling me a liar, saying that he found it hard to believe that someone of my youthful age could have learnt such skills. Writing this now I suppose he just couldn't comprehend that I had started my real apprenticeship at about the age of eight. Thankfully I didn't get the apprenticeship.

The attitude of that lecturer and that of most of my teachers has ingrained in me a hatred of our education system. They all, especially in the 1960s, had a superior holier than thou attitude towards their students, expecting you accept everything they say as gospel. They just could not tolerate anyone that was a free thinker. They caused me to believe then and I still do to this day, that on the job training is much better than in the classroom for vocational careers. Lecturers have rarely run their own businesses, and they operate in the cloistered environment of the educational establishment with little knowledge of what goes on in the real outside world.

Sadly, this attitude prevailed in the British Horse Society with their exam systems as well, and was the reason that dad broke his links with them. It was a standing joke amongst the riding schools that if you wanted to ruin your business, employ a newly qualified person with the British Horse Society Assistant Instructors qualification. This sad state of affairs led to the formation of the Association of British Riding Schools who advocated practical workplace exams. Both types of exams were very popular and very different during the late sixties and seventies but constant changes in government policies, introducing NVQs and then UK coaching levels and now we are back to Apprenticeships, have caused even further confusion. Yet another totally unforeseen action and I am not sure who started it, the colleges or the government. Was that Agricultural colleges started to offer a whole raft of equine courses right up to degree courses. This has been the go-to place for every horsey girl wishing to avoid getting a job for another two or three years. Although many of these students get jobs in industries that service the equestrian industry, hardly any of them come back to the industry as grooms which is what we really need. Sadly, the racing industry in particular are having to import grooms from abroad, which is a crazy state of affairs.

During the spring and early summer of 1968, I did everything and anything to earn a bit of money. The National Insurance office was still chasing me for my stamp arrears, so a lot of my ad hoc earnings had to go on buying stamps to keep them off my back.

Our neighbour in Bunny Wood was Harry Murfitt. Harry who was a successful dealer in most goods had made enough money to buy the woodland that bordered our property to the north known as Bunny New Wood. Harry was trying to get planning permission to build a house in the wood. He had bought an old Drott (a tracked bulldozer) to clear his plot of trees and scrub. Like most things that Harry dealt in there was always a rub. The Drott had a blown cylinder head gasket and one of the tracks had a habit of coming off when you slewed to the right due to a worn drive cog that drove the left-hand track. To be honest nearly everything was about worn out on this machine.

Dad had several jobs that required a tracked bulldozer, so he and Harry did a deal. Like all deals between dealers, each thought that they had conned the other party and got the better side of the bargain. Dad and Harry did loads of vague deals and always ended up falling out when the deal actually happened as both of them had a radical differing view of what they had agreed to. In this case Dad had agreed to help Harry mend his Drott in exchange for him using it for free. What this actually meant was that I was dispatched into the woods to help Harry mend his Drott. However, it turned out that Harry had no mechanical knowledge, so it was me on my own. Harry's part of the bargain in his mind was that he would go and get the new or second-hand bits that I required. That was his part of the bargain, so you can see where this was going. Dad supplies me, Harry gets the parts, neither does any actual work. Me, I do all the work and get paid? Well not exactly, it turns out I get the privilege of driving the Drott which according to Dad and Harry will bring me riches beyond my belief. The fitting of the new cylinder head gasket was straightforward and easier than I had expected. It turned out that the Drott was powered by a small three-cylinder tractor engine similar to those that power the small Massey Ferguson 165 but the Drott's very low gearing meant the engine was powerful enough to get the job done.

Removing the steel track, however, was way beyond my know-

ledge, as was the removal of the main drive cog, so a more knowledgeable person was found, with me assisting him and Harry
watching as we struggled to split and remove the steel track. It
was at this moment that a car pulled into the gateway at the
bottom of the muddy track. Harry became very uneasy and I
thought that he was going to make a run for the trees but that
seemed very unlikely as I had never seen Harry move any faster
than a slow walk. "Oh shit! It's that bloody building inspector
again, don't say a word while I deal with this little pratt" said
Harry. The suited young man opened the car boot and changed
his highly polished shoes for a pristine pair of wellingtons before trudging up the slippery muddy track. All work ceased as
we watched him proceed towards us. We all hoped he would
fall flat on his face as everybody in the building trade hated
the building inspector. Unfortunately, he safely made it up the
hill and greeted Harry by saying, "Good morning Mr Brown is
Mr Murfitt about?" Harry replied by saying "Unfortunately you
have just missed him" the young inspector looked deflated and
enquired "You did give him the message that I was coming to
see him this morning" "Oh yes, but he is a very busy man, he
asked me to apologise to you. It was a real emergency." He
thanked Harry and trudged off down the hill back to the car.
Harry turned towards us grinning like a Cheshire Cat while we
retreated behind the Drott before breaking into muffled laughter. "Dozy B***er, that's the fourth time I've sent him away," said
Harry and making us laugh even more.

As the young inspector reached the car, another man got out
and confronted him, his load deep voice clearly audible to us at
the top of the hill. "Well what's Murfitt's excuse this time?" "Mr
Murfitt is away again," replied the young man. "But that is Mr
Mufitt you have just been talking to you idiot!" Boomed the man
that I now recognised as the Chief Building Inspector. I glanced
across at Harry, but Harry was gone! I thought what a shame, I
would have loved to hear him try and talk his way out of that
pickle.

After much cursing and a lot of big hammer use, we finally got the left track working properly and I got to drive the Drott. It was a revelation as I had never driven a tracked vehicle in my life before this. There was no accelerator you had to set your revs on a Rachet throttle. You steered the beast by disengaging the drive on the left track to turn left and vice-versa to turn right. To go forward or backwards you selected either high or low speed forward or reverse using a clutch. Finally, there was another lever that lifted and lowered the dozer blade. Once you got the hang of all the levers it was easy to drive. After two days of levelling piles of brick hardcore and knocking a few trees over on Harry's plot, I declared myself competent to do paying jobs.

Everything that Dad and Harry did was a bit dodgy, so things were never going to go smoothly. The first job was for a friend of a friend in a village near Melton Mowbray. The site had been a farmyard in the middle of the village which was now destined to become a luxury house. I started very slowly and carefully as it was a small plot surrounded by neighbouring houses and bungalows. I soon realised that I had been a little hasty in declaring my competence as I had to work right up the neighbours' garden fences. One mistake and I could easily take out a garden fence or even worse a whole flower garden in seconds. It was steady as she goes as I demolished some sheds and levelled the site ready for the next building stage. It was mid-afternoon when I got to the final stage of my job. It is called tracking in and you drive backwards and forwards to roll and compact the ground with the Drott's wide steel tracks. It is a very time-consuming job and I soon became I little bored, so I decided to speed things up a bit by moving up into high ratio. When I let the clutch out the Drott did a mini rear as it lurched forward throwing me back violently.

I looked at my hand in horror, it held the gear stick and my hand was high above my head. The screw top cover that held the gearstick into the gear box was so rusty and worn so it was not no longer doing its job. I pushed hard on the clutch the beast slowed but didn't stop; the clutch was so old it wasn't functioning properly. I was heading straight for the bungalow of the nice elderly couple who had kindly brought me a cup of tea earlier in the day. Now I was about to crush their lovely little bungalow and most likely them as well. My whole body was suddenly drenched in cold sweat. The Drott trudged on remorselessly as I tried to push the gearstick back into the hole, but it was a very complex procedure and require exact alignment, not easy as you chugged over rough ground. I was about five yards from next doors fence, visions of being arrested for manslaughter and life in prison spun through my head. Then suddenly, "Click" the gearstick popped into position. Pushing down hard on the gearstick so that it didn't come out again, I pulled it back and selected neutral. I collapsed hunched over the gearstick shaking, sobbing, and drenched in sweat. It took me over ten minutes to recover my composure. When I restarted my work, it was low gear and low revs, very steady as she goes. Guess what, I never got paid. Thinking back now, in my panic, it never occurred to me to pull the engine stop button.

Over the next year or so, the gearstick came out several times, but I became quite adept at relocating it and I avoided high ratio and high revs at all times. I tried to get both Harry and Dad to replace the gearstick but getting them to spend money was like getting blood out of a stone.

I had another close shave driving the Drott and this one was just down to my stupidity. The land across the road is a tenancy and belongs to British Gypsum. We had always called the land Coopers because a family called cooper lived there. They had a house and barn in the second field where our muck heap is today.

The whole of the area underneath Bunny Hill has been mined for Gypsum and the company wanted the house and barns demolished so that they were not liable for any damage caused by subsidence. They would pay Dad to knock them down, so I got the job with Harry's Drott.

I had seen loads of war films where Tanks drove straight through houses and came out the other side. It looked an awesome thing to do but I was not planning on going right through the house as the Drott didn't have a cab and there was no protection at all for the driver.

I aimed for the middle of the long side of the house and crashed headlong into it and the Drott went straight through the wall. It was amazing, the brute power, it gave me a real buzz. The buzz lasted less than a second! The wall above the hole I had made was collapsing and bricks were crashing down onto the bonnet of the Drott and bouncing everywhere, several nearly hit me. Shit I was in serious trouble! I selected high ratio reverse in a flash to get out as quick as possible. Wrong decision! As I reversed so quickly, it pulled more brickwork down but worse still the roof was sliding back towards me! I hit neutral and bailed out as fast as I could.

After a few minutes, bricks stopped falling and the dust cleared to reveal a large hole in the side of the house and a sagging roof above the hole, but it looked reasonably stable. I crept into the hole and cleared the rubble off the bonnet of the Drott. Luckily the bonnet was very sturdy and already well dented from its long hard life. I carefully removed anything around the dozer blade that might disturb the fragile roof and walls.

I did this with bare hands and no safety hat or gloves, this was pre-health and safety. When I was satisfied that I had done all I could to make it safer to get the Drott out the hole, I remounted the Drott that was still ticking over, all the time keeping an eye on the precariously balanced roof. I gently lifted the dozer blade up clear of the rubble and then started to inch back very gently, still with the engine on tick over. I had to stop several times as bricks fell and bounced off the bonnet. Finally, sweating profusely from nerves, I got the machine clear of the building. It was time to sit down, have a fag and contemplate how I could do this job without killing myself.

A Drott was really the wrong tool for the job, but I improvised by putting a long chain through windows and out through the hole and then pulling sections of the wall out from a distance with the chain attached to the Drott. Once the roof collapsed, it was plain sailing after that. I kept my near disaster secret for many years as I was embarrassed by my stupidity. Sometimes smoking a cigarette and doing a bit of thinking can be good for your health.

For those of you who know me today you will probably be surprised that I used to smoke. Both Louise and I gave up smoking on our honeymoon in Ibiza. We both went away with heavy colds and neither of us was prepared for the hot weather, it was my first trip abroad on a plane and I think it was Lou's second. We felt pretty awful all holiday and never smoked any of the duty-free cigarettes that we had excitedly bought on the plane. When we returned home, we were very short of money, so we decided to give up smoking and sell our duty-free cigarettes.

The Clubroom and Bar opened in the autumn of 1967 and became more and more successful. With the help of the Riding Club we started to have social events similar to the ones that we had had in the old clubroom but on a grander and more refined scale. The buffets that we put on at these events were of a high standard for that period in time and catered for the type of clientele that we were now attracting to the Riding Stables, wealthy middle-aged businesspeople.

In the late sixties everything was changing, social attitudes, music, dress codes and the way people socialised. Instead of going out two or three times a year to a ball or a dinner dance, people were starting to go out every weekend. The age of the Disco was upon us. That meant loud pop music in a room with minimal lighting and if it was really upmarket, a coloured light. They were hot, sweaty and very smokey. Skirts got shorter every year and what happened in the darker corners of the room is best not written down but left to your imagination.

Our big social events at Christmas and the New Year gradually became more Disco orientated and the more we went that way the more successful they became. They were so successful that they sold out weeks before the event. The bar and clubroom had a maximum capacity of one hundred customers. I remember one New Year having a capacity crowd and Dad and I having to man the door to stop any more people coming in. They weren't trying to gate crash the party they were just trying to pay to come in. At one stage we had over fifty people queuing in the car par just hoping to get in.

The pace of change was beyond my parent's comprehension and it fell to me to suggest more modern food and music for these events. Buying up-to-date records was always contentious as they could not understand why they couldn't play the same old records year after year. Dad in particular could not cope with the idea of spending money on such frivolous things such as records but as the events became more popular and the money kept rolling in even, he acquiesced. I even got money to have a state-of-the-art set of twin deck turntables built to provide non-stop Disco music. The role of Disc Jockey fell to me. It was a role that was forced onto me out of necessity rather than desire, although I did enjoy building up a record collection. At this point in my life I was very shy and lacked self-confidence so standing up into front of an audience playing records and announcing them over a microphone was absolute torture for me. The younger Club members loved the Disco part of the big events and started asking to have more just Disco nights. The precursor to starting regular Discos was my seventeenth birthday party in the clubhouse. We turned all the lights out except for a light over the Disco decks. Everyone brought their own drink and I persuaded mum and dad to fund a barrel of beer. Everyone got very drunk and several people passed out from drinking too much. A couple of girls were unconscious for nearly two hours which was very frightening, but we hushed it all up and none of our elders were any the wiser thank god.

News of this wild party quickly spread through the local teen-age community and rapidly gained cult status with people asking me when the next one was going to happen. Some of the things that happened that night really frightened me and the consequences of what might have, been didn't bear thinking about. However, it was very clear that there was a real demand from the local younger generation for somewhere to go at the weekends to dance, listen to loud pop music and have a drink.

We tried a few monthly Saturday nights of Disco music in the bar and they were extremely successful, I did the Disc Jockeying and mum and dad plus friends did the bar.

These were exciting times for me and for the younger generation. If you had an idea or just a dream you could just go ahead and do it! People were enthusiastic about any new ideas and they supported them however crazy they were. I wonder how different things really were back then compared with the beginning of the twenty first century with all its technological innovations and social media. I supposed most generations feel that their teenager decade was the most radical decade ever.

Even so, the sixties are still talked about today as the start of the modern era. It was a decade of great social and political change, so great that it took the establishment nearly two decades to pass laws to suppress and control those new-found freedoms and stifle it all in what is now referred to as red tape. If you had an idea for starting a business you just did it, there was no public liability Insurance, no Health and Safety, no Employment Law and what Laws that were in place were either ignored or ducked and dived around. It was great fun to do business in those days. People like Richard Branson and his Virgin Record Company were a typical example of starting out with nothing and becoming a multi-millionaire.

From my sixteenth birthday, when I got to enjoy to the freedom of driving everywhere and anywhere, I stopped riding and lost interest in riding and the riding school. This caused a lot of friction with my dad. The Riding School and farm were seven days a week and long days at that. I had made new friends at school and at youth clubs in West Bridgford and Ruddington. They all worked five or five and a half day weeks with weekends off. Everyone was always planning nice things to do whilst I was stuck at home working. Every time I did anything but work dad would say "You're a lazy good for nothing, I don't know why I ever bothered having you".

I wanted something more than catching, mucking out and tacking up horses. Mum understood my frustration and secretly encouraged me to think about pursuing a different career. She kept reminding me I had left school with seven GCEs, all with good grades and that there were lots of opportunities out there for me. The trouble was that I had no idea what I wanted to do. After my failed attempt to get an Agricultural Engineering Apprenticeship, I had lost confidence and was convinced that nobody would take on a country bumpkin like me.

My mother had a friend that worked in the laboratories at British Gypsum in East Leake, she also had horses and rode out hacking with mum. She must have discussed my predicament with her because one day mum announced that there was a job vacancy in the Research Dept at British Gypsum. Chemistry had been my best subject at school and one of the job requisites was that the applicant held an O Level in chemistry. The job sounded wildly exciting and for once I felt this was a job that would suit me. I had to apply in writing stating all my qualifications. To be honest I didn't hold out any hope that they would be interested in me so when a letter arrived back I expected it to say "Thanks for applying but no thank you" the fact that they had asked me to go for an interview was such a boost to my self-esteem but I was quickly brought back down to earth when I tried to recall the periodic table that I had not thought about at all during the past year and a half since l left school.

I attended the interview dressed in my best clothes and with a new haircut. Dad said he didn't know why I was bothering to even go. I had a perfectly good job here at home and what the hell did I know about laboratories and research. It would be a total waste of time. To my astonishment the people that interviewed me were very pleasant and gave me a tour of the laboratories and the half-size plaster board production plant that was used for testing new products and machinery. The only thing that I could compare it with was the Pedigree Pet Foods plant that I had worked in with dad during the summer holidays when I was fifteen. I didn't think my interview went very well as I had struggled to fully understand the chemical structure of gypsum and plaster when I was questioned. I left thinking that it had been an interesting afternoon out but that I had blown any chance of a job by not preparing and researching what British Gypsum did. I was very cross with myself for my ignorance and stupidity. I really would have liked to get that job. It sounded really interesting.

I was stunned when I got a letter offering me the job, mum was so pleased and excited for me, dad was furious!

My first month was spent in the main analytical laboratories that tested samples from the main plasterboard production plant and the bagged plaster plant. It was here that I was taught all the various techniques used for the quality control of all the various products that they made at East Leake and the sister plant just two miles down the road at Gotham. I had to stay in the main laboratories until all my analysis results consistently matched those of the main laboratory. When I was first taken down to the labs, a pungent smell of ammonia hit me as we entered the corridor that led to the labs. It was so strong that it made my eyes run and I was almost sick. I could feel my stomach heaving as I approached the laboratory door, only intense concentration and the thought of spewing up in front of my new boss at our first meeting conquered the spasming stomach muscles.

I was glad to leave the laboratory as I soon found the work to be repetitive and rather boring after a few weeks. The people working in the labs were really nice and it was a refreshing change to talk to people about things other than horses. Another thing that made me want to leave the labs was that after a week or so, I suddenly noticed that I could not smell the boiling ammonia that had so affected me on my first day. I had always been used to the clean air of Bunny Hill and I couldn't stop wondering what those fumes were doing to my lungs.

My new place of work was called The Experimental Mill and Board Plant which housed two separate departments, which I quickly discovered had an us and them relationship. I had imagined that that it would be a sort of toy plant, but this looked huge to me and produced proper sheets of plasterboard that were half the size of the ones produced on the main production line and quite usable. The boards were much easier to handle measuring two feet by four feet instead of the industry standard of eight feet by four feet.

There were two floors in the building. The ground floor housed the board making machinery, a drying plant that sort of cooked the plasterboard and an area to the store the completed boards. The second floor housed an office block which consisted of a private office for the plant manager, an open plan office for the other six staff and a separate laboratory room for me to do my testing. I was extremely proud of having my own desk in the main office area.

I arrived all fired up and ready to start doing all the tests that I had been trained to do but was dumbfounded when I was told that there would be nothing to do for several weeks to come.

I eventually discovered that this was very much the norm for the experimental plant. They had just finished one project just before I arrived and most of the office staff were now busy collating results or writing reports for those higher up command chain. I had been recruited because the company was developing a new gypsum mine at a place called Sherburn in Elmet near Leeds. It was a massive project and would dominate most of the work I did for the years that I worked there.

There were several other experimental departments on site and also some very specialist labs, such as a spectrometry lab that could measure tiny amounts of impurities. To keep me out of their hair whilst they wrote their reports, I was despatched to wander around the whole of the research area and introduce myself. I started out very nervous of interrupting people doing all kinds of important and complex work but soon discovered most people had plenty of time to have a coffee and biscuit with me and a good chat. When I explained my mission, they would ask had I met so and so from this or that department. If I had not met them, they would ring them and make an appointment for me to visit them. There were so many interesting projects going on, many of them had little to do with gypsum and more to do with the development of new and better ways to make or handle their products. I loved it all and the people I met were happy to spend time explaining what they were trying to achieve. I even spent time chatting to the head of accounts and people in the typing pool. It was time well spent and stood me in good stead over the next two and a half years that I spent there.

The hours that I had to work were 37.5 hrs per week and I had paid holidays, compared with 60 plus hours at the stables and no holidays, let alone paid holidays. It felt like I was on holiday, all the time. I went to work in a jacket and tie, we had tea and biscuits delivered twice a day, a canteen that served highly subsidised meals all day, a works club that sold drinks at half the price of pubs and was open at lunch times so that you could have a couple of pints after lunch in the canteen. All very civilised! We often skipped lunch in the canteen to get a break from the work environment and had beer and sandwiches at the Nags Head in East Leake or in the summer we would pop up to Stanford Hall for a swim in the bracing waters of the Lido that was situated there.

I was very naïve to the ways of working for a large company and soon became aware that there were lots of perks to be had if you got to know the ropes. My trips to the accounts department enlightened me to a myriad of expenses that could be claimed if I went on training courses or to college. There was also compassionate leave which if used in a clever way could add another 14 days to your holiday entitlement. One member of our office would regularly have a doctors or dental appointment on a Friday. Because he travelled by bus everywhere, he claimed it took him hours to get from work to his appointment because it required several changes of buses. He always had appointments around one o'clock, so he would come to work at 9am leave at 10am and then not return as it would be time to go home by the time he got back. When I commented to my fellow workers that he must be in very poor health, they all laughed. They explained that he was nearing retirement with no hope of promotion, so he was just milking the system for all it was worth.

If you went on a training course, you got travel expenses plus hotel and subsistence payments. Bills were nearly always handwritten in those days, so your food bill could include beer or wine but not be shown on the bill. It was head of department who showed us this little trick. I soon learnt that although the wages were not great, you were still able to live well. These perks were used by everyone from the top to the bottom. One perk was so popular, that when I first started work at the plant, I was asked to fill bottles of Teepol for people in other departments to collect on Friday afternoon just before we closed for the weekend. Teepol is a highly concentrated soap solution probably three or four times stronger than the best washing up liquid. It was used to make the plaster flow better when making plasterboard and we used huge amounts of it, so nobody noticed if a few gallons went missing from a fifty-gallon drum. Another thing that people sought from us was Acetone. This was a very strong solvent which we used for various procedures in the Lab and on the plant. It also happened to be the main constituent of ladies nail varnish remover and very good at dissolving oil when cleaning car engines, need I say more. Every department had something to trade, be it photo copying from the office department to nuts and bolts from the engineering department. We would often get orders for twenty or thirty odd plasterboards when somebody was planning a house extension and these requests usually came from high up the management chain such as department heads. In all you had a major sub-economy operating.

The lure of expenses and wanting to better myself led me to enthusiastically embrace taking college courses. I really enjoyed college, it got me a day off every week from the plant and I got to spend a day in Nottingham. I soon discovered that my food allowance more than covered a cheap Chinese business lunch. Chinese food during the sixties was considered very chic and people were well impressed when I mentioned that I had eaten a Chinese lunch but best of all it was very filling and was probably the most nutritious meal I ate all week. This was because I had now left home and was now sharing a house with two other lads.

My relationship with dad quickly deteriorated after getting the job at British Gypsum. I think he thought I would fail, get sacked or not like the job and come back to the riding school with my tail between my legs, but that didn't happen, so he resorted to verbal abuse. He would stare at me when we were at the table for a meal and say, "Has he paid his board this week because I'll not have that good for nothing sitting at my table eating my food for free?" or "Look at the Nancy boy going to work in a jacket and tie, nobody does a proper day's work dressed like that."

Being independent meant a lot to me and I think I came to realise that I would never be my own man if I didn't make a clean break from home. Feeding myself and paying rent on my small wage meant it was very hard to make ends meet. I remember clearly to this day, at the end of the month a couple of days before my salary was paid into my bank, I had less than one pound to my name. It was enough to buy a couple of subsidised meals at work with enough change to buy either fish and chips or a tube of toothpaste. The toothpaste was important for my love life and the fish and chips important for my rumbling empty stomach. After half an hour's careful deliberation I decided to put my love life on hold until pay day and fill my stomach with fish and chips. Dad had made it very clear that if I left home there was no coming back, in fact he didn't want me to set foot on his property every again. This upset mum greatly and to see her so upset caused me to waiver, but I knew I had to getaway. I knew dad's routine and would phone to let her know I was ok when I knew dad would be out and often popped back when I knew the coast was clear to see mum. I would always leave with a much-treasured goody bag of cakes and biscuits.

After about six months away mum told me dad had mellowed and invited me to come for a meal one evening. Dad wasn't there when I arrived, and I sat nervously awaiting his arrival. When he arrived, he glared at me and shouted, "What the bloody hell is he doing at my table?"

I stood up with tears welling up in my eyes and took a deep breath before saying straight to his face, "I thought I had been invited but obviously I was mistaken," and I walked out.

The house I shared was owned by Mick Dyer-Greaves who had split up with his partner and needed extra income to keep up the mortgage payments. Geoff Watson and I both rented a room each in the three bedroomed bungalow. The bungalow was situated in a small estate on the edge of East Leake and about half a mile from where I worked so it was very convenient for me. We were strange bedfellows and had virtually nothing in common with each other. Geoff was an engineer at the Brush engineering factory and left for work very early in the morning. He was a very quiet person who would spend hours in his bedroom playing the guitar. Although we lived in the same house, I saw very little of Geoff except for occasional short periods over the weekends. Neither our lifestyles nor body clocks seemed to be in sync. Mick was a car salesman and started work at about the same time as I did. We both had to be smartly dressed for our work and it was Mick who showed me the art of just ironing the front of your shirt if you were late for work. The thing you had to remember was not to take your jacket off in public. We always said that we would do all our washing and ironing over the weekend, but it never happened with our wild social life.

When I moved in with Mick and Geoff, I could not afford a bed but managed to acquire a mattress from someone at the stables who had just brought a new one and was giving it away. In fact, I had virtually no possessions during this period of my life just my van and two mattresses. One mattress was on the floor of my bedroom as I didn't possess a bed. The other mattress was in the back of my van which was my mobile bedroom. I had very few clothes but I was happy with that and spent all my money in the pub or watching bands.

At this particular time, West Bridgford and the boat clubs along the banks of the River Trent were a mecca for some of the finest bands of that period such as the Who, John Mayall, Eric Clapton, Rory Gallagher and Fleetwood Mac when it was still a blues band and fronted by the legendary guitarist Peter Green. We were also lucky enough to see some of the great Black American blues artists that were touring the UK in the late sixties. One of my favourites was Champion Jack Dupree who I saw at the Dancing Slipper that was on central avenue in West Bridgford. Champion Jack was an amazing piano player with an unusual playing style of flicking his hands high in the air between notes, especially when playing Boogie.

My years at British Gypsum gave me confidence and a feeling of self-worth. My superiors treated me as an equal and one of the team, although they were much older than me. They broadened my horizons by sending me on courses and visiting other company plants in various parts of the country. I did courses on industrial relations, trade union law, and even health and safety. I attained my first aid at work certificate and became the Safety Officer for the offices and laboratory in the plant. I retook my GCE in maths and passed it easily in one term. College tuition was different from school and I loved the way you were encouraged to ask questions. I had to re-sit my maths GCE maths as it was prerequisite for me take an ONC Science course.

The work was easy and was perfect for my late-night clubbing lifestyle but the long periods of waiting for the next project to come in and nothing to do drove me mad. Using the network of people, I had met in other departments during my induction I would put some plaster into a couple of sample bottles and take a sheet of A4 paper in my hand and set off for tea and biscuits in all the different departments. With my sample bottles and paper nobody ever questioned me as to why I was in another department. On these rounds I made a lifelong friend with the research department's electrician. His name was John Birch. John and I would spend hours talking about our plans for the future. John like me had been subjected to some unsavoury business experiences, in particular not getting paid for jobs. We were both in a sort of hibernation recharging our batteries gathering knowledge and the energy to go back into the fray and re-join the ranks of the self-employed. John was slightly older than me and mentored me greatly about the pitfalls of working for yourself. It was great advice that helped me avoid potential disasters many times through my business career.

We both had big ambitious plans which we discussed over and over again during our passing the time meetings. Curiously we both left British Gypsum almost at the same time. John went on to build a very successful electrical business with his electricians working all over the UK. John has now retired but the business is still based in my home village of Costock and continues to flourish with his son Dave Birch at the helm. Dave is a keen horseman and was an amateur whipper-in for the Quorn Hunt for many years. The company has been doing our electrical work since John restarted his business and they continue to do so with my son Mark who is now at the helm of the riding stables.

In 1969 there was a lot of talk about the Isle of Wight pop festival that was to take place at the end of August. There had been a very successful pop festival there the previous year but this year it was going to be much bigger with some of the biggest bands of the time performing there. In particular my long-time favourite artist Bob Dylan. On a whim I decided that I would go to the festival and watch my hero live on stage. I had no idea how to get to the Isle of Wight or its precise location just that it was off the south coast of England. There was no internet in those days and the only information I could get was from newspaper articles and adverts in Rolling-stone magazine and the New Musical Express.

The event was at Ryde but that was not quite true as I was to discover when I arrived.

Because I was now working for a company, I could book holidays as and when I wanted. I would have never had gone to The Isle of Wight if I had stayed at home but now, I was free to do whatever I wanted, although the lack of money put a restraint on many of my desires.

This trip was going to require a lot of money, so I started saving hard and almost disappeared from the social scene all together. I estimated that the Isle of Wight was about 200miles away after studying an old very creased road map of Great Britain. Motorways were still a rarity and my planned route was all on A and B roads. My Ford Anglia van had over 50,000 miles on the clock which in those days was considered terminal for engines. It had a top speed of about sixty miles an hour, but you would have been reckless if you did that sort of speed for more than a couple of minutes. Forty miles per hour was a much safer speed for both the driver and longevity of the engine. I estimated that if I was lucky I could maybe average about 30mph which meant about four hours driving time and another hour for refuelling and rest.

Slowly, over the preceding weeks, I prepared my van for this monumental trip. My biggest expense was buying oil and a filter so that I could do an oil change on the engine and also buying a spare fan belt. In those days fan belts were not so durable as they are today, and a broken fan belt was a common cause of breakdowns. I borrowed extra tools from my mates so that I could perform roadside repairs.

In those days there were no roadside assistance companies except the RAC and the AA which were clubs in those days and only for the wealthy. If you had a serious breakdown that you could not mend yourself then you thumbed a lift in a passing car to the nearest garage. The garage would then go out and tow you back to their workshop. In the sixties there were hardly any petrol stations that were not attached to a garage workshop, nearly every village had a garage that mended cars and dispensed petrol. Locally Bunny and East Leake both had two and Costock and Rempstone both had one, so you were probably safer traveling by car in those days than using the breakdown insurance companies of today. The garages/petrol stations were owned by mechanics who could mend just about anything and held a wide stock of vehicle parts on site. So as long as you had a few quid in your pocket this was not such a reckless trip as it may seem.

I set off with a mattress in the back of the van for a bed, a sleeping bag and haversack full of food and water. I could not afford a tent, but the weather forecast was good, and I was used to sleeping rough in the woods from my earlier adventures. I did take my sleeping bag and a ground sheet which would give me a bit of protection if the weather turned wet.

My drive down to Portsmouth where the ferry terminal was

situated, was uneventful but very tiring as I had never driven such a long distance before. I had to stop a couple of times to allow the engine to cool down and also check if the engine oil level was ok.

The ferry car park was huge and looked full, but I eventually found a space and parked up. Parking was free of charge, which was normal everywhere in the sixties, unlike today. I took my rolled-up ground sheet and sleeping bag which was tied up with some old washing line so that I could carry it slung across my back, like the soldiers of the American Civil War. I also had an ex-ww2 army haversack with emergency food and clothing which I also took from the van and headed for the ferry.

The ferry was packed with moustached long-haired people just like me who were very friendly. They came from all over the world, but we were all united in our love of the music. By the time we reached Ryde on the Isle of Wight I had hooked up with a couple of lads and we stayed together as a group for the whole of the festival.

I was not prepared at all for what greeted us on our arrival. Everywhere was clogged with people. My plan was to find a café and have some lunch, then go into the festival after lunch. The scene that greeted me was more akin to a film scene from Dunkirk. Everywhere was jammed with people roads, cafes, pubs, shops, people were queuing for everything, many food and drink outlets already had "sold out" signs outside or just closed down. I searched the little town with my new-found friends for food, but we were too late. 150,000 people had descended on this unprepared town and stripped it bare of food and drink. We asked people where the festival was, and the answer was always the same, "Somewhere up that road Man" as they pointed to a road jammed full of people shuffling forward at less than a snail's pace.

We decided to give up on lunch and joined the shuffle, we had no idea where we were heading but like lemmings followed those in front. The sound of loud heavy rock music wafted over us on occasions when the wind dropped giving us hope that we would soon arrive at the festival. It was dark when we finally arrived at the festival and all the ticket gates were closed. The site was enclosed by a high boarded wall about fifteen feet high, from behind the wall a huge dome of light emanated into the night sky. It was as if some ex-terrestrial spaceship had landed, but the deafening heavy rock music quickly brought you back to reality.

Barred access, we settled down in the field outside of the wall to listen to some of the top bands from around the world. Our night in the field was topped off by listening to Who performing their "Tommy" set, the same set as they had played just eleven days before at the iconic Woodstock festival in the States.

The previous year's festival on the Isle of Wight had an attendance of 10,000 and I think that the organisers had seriously underestimated the draw of Bob Dylan doing his first live performance in three years, following his near fatal motorcycle accident. The official attendance was 150,000 but other sources have put it as high as 250,000. Whatever the numbers were, food and sanitation just could not cope with such massive numbers and appeared to most of us as non-existent. Me and my new friends shared some of the food that we had brought with us but held some of it back as the gravity of the situation started to dawn on us. It now looked like the food we had packed to travel down with might have to last us for three days.

Next morning a search for food or sanitation proved our worries from the night before, however, we did manage to gain access to the festival, buying tickets for the final two days and hoping that food and sanitation would be much better inside the walled off area. Sadly, we were greeted to hundred yard plus queues for both toilets and burger vans. It was not yet midday and some catering vans had already sold out. People also queued to get water from a few standpipes that were dotted around the outskirts of the arena, for both drinking and washing. People were getting annoyed but in the nicest possible way, for this was the time of "Love and Peace". The crowd started spontaneously to chant with chants such as "We want food" and when a 100,000 plus start chanting it makes a point.

The organisers came on stage and apologised saying that they had completely underestimated the amount of people that would attend the festival and that every effort was being made to get more food, drink and sanitation, but unfortunately being an island, everything had to come in by ferry and all the ferries were full to capacity. They were scouring the island for extra food vans and mobile toilets. The only food that seemed to be available at an affordable price was something called Yogurt and although nowadays it is a mainstream food that is readily available everywhere, in 1969 it was still virtually unknown. I had tried some back in 1967 when I worked at Pedigree Pet foods which is owned by the Dutch Company Mars and presumably it was liked by Dutch people. I tried to eat a teaspoonful but spat it out as it tasted like gone-off milk.

At the festival it was not going down very well, even at the promotional half price and the queue was a mere thirty yards long. It still tasted foul but when you are hungry and short of money it is amazing what you can force down your neck.

The music and the atmosphere was something I had never experienced before or ever again. The first night concluded with the Moody Blues who were so much better live rather than seeing them on Top of the Pops. After a standing ovation at the end of their set there were chants for more, they seemed to come reluctantly back onto the stage. The lead singer explained that it had taken over a year to perfect the songs that they had already played, and they didn't know any more. However, they would repeat one that they had just played. I think it was "Nights in White Satin" which remains one of my favourite songs to this day. Little did I know then that I would be asked to do some riding stunts for a video to accompany the song for "The Dave Lee Travis Golden Oldie Picture Show" in the mid-1980s.

The final night was concluded by Bob Dylan who for me was a disappointment. First there was a delay of over one hour which was supposedly for technical reasons but there were rumours that he might not perform at all as he had been a virtual recluse for the past three years since his near fatal motorcycle accident. Eventually he did perform, but it was not what I was expecting. I was expecting all his hit protest songs but what he performed was mainly electric/rock, it was a shock to the system, and you could sense an uneasiness in the audience. Not only was the music different but Dylan's voice was completely different. I later learned that this was due to him suffering a broken neck when he had his accident. At the end of the night I felt disheartened although I later came to love the songs that he showcased that night.

For me the bands I enjoyed most were The Moody Blues and two folk singers that really captured the audiences' hearts and soul. First was Julie Felix who had the whole audience singing along to her annoying hit song "we're going to the Zoo" I still recall clearly her asking the audience "Where are we going?" and 150,000 voices shouting, "To the F**king Zoo". The other artist was Tom Paxton who just held the audience in the palm of his hand for the whole of his performance of hauntingly beautiful folk songs.

Bob Dylan's set closed the festival and due to the delays, it was well past midnight when the performance finished. It was then that a new problem arose. The audience had slowly grown over the three days and even then, there were massive queues at the entrance gates. Now the whole 150,000 all wanted to leave at the same time and the only exits were the entrance gates. It appeared that nothing was moving and after an hour or so frustration set in and people started to push at the perimeter fence. Within minutes it turned into a stampede as thousands started to push at the fencing rocking it back and forwards until great sections of it collapsed allowing thousands to burst forth like water from a fractured dam. How people were not seriously injured is beyond me, but I can only think that I was the love and peace mentality of the audience that saved it becoming a mass disaster like the football disaster at Hillsborough.

Our escape was short lived as the only lane back to the ferry was completely blocked by a solid mass of shuffling people. We followed the road back to the terminal where we had disembarked three days previously. It was morning when we arrived, and pandemonium raged, everyone wanted to leave at the same time. A big problem was that the ferries were calling at another terminal first. This terminal was also swamped with festival goers who wanted to get home and were filling the ferries to capacity. When the ferries docked at our dock only a few locals got off, so the ferries could only load ten or so people onto each ferry. By lunchtime the crowd was getting out of hand as people started to jump off the pier onto the ferries in a desperate attempt to leave the island. Two beleaguered police officers tried to keep order but with tens of thousands of angry and frustrated people all pushing to get onto the ferries, it was a suicide mission. I think someone eventually fell into the sea and this jolted the head in the sand mentally of the ferry owners to take some decisive action and divert some empty ferries to our dock first. I finally made it back to the mainland in the late afternoon. Thankfully my van started, and I headed for the first transport café outside Portsmouth. I was ravenous I hadn't eaten or drunk anything for over 24 hours and eaten very little for the past three days. I ordered a big fry up and a pot of tea when I reached the transport café but struggled to finish my meal, I think my stomach had shrunk after my near starvation diet of the last three days.

I returned home a wiser and worldlier person with some fantastic memories that are still with me to this day. I also learnt never to believe what you read in the newspapers. Friends were desperate to hear about my travels and the festival and showed me the headlines in the newspapers. According to journalists anyone who attended the festival was a drug crazed, scum of the earth who never washed and made love in public. I was never aware of any drug taking although with the vast numbers involved, there must have been some drugs taken. The long queues at the water standpoints in the mornings of people waiting to wash, and clean their teeth was testimony to people's cleanliness. There was no trouble at all that I saw over the whole weekend except frustration with the lack of facilities and planning to cope with such vast numbers. All I witnessed was happy easy-going young people that were enjoying themselves and the music despite all the problems. A million miles away from the newspaper accounts.

It is amazing how technology has changed our lives since the late sixties. When I joined British Gypsum in the late sixties all our complex steam evaporation rate calculations were done using a Facit machine which I can only describe as a manual hand cranked calculator. Adding, subtracting, dividing and multiplying were all done by moving levers and then cranking the handle the number of times that you were multiplying or dividing. It was a very complicated machine and it took me weeks to learn how to work it correctly. Using the Facit to do a steam calculation could take up to twenty minutes for each one and we had loads of them to do every day. It was also very easy to miscount the number of cranks forward or backwards if distracted. One day we were presented with a large electrical box, it was about the size of a big briefcase. It also came with an assortment of white plastic cards the same size as our modern-day credit cards, but of course these had yet to be invented, as we lived in a cash and cheque society. It turned out to be the forerunner of the computer/calculator. Each card performed a specific calculation, all we had to do was type in the reading, insert the white card and hey presto we got the answer in about one minute instead of twenty. It saved hours of monotonous work every day and with no mistakes.

Facit was a very successful Swedish company with massive worldwide sales of its mechanical calculating machine. The invention of the electronic calculator in the late sixties completely destroyed the company in a matter of a couple of years. The pros and cons of new technology.

Another new technology I was involved with was Fluidics. I can only describe it as a type of hydraulics where the oil has been replaced by compressed air that was triggered by micro-switches. It was quicker, much smaller and cleaner than a conventional oil-based system. However, it was prone to leaks and had several other problems when we scaled it up to the harsh environment of the production line. It was still being perfected when I left the company and I have never heard of it since so I have no idea if they ever got into mainstream production.

British Gypsum had a regular yearly intake of university graduates and part of their induction was to send them to work in all the many differing arms of the company so that they gained a broad understanding of how the company functioned. We often had these graduates assigned to our facility for two to three weeks at a time. They came with a variety of skills but with the short time scale it was hard to find them useful or meaningful jobs to do. One graduate taught me not to be too quick to judge a person's character or worth. This particular graduate was an honours graduate in maths.

When he arrived, we found him very introvert and completely lacking in any practical skills. Every task he was given in the production plant ended in a total disaster. The plant manager decided that he might be safer in the Lab with more scientific jobs to occupy his mind and so he became my responsibility. There was very little work to do in the Lab at that particular moment and I scoured my brains to try and find a useful but safe job that he could do. I had a dodgy screened electrical cable on one of the electronic instruments in the Lab. The steel screening wire had become detached from the metal plug and needed to be re-soldered, a relatively simple job. I asked him if he could solder, his answer was negative, but he was really excited about the prospect of learning this new skill. I got out the soldering kit and showed him how to do it. He assured me he understood the process and as he had such I high IQ never thought to doubt it.

I left him in the Lab excitedly preparing to perform his task and went off to do some work in the main plant. I estimated that it might take him about fifteen minutes to complete the job which would take us up to the lunch break. When I returned to take him to lunch, he cheerfully announced that it was taking a little longer than expected but was happy to skip lunch as he was really enjoying himself. Overjoyed at not having to chaperone him over lunch I dashed off to join my pals who were all off to the village pub for a liquid lunch.

When I returned after an hour, I found my graduate still hard at it. I could not believe that after one and a quarter hours he still hadn't managed to complete this five-minute task. When I asked what the problem was, he explained that the soldering iron didn't seem to be getting hot enough to melt the steel wire that screened the cable. We were all flabbergasted that a person of his intelligence didn't know that you couldn't melt steel with a soldering iron.

However, a few days later we had a major power cut. This was a common occurrence during this period as there was a shortage of electricity due to strikes by miners and railway workers that affected the supply of coal to the power stations. This in turn rendered our new calculating box useless. Our Facit machine had been scrapped and nobody in the office felt confident to attempt the huge string of equations long hand.

Suddenly our graduate came to life asking if he might help. We showed him this huge formula of this over that in brackets plus something else in bracket divided by something else and so on and so on, you get the picture. After studying the formula for a matter of seconds he announced that it was very easy and if we gave him all the readings from the meters, he would happily do them for us. The whole office watched in amazement as he worked out the steam evaporation rates of the cooking plaster-boards almost as quick as our new calculator box.

At that moment I started to understand that there were many different types of intelligence and all have their worth in society. It sparked an interest in me to notice how different people's minds work and has become the cornerstone of my teaching and coaching to this day.

I left British Gypsum in the early 1970s, I had just been given the highest pay rise in the whole of the research department. When I handed my notice in, I was summoned to go and report to the Director of Research. Although I had seen the Director, I had never spoken to him ever, in the whole time that I had worked there. He was bemused by my letter of resignation and wondered if I had a problem with any of my colleagues. He explained that they had given me the generous pay rise because they had high hopes for me and wanted me to stay on. I was overcome by emotion and tears started to well up in my eyes. For a long moment I thought about what I could achieve here, and I considered everything that my superiors received including the high and mighty Director sitting in front of me. After a long moment I realised that even if I were to rise higher in the company than my wildest dreams this was not what I wanted for my life. I saw very clearly at that moment in time it was time for me to leave and search for new challenges for better or worse. It was time to move on

Chapter 16

Moving on

I left British Gypsum with no job to go to and no house to live in. I had saved very little money during my time at Gypsum and now with no income, I could not afford the rent on my shared house in East Leake.

However, all was not that bad, there was the dole money you could claim from the government (today it is called unemployment benefit). In the late sixties and early seventies unemployment was very high and leaving school and going straight on the dole became the norm. This had two very different effects, some people were happy to live a subsistence life payed for by the government and do nothing at all, while others used the dole to pay the rent and buy food but also worked for cash doing anything and everything to top up their dole money into a nice income. This is turn spawned a free-wheeling younger generation that worked when they were short of money but if they felt like going off to a pop festival or a wander around Europe, they would just drop everything and go knowing that the dole would cover their basic expenses. Of course, this was illegal but with over six million unemployed and no computers to keep a track on things the chance of getting caught were very minimal.

The dole helped greatly in creating and supporting the hippy culture of that period but much more importantly it spawned a generation of wheeler dealer entrepreneurs that would become the backbone of the boom times that came a decade later.

I don't think the government foresaw either of these consequences when introducing the dole.

I never claimed the dole, but I did have to go to the dole office in Nottingham to register as unemployed. I sat in a crowded room for over three hours waiting for my number to be called, by which time I was climbing up the walls. I had intended to claim the dole but the thought of going through this purgatory every month just to get a few quid from the government quickly changed my mind.

After helping Dad out by doing a jousting show at Wollaton Park in Nottingham relations had improved greatly and I knew I would be welcomed back home, and it would be on my own terms. (The story of my involvement with jousting is a story on its own and is the subject of my first book The Knights Errant and will not be covered in this book).

It took some time for me to agree the ground rules to return home and keep my independence. Luckily for me, mum and dad needed my help, the business was growing faster than either of them could cope with. There was also a raft of new legislation regarding accounting, health and safety, and VAT coming into force and much of this beyond their comprehension. To make matters worse dad's partnership with Major Richie had not gone well and dad had had to re-mortgage the property to buy him out of the partnership and the bank was demanding credible accounts for the loan.

Dad buried his head in the sand, but mum knew we needed to sort things out and quick if we were going to be able to keep hold of the place. Dad was prepared to work night and day to keep the place but spending time with solicitors and accountants just wasn't on his radar. However, for me, this is what I had been doing down at British Gypsum for the past years, sitting in planning meetings and writing reports. My time at college doing management studies and health and safety had given me the tools to get things sorted out. The business as I have already said was basically good, but it needed to change quickly if it was to survive the 70s. Along with what I have already mentioned, employment laws, tax and national insurance were all being updated and enforced much more rigorously. The days of paying grooms cash in hand and working seven days a week were ending.

Luckily, the riding school and bar had attracted both wealthy and academic people who were more than prepared to give advice and drop a good word in for us in the right places. It was to these people that we owe a great debt of gratitude. Thankfully, we had not reached the age of the computer and loans were still given on a man's reputation or someone of note recommending them.

It was not an easy time for mum and dad, people always talk about the sixties being the decade of change, and it was because people started to think differently and old attitudes were challenged but it was in the seventies that the establishment accepted that change was needed and acted to implement radical new ideas, but as usual the law of unintended consequences produced many unpleasant problems as well welcome changes. VAT was the biggest change and for small businesses, it caused a lot of pain, sorrow and stress for the older generations with many good small businesses closing down because of the complicated paperwork that was required. The new legions of Vat inspectors were of the old school inflexible and intolerant demanding that paperwork be perfect and the books balance to the penny. People I knew and respected had nervous breakdowns and I witnessed hard men reduced to tears by the soulless Vat inspectors. It was Vat that terrified mum and dad. I now understand how they must have felt because Lou and I felt the same just before we retired trying to grapple with ever more complicated health and safety, business rates, the workplace pension and endless other new legal requirements. As you get older you just seem to run out energy to take on these new challenges.

Although VAT was not introduced into the UK until 1973 accountants were preparing their clients for the change long before that date. By the end of the sixties the Inland Revenue were demanding more accurate and up to date accounts from small businesses. The days of dad taking his box of random bills into the accountant once a year were coming to an end. Dad found it impossible to remember to ask for a proper invoice let alone record daily income and this worried mum greatly. Every year brought more complaints from the accountants and warnings of dire consequences if things didn't radically improve.

In order to keep my independence, I didn't move back into the family house but chose to move into and old caravan that dad had bought for staff accommodation. It was not a touring caravan but an old-fashioned living van, rectangular in shape with sleeping areas at either ends, a small kitchen and a coal/wood burning stove for heating. If asked to describe it, you would say very old and basic! My bit of luxury was an old extension lead poked through the corner of one of the windows that gave me mains electricity to power my all-important record player and a couple of old table lamps. Except for making early morning tea and late-night coffee and toast the small gas cooker was mainly redundant as I ate with my family in exchange for work at the stables.

I tried to avoid anything to do with the horses if at all possible, by volunteering to do mainly tractor driving and mechanical work. There was always plenty of mechanical work to do as all our machinery was very old and well past its sell by date. Having said that dad was very good at modifying old tractor belt powered machinery and hand powered to electric power. He successfully converted a hand cranked horse clipping machine to an electric motor as well as our chaff cutter, saw bench, cement mixer and various other yard tools. The hand powered chaff cutter was by far the scariest conversion. The chaff cutter must have been manufactured in Victorian times; it had a large cast wheel about three feet in diameter that had two scimitar shaped blades that were fitted to the two spokes of the wheel. The blades were made of thin metal like a scythe and were razor sharp. The wheel was turned by a large handle that could take the hands of two people as this monster required serious muscle power. The handle also powered a gearbox that worked two sets of rotating crimpers that pulled in and also compressed the hay or straw before it was chopped. In all it required three people to work the machine just to produce some chaff to mix with the horses hard feed. When it was hand powered the wheel and blades were covered with a wooden box for safety even though it was rare to manage one complete revolution without the blade getting stuck halfway through the cutting process. During the electrification process the wheel cover was broken and never replaced leaving the wheel and blades exposed. To make matters worse when dad fitted the huge electric motor, he omitted to fit any guards over the rotating pulleys or the vee-belts that connected them. Both of the above-mentioned hazards were capable of chopping off a limb in a mille-second. To make matters even worse the machine now operated at over ten times its design speed causing the crimpers to drag the hay in at an alarming rate and snatch your hand towards the crimpers and the rotating knives. There were several times that I felt the hay suck my hand towards those crimpers and a thought I was going to get my hand or even arm chopped off.

The horse clippers were not so dangerous, but they also worked at about ten times their design speed and you needed a strong grip and a strong arm to keep hold of the juddering, vibrating cutter head. The loud whirring noise terrified most horses making them impossible to clip. Not the best of dad's inventions.

Probably his most successful modification was the electric concrete mixer which was at least fifteen years ahead of its time and I always wonder how much it would have made dad if he had thought of patenting it. The only drawback the electric cement mixer had was that the electric motor was not waterproof which is not a good idea when buckets of water are being continually thrown at it. Remarkably the motor never gave us any problems despite it being regularly doused in water due to mis-aimed buckets. It was so good and reliable that it mixed all the mortar and concrete used to build the club room, the three-bed extension to our bungalow and many other projects. One more major benefit over the Diesel engine that it replaced was that it was so much quieter.

I was constantly aware that dad was trying to drag me back into the riding school business, but I knew it was a non-starter as dad's mentality was firmly set in the past when it came to labour relations and he still thought of his children as free or cheap labour. Having experienced corporate working and a regular pay packet I was determined not to go back to the old days. In the end dad and I reached a compromise in exchange for the use of the old club room as a workshop cum spray booth, I would do a few hours per week working for dad.

These duties included general maintenance and bringing the daily requirement of hay and straw down into the yard. Today it takes less than five minutes to bring hay and straw down into the yard using the big round bales and a telescopic handler, but in those days, we were still using small square bales that had to be loaded onto a trailer from the barn and then taken down to the yard and dropped off outside the stable doors. This was done twice a day mornings and late afternoons taking about forty-five minutes each time if the tractor decided to start. On cold mornings you could waste another hour trying to start the tractor. Usually, it was a flat battery, nearly every vehicle on the place had a defective battery but they were expensive to replace. The first option was to try and jump-start it from a car. If that failed, we had to round up every able-bodied person on the premises and push the tractor out of the yard onto the slip-road and roll it down the extremely steep road towards the main A60 road. The tractor had very poor brakes and if it didn't fire up quickly the driver (usually me!) would have to veer off the road onto the verge and into the brambles as means of extra breaking, the alternative was to shoot straight out onto the main road and almost certain death. Thankfully on most occasions the tractor would start within the first twenty yards giving you plenty of braking time. We also used the steep slip road to start cars and lorries. In the case of lorries, we first had to start the tractor and then tow the lorry out onto the slip road before launching them down the slip road, sometimes with the aid of the tractor pushing from behind. This practice was severely curtailed by the introduction of air brakes on lorries as they had a fail-safe system that locked the brakes until the engine powered compressor could raise the air pressure high enough to work the brakes safely. It was not uncommon to waste a whole morning just starting vehicles.

Writing this last section has reminded me of several other incidents where we diced with near death incidents due to near obsolete machinery or lack of safety barriers. It was not just us that operated in this way nearly everyone in the farming/ rural world operated in this way, even the local council.

I mention the local council because of the slip road that runs past the front of our property along the top of an embankment that falls steeply down to the busy main road below, it is a drop of sixty feet. We contacted the council on many occasions about having a safety fence erected in case a car or horse went over the edge, it was not until about ten years later when my uncle Ron came out of our stables on a runaway horse straight down the bank onto the main road did, they finally agree to fence it.

During the seventies and eighties, we farmed some land on the north side of Bunny Hill where the hill is at its steepest. On two occasions I was working in these fields on my own collecting hay bales, I was zigzagging across the face of the hill and had collected about half a trailer full when I turned downhill for another run across the hill face. Suddenly I felt the trailer start to push me down the hill at an alarming rate, the engine revs increased to a high-pitched whine as the wheels started to drive the engine rather than the engine driving the wheels and then suddenly, we lurched forward with massive acceleration as the clutch failed and we started to freewheel down the hill at an alarming rate. I slammed my foot on the brake, only the rear wheels of the tractor were braked and there were no brakes at all on the trailer. The back wheels of the tractor locked up and I continued to skid down the hill at exactly the same speed, unfortunately, the loaded un-braked trailer continued to pick even more speed and the combination started to jack-knife. I looked back in horror as the trailer pushed the tractor sideways and I thought we were going to roll over. I thought this was the end! I don't know what caused me to take my foot off the brake and put the opposite lock on the wheels, but it straightened the tractor and trailer out and averted us rolling over. It must have been my earlier years of skidding old bangers around on greasy wet fields that kick-started my instinctive response. We continued to snake down the hill with me changing the tractor wheel direction like a professional rally driver. At the bottom of the hill, the ground levelled out into another paddock enclosed by a wire fence. We smashed straight through the fence and into the flat paddock where I finally managed to bring things under control. When we finally stopped, I jumped off the tractor was instantly sick and could not stop shaking. When I returned to the stables, I never told anyone what had happened as I knew I would get a good bollocking from dad for letting it happen. I was always ultra-careful in that field after that and never put too many bales onto the trailer.

It did happen again next year but this time there was far less weight behind me, the engine braking held, and I quickly regained control although it brought me out in a nervous sweat.

That hill was so dangerous, it almost got me again a couple of years later. We had recently bought our first Massey Ferguson tractor which although quite old had a new kind of gear system called Multi-Power. You could flick a lever up or down on the dashboard and it split each gear into two, effectively doubling your gears from ten up to twenty. The problem with the system was that if the Multi-Power was in high you had engine breaking but in low, the tractor would freewheel down a hill. Although I was aware of this, turning a large field of hay with a hay-bob on a blistering hot summers afternoon tends to dull the senses or even cause you to nod off at the wheel. Changing gear in low multi-power was much easier and on such a steep hill you had to make numerous changes on every row. Keeping it in low going uphill was fine so long as you remembered to change back to high before you turned down the hill. Half asleep I forgot and suddenly we were flying down the dreaded hill yet again. I must say it is amazing how quickly you come to your senses when something like that happens. This time a quick flick of the switch brought back the engine breaking and we were back in control within thirty yards.

Dad also had a close shave driving a tractor up Bunny Hill from Costock with a trailer of straw behind him. Near to the top of the hill there is a left-hand bend, halfway around the bend the tractor veered off the road and ploughed into the hedge. Luckily, the hedge was very thick at that point, in fact it was about thirty feet wide. The tractor went about twenty feet into the hedge before dad had time to pull the engine stop. The thick hedge saved dad from serious injury. When I arrived at the accident scene to help recover the vehicles all I could see was half of the trailer protruding out into the road, the rest of the tractor and trailer were completely buried in the hedge. A farmer friend helped us recover the trailer first and finally the tractor. It was a difficult operation as we had to un-hitch the trailer and let it roll back into the main road before we could hitch it onto the new tractor. Thankfully, nobody called the police and we were able to recover both the tractor and trailer without having to answer any awkward questions. When we investigated what had happened it turned out that the retaining clip for the main steering pin had corroded away and allowed the pin to fall out.

This meant that the two front wheels were no longer linked together or linked to the steering wheel. Luckily the steep camber on the road caused the tractor to veer left into the hedge. If the pin had dropped out going down the hill the camber would have taken the tractor to the right, head on into oncoming traffic on a high-speed blind bend and probably caused a multiple pile up.

Another lucky escape from old machinery!

So back to the main story. After leaving Gypsum I was earning my living by doing some work at the stables, doing some mechanical work, repairing damaged bodywork, re-spraying vehicles and running discos in the clubroom. I was also doing some jousting but that was for fun, the Nottingham Jousting Association was a non-profit making organisation in its first two years. It was a time of haphazard earnings, but it opened up a lot of different opportunities. During the next three years I would do a master's degree at the university of life. My varied occupations brought me into contact with all sorts of people from the highest down to the seriously dodgy. I made some appalling mistakes and learned the hard way just how hard life can be. Many of my mistakes are still too painful to put down on paper and be shared, they need to be kept locked up in the painful memories box never to be reopened.

My motor repair business led me into buying old cars and doing them up to resell. You may wonder how I made this quantum leap in lifestyle, but it was all down to my uncle Johnny, dad's youngest brother. His real name was Ian, but the family all called him Johnny. He was one of my two favourite uncles and was very much a role model to me as was my mum's brother Ron. Uncle Johnny had built up a very successful business dealing in second-hand cars and had sent me some cars to repair and respray, so I thought I would try to emulate his success. As with many cottage industries buying and selling the first few items was easy but to do it on a regular basis required a lot more dogged work. Finding the next restoration project became harder as did selling the end product. I resolved this problem by forming a loose partnership with a friend from the local village of Bunny called Arthur Evison.

Arthur was married to a horse dealer and that is how we met. Arthur dealt in cars for many years and had many contacts in motor trade. He introduced me to the motor auctions and to buying traded in cars from main motor dealerships. This was a tough world and you could buy yourself a lot of expensive trouble if you were not carful and I have to admit we got caught on several occasions. A friend of my father Max Rumph who had a garage and car dealership in Bunny gave some valuable advice at this time. He told me that we all get caught every now and then with a bad deal. Don't throw good money after bad take a loss and put it down to experience, turn your money over and move on. That advice has stood me in good stead all my life.

Arthur and I lived an up and down existence paying out to buy cars and doing them up and then advertising them for sale. Only when we sold a car did we get a pay day. We were also always trying to trade up to better cars, so part of our profit was always ploughed back into our next purchase. One day we bought a Ford Counsel which was larger than our usual purchases, but it had a long mot and only needed a good valeting to make ready to sell. We had been working together for about a year and Arthur suggested we take a holiday in the nice car we had just bought. I have no recollection where the idea came from, but we decided to rent a boat on the Norfolk Broads.

We felt very grand in our big car, it had large leather bench seats front and back capable of comfortably seating six people and a column gear change, all very American in style. Arthur had split up with his wife and was taking his new girlfriend Liz who later became his wife. I went on my own as I couldn't afford to take a girlfriend.

It was out of season, so we got a six-berth cruiser and a sailing dinghy for the price of a standard four berth boat. None of us had any experience with boats but after a quick explanation of the controls the boatyard gave us the all clear to cast off and set off, towing our sailing dingy behind. It was a bit scary at first, but we gradually got the hang of things and safely made our way to the Broads and dropped anchor for the night. It was heavenly, not a soul in sight, there was no wind and the water on the Broads was flat calm, reflecting the deep red autumn sunset. The only sounds that could be heard were occasional calls from wildfowl and the lowing of some distant cattle. I cannot describe my joy, all my troubles just melted away.

We had brought all our food with us including a plentiful supply of beer. Arthur had also managed to borrow two fishing rods and all the tackle. I settled myself into a deckchair at the back of the boat cast my fishing line out into the Broad, took a swig of beer and soaked up my surroundings, as David Jason used to say in the TV series Darling Buds of May "Just Perfick".

I had only two problems with my fishing. The first was that I never caught anything all week and the second was that every time I made a cast I was mobbed by ducks and geese at the point where my bait entered the water and although being very annoying it would prove to be very helpful later in the week. We had started our holiday mid-week and by the time we got to Sunday both supplies and money were starting to run low. Liz, who I think was wanting to impress Arthur with her cooking skills, suggested that she would cook a traditional Sunday roast for us all. The big problem was that none of the moorings had any shops, most were associated with a riverside pub that might be in the vicinity of a small village that maybe had a small shop selling, basic essentials, but we had no idea where to find a butcher also we didn't have the money to buy a joint of beef. That's not quite true as both Arthur and I had some money left but that was our beer money, so it came down to beer or beef.

As I pondered the predicament seated in my deckchair, I cast my line once more into dark black water harassed by the usual flock of ducks trying to grab my bait. As soon as my bait hit the water, my line snatched, and the fishing rod bent to almost snapping point. A fish at last, and a monster I quickly paid out some line to take pressure off the line and rod working instinctively and at great speed. It was probably a few seconds before I looked at the end of my line and saw my catch. One of the Ducks had taken the bait before it had time to sink, I now had a big mallard drake on the end of my line well and truly hooked. Luckily, I had been fishing for pike so had a strong line and a three-pronged pike hook on the end. The duck was doomed as it had completely swallowed the hook, so i reeled it in and dispatched it to put it out of its misery. On the brighter side we could now have roast duck for Sunday lunch and still have beer!

We were anchored in the middle of one of the Broads along with several other boats and Arthur wasn't sure if ducks were a protected species on the Broads, so we decided to up anchor and quickly move on in case someone had seen what had happened. We decided it would be best if we plucked and drew out the innards straight away, so if stopped we could say we had bought it oven ready. Arthur was driving while Liz and me frantically plucked and prepared the duck, we were trying to keep all the feathers together in a bag, but a strong breeze was blowing through the galley and evidence of our misdemeanor was blowing all over the boat. We had just finished when there was a shout from Arthur up top at the wheel, there was a police launch bearing down on us head on. I had to look out and see for myself as Arthur was a great practical joker but sure enough, no more than three hundred yards away was a police launch coming our way. Liz and I were in panic mode our first thoughts were to throw the feathers overboard but then we realized that the feathers would float on the water, bad idea. Arthur had cut the engine to slow down the closing speed and give us a little more time. We decided to light the oven and start cooking the evidence and to flush the feathers down the toilet. In the toilet, I was completely blind to what was happening outside. I was having great trouble flushing the duck feathers down the toilet and it took four or five flushes before they were all disposed of.

I emerged from the toilet expecting to be confronted by a police officer only to be told by a grinning Liz "Panic over they went straight past us". I dashed upstairs to see for myself and sure enough the police had just passed us. It was at that moment relief turned to panic once more as I saw a Long line of feathers bubbling up at the back our boat and slowly spreading across the surface. Unbeknown to us the toilets on boats in those days flushed directly into the river and now the feathers were floating across the river for all to see! Unbelievably nobody looked back on the Police launch and they continued their way. We had brought a bottle of whisky with us courtesy of Liz's father who owned an off license, we poured three large ones both to celebrate but also to calm our nerves.

Sunday brought us to Rollesby Broad and a quick reconnaissance circuit of the Broad revealed a bar at the sailing club with a large sign outside stating that visitors were welcome. A Sunday drink at the sailing club followed by roast duck for Sunday lunch sounded perfect. Unfortunately, there were no available berths at the sailing club, so we had to drop anchor on the other side of the Broad. Liz declined to go for a drink as she had too much to do preparing lunch but insisted that we went so that she had room to work in the cramped conditions. We hadn't used the dinghy at all during the holiday so far, so with great excitement and sense of adventure we climbed in and cast off. The breeze was gently blowing towards the club, so we raised the mast and hoisted the sail, neither of us had ever sailed before but "Hey ho" how hard could it be. After a few wobbles we caught the wind and sailed straight across to the club it was exhilarating and we were buzzing. We were under strict instructions not to be late for lunch so after three pints we decided to return. As we came out of the bar, we noticed that the wind had picked up and was blowing strongly into our face we looked across the Broad towards our boat.

It had never occurred to us that we may have a problem return-ing to back to the boat as we raced across the broad with only beer on our minds. A plan of action was required and after much arguing and debate it was decided that we would row out into clear water before attempting to raise the sail. We raised the sail and quickly returned to the sailing club, crashing into to wharf much to the amusement of the clients of the boat club bar who were watching us through the large panoramic windows. We de-cided to catch our breath and watch some of the people sailing out on the Broad. We sought of got the idea of how to sail against the wind by zig zagging or as I found out later tacking. After nearly capsizing several times we finally got going and picked up some speed, we were busy congratulating each other until we reached the other side of the broad when realized we had landed over a quarter of a mile away from our boat. By this time, we could see Liz on deck watching our antics. We turned around crossed back towards the club but this time we missed it by about one hundred yards. We repeated this several more times never getting any closer to our boat. In the end we dropped our sail when we were at our closest point to the boat and slowing rowed the rest of the way. Unfortunately, our rowing was not much better than our sailing skills. We were very late for our Sunday roast and expected a good bollocking from Liz. When we arrived, she was laughing her head off, she said it was the funniest thing she had ever seen, it was just like watching a live "Carry On" film. A truly memorable holiday!

My other revenue came from running the bar. When I came back home, the bar was being run by someone who had talked his way into the job with wildly inflated predictions of making the bar into a goldmine. When I looked at the accounts, the bar was barely breaking even. I told my parents something was wrong. Dad would have none of it as he had appointed the guy and dad never admitted being wrong, mum didn't want to go against dad. However, they did agree to let me check the bar accounts in detail. I secretly did a stock check and then added up the invoices for bar purchases. From these figures it was relatively easy to work out what the bar receipts should have been.

The figures were damning, far worse than expected. Thousands of pounds were missing. Mum and dad now realized that the bar man had to go, but they wanted the embezzlement kept quiet as they did not want people to know what had happened. It was decided to tell the barman that now I had returned I would be taking over. The missing money was discussed with the bar-man but he of course blamed other people, but he knew that we knew he was responsible. He was given a weeks' notice and I spent every day with him, supposedly learning the ropes. The day after he was fired, we had a big party organized and he asked if it was ok for to come to the party. He had a bit of a following at the stables so to keep things sweet we agreed to let him come. About halfway through the evening we ran short of change, so I went down to the house to get some more from the safe that was in dad's bedroom. In those days country people never locked their house.

As I entered the dark bedroom and fumbled for the light switch, I saw a blur of movement. When I switched the light on, I found our barman with a bag of money in his hand rubbing is head. The safe was wide open with the keys still in the door. He claimed that he had seen a stranger enter the house caught them rob-bing the safe, tackled the robber and had managed to snatch the money from him before he was hit over the head and stunned. I never saw anyone leave the property and the barman was the only person who knew where the safe was hidden and where the key was kept. Nobody believed him, we retrieved all the money and then threw him off the premises, never to be seen again.

I took over the day to day running of the bar and started run-ning a disco on Saturday nights. The discos were very popular and the number of people attending grew steadily. I worked on the interior of the bar, constantly fitting plywood arches over the windows and put ultra-violet lights everywhere to create a night club feel. Ultra-violet light was a new innovation when I fitted it and it made everything white glow in the dark. Many a girl was caught out in the early days wearing white underwear under a darker dress as it made them appear to be wearing nothing at all except there glowing white underwear, much to their horror and the delight of the male clients.

One evening two lads approached me at the end of the evening and asked if they could have a word with me. Their names were Chris Parry and Terry Harris, Terry was a DJ who went under the stage name of Terry Gee, Chris was his manager/promoter. Chris proposed that Terry would be our resident DJ and to pay for him we would charge an entrance fee on the door which would be collected on the door by Chris and divided between us. After discussing the proposal with my parents, we decided to give it a go for a trial period. The trial period was a success and we gradually built it up to opening Friday, Saturday and Sunday. We called it the Rodeo club. As our audience increased, I upgraded the lighting effects and sound system on a regular basis. We even had a big event in the indoor school with a top-class band. Although we had posters printed and plastered the all over the area we clashed with a couple of other local big events and only just broke even. If you factored in the time setting it all up it was not profitable. I remember going to the doctor and asking him for some pills so that I could stay awake and not have to sleep because I had so much to organise, not surprisingly he refused. It was a great night; several hundred people came and the band which was called the Jaffa Band was amazing. Although we didn't make our fortune it became the blueprint for several great events held in the indoor school some years later.

And so, I became a night club manager and a promoter which sounds great, but it was a hard, wild, life. We closed at eleven and it would be midnight before we had washed the glasses and cashed up. Although it was late, we were all buzzing, so we would head off to other clubs that stayed open later. Our closest venue was the Flying Club situated at Tollerton Airfield, but there were numerous other clubs in Nottingham that stayed open much later some legally and some not so legal. On Saturday and Sunday mornings I had an early start even though I rarely got home before three in the morning as I had to mop all the floors and open all the doors to clear the air of stale beer and cigarette smoke before the riding school clients arrived.

The Rodeo club ran very successfully for about two years until there was a mass brawl at closing time, Dad, me and several staff were injured, and we never reopened, our success was our downfall we no longer knew all our clientele personally anymore.

By the time we closed the doors to the night club, other things were starting to happen at the stables. The jousting had taken an interesting turn following us working with the London stuntmen once again in a three-day jousting tournament to commemorate the Battle of Hastings at Battle Abbey. We worked with a lot of celebrities and met some important players in the finance and entertainment industry. Dad and I travelled to London on a regular basis mainly to meet Sir Trevor Lloyd-Hughes who was a PR consultant and had until recently been prime minister Harold Wilson's press secretary. The jousting was about to change from a hobby into a major part of our business.

During my time working with Chris Parry at the Rodeo club we had a slight misadventure. Chris like me dabbled in the motor trade buying and selling the odd car and also renovating them. His pride and joy was an early model of a Ford Thunderbird or better known as the T- Bird which featured in the lyrics of the Beach Boys hit "Fun, Fun, Fun." Unfortunately, he rarely had it on the road due to its excessive thirst for petrol.

One afternoon Chris asked me if I fancied a trip to Cornwall, he had been asked to deliver a minibus down to Launceston and bring a full size 52-seater coach back to Loughborough. The plan was to leave that evening about ten o' clock drive through the night and then a steady drive back arriving home mid-afternoon. As usual we never managed to leave the pub until closing time and although the pub closing time was 10.30pm it was nearer to eleven pm before we were on the road. The minibus was a Leyland 15cwt van that had crudely been converted into a minibus by fitting windows into the rear side panels, the seats were tubular steel framed double bench seats. It was basic, slow and noisy, designed to transport workers short distances.

There were no motorways to the West Country in those days, so it was A roads all the way. This also meant that we had to drive through many towns on our journey. I think it was driving through Tamworth that we hit a pothole and the exhaust system fell off. It wasn't the silencer that fell off which was the usual problem. This exhaust system had detached itself at the engine manifold and the noise was horrendous.

The plan had been to share the driving through the night so that each of us could get some sleep but the loud noise from the engine and the uncomfortable seats made this impossible. When we left Loughborough, the weather was warm and balmy but by the time dawn broke the temperature had dropped and it was drizzling. Neither of us had thought to bring a coat! By the time we reached our destination the drizzle had turned to heavy fine rain, the sort of rain that soaks you in seconds. We had expected to be gratefully received and hopefully be offered tea or coffee and maybe even breakfast but nothing at all was offered. Our destination was not a garage or showroom as we had expected but a smallholding that closely resembled a scrapyard. The proprietor of these salubrious premises was an overweight grumpy man who wore a boiler suit that had probably never ever been washed. The ingrained oil and grease on it was so thick that it had polished itself and patches of the fabric now shone like newly polished boots. His means of communication seemed to a series of grunts and growls.

By the time we had exchanged paperwork and vehicles we were soaked to the skin. Chris was much stockier than me and didn't seem to feel the cold, I was less than ten stone and always felt the cold. I was shivering badly by the time we started the coach and I was dreaming of drying out and warming up in front of the bus heater. Twenty minutes later I realised that the heater wasn't working, and my shivering was getting worse. I was starting to feel unwell.

We pulled into the first garage we could find for fuel as the fuel gauge barley rose past the empty marker. No doubt our friendly vendor had syphoned off any spare diesel. Garages in those days repaired vehicles and sold fuel, if you were lucky, they might sell cigarettes. This garage was somewhat unique in that it sold gallon jars of farm made scrumpy cider. It was very cheap so we each bought a gallon as a souvenir of our trip. I started mine immediately in place of medicine. I do not know how strong it was, but it gave you a warming glow as it went down your throat and certainly dulled my aches and shivers. Things were looking up; the rain had stopped, and the sun was starting to occasionally break through the clouds. The only downside was that there were no cafés on our route, and we were starving hungry.

We made good progress for the next hour and our spirits were lifting, mainly due to regular sips from our scrumpy bottles. Then the sound of a distant woodpecker started to emerge from the engine and quickly changed to the sound of a machine gun, a sound so loud that we could not hear each other speak. We ground to a halt and the engine died. This was a major engine breakdown, probably the big end bearings, the bus was going nowhere for some considerable time.

I stayed with the bus while Chris trudged off to find a phone box to inform the new owner. When he returned, he told me that he had to stay with the bus and then come back home in the recovery vehicle which might not arrive until the next day. He would be reimbursed for a hotel room or could sleep on the bus. As I was not supposed to be on the trip, I didn't feature in any of these arrangements. Also, I needed to get home as I had things that I had promised to do the following day and to make matters worse I was running a high temperature.

I decided to try my luck thumbing lifts back to Nottingham. I had only light clothing and just a small amount of loose change in my pocket not the best way to try and thumb your way halfway up the country. I asked Chris if he could lend me some money, but he had barely enough for a hotel room and nothing spare for him to buy any food. We were both very ill prepared for unexpected problems.

I walked a couple of miles with no luck thumbing and came to a traffic island. I positioned myself on the exit for the road to the Midlands and half an hour later a lorry picked me up and took me to the edge of Birmingham. Again, I positioned myself on the exit road of an island this time signposted to Leicester. I was at this island for over an hour and was feeling quite despondent when I finally got a lift in a lorry going towards Leicester. The lorry driver knew the area well and dropped me off close to Loughborough. It was at this point I decided to find a phone box and use what change I had to call home and ask to be picked up. A little over an hour later I was home just in time for Tea. Remarkably the journey had only taken about three hours longer than it had taken us to drive down. After a hearty hot meal and several cups of hot tea I retired to bed and sweated out my chill.

I had been stupid, totally unprepared for the unexpected events of the last twenty-four hours. This and a few other similar cockups, taught me to prepare for the worst whenever undertaking long journeys, something that would stand me in good stead for what life was going to throw at me in the not too distant future.

Chapter 17

Returning to the fold

There had been a gradual softening of relations with Dad since my return to Bunny Hill, but it was the jousting tournament at Battle on the south coast really started a reconciliation. Just four of us went to Battle Dad and I rode in the tournament and Brian Hinksman and Brent Haddon went as squires. Brent was also there as first reserve in case Dad or I got injured. Brent travelled down on his own in his E type Jaguar and booked himself into a fine hotel; Brent did things in style. Dad drove the lorry down with Brian and I crammed onto the Tk Bedford's small bench seat. The trip took over five hours. Dad slept in the lorry whilst Bri and shared a tent. We worked ate and slept together for five days, you just had to make compromises and get along in these circumstances. I met people that were making a living out of doing exciting and creative things. They had money and flair so different to our lives in the north.

I already knew Max Diamond, as he had hired the horses from Dad for the famous first jousting show at Wollaton Park in Nottingham. I now also got to know the Powell family who were an institution within the film stunt world. There was Nosher Powell, his brother Dinny. Nosher's son Greg was about my age. Greg was an amazing horseman and I was mesmerised seeing him standing on the back of two galloping horses controlling them with just one hand and waving the other hand high in the air. Greg later went on to be top stunt man specialising in horses, cars, and battle scenes. He later became a stunt coordinator and is now a film director. My brother Stuart worked with him recently on films in Hungary and in India.

People were desperate to meet and be seen with the dashing brave Knights who were the main attraction of the festival. The jousting was not a show in those days, and we were pitching our lances at complete strangers. During one of these jousts I was lucky not to have been killed when a lance hit me on my head and ripped my metal helm clean off my head. For a moment, both the crowd and the participants were stunned into silence as it looked as if my head had been completely knocked off and was bouncing across the arena. I was briefly knocked out but was allowed to continue after a few minutes rest. Oh, how health and safety has changed these days!

In the evenings we were wined and dined in pubs and restaurants. We were even made Honorary Members of a private dining club in the town of Battle and treated to some of the finest food and wine that I have ever had in my life. It was during one of these nights out that I met a guy who was a year or so older than me, he was helping out with the accounting side of the show as a favour to his girlfriend's father. His name was Graham Lucking, and his girlfriend was Katie Lloyd-Hughes daughter of Sir Trevor Lloyd-Hughes who had been Prime Minister Harold Wilson's Press Secretary and now had his own consultancy firm that specialised in linking big business with government. I think that he would be called a lobbyist in today's world.

Although we only met a couple of times, Graham and I got on very well and he was extremely enthusiastic about developing the jousting into a major spectator event. I was getting used to people singing our praises to try and be seen with us at events but after the event you never saw them again. I had Graham down as one of them, but he insisted swapping telephone numbers and told me that he would be in touch. Dad had similar experiences with people more of his own age and again thought nothing of their promises. I made another contact that weekend that was to slowly develop into a long business relationship that continues to this day albeit now mainly through my son Mark and his son Dean. His name is Terry Goulden, and in 1971 like me he was starting to find his business feet in the world of medieval re-enactment. His name crops up quite regularly in my book The Knights Errant.

About two weeks after returning home I got a phone call from Graham inviting me to visit him in London. He had just managed to get a flat in Clapham and was very excited about it, apparently it was the new up and coming location in London. The best thing was it had two bedrooms so I could stay in London without having to pay for accommodation.

I couldn't wait to go to London and see Graham's new flat. Graham was an accountant and he worked for The Ford Motor Co. at their head office. His new flat was costing more for a week than I earned in a month, so it had to be something like James Bond had in the movies. After all, he was dating a Knight of the realm's daughter. I went down on the train to St Pancras and then took the tube following his detailed instructions which finally took me to a pub where I met up with him. It was quite an adventure as there were no mobile phones in those days and I had no way of contacting him from the moment I left home until we met in the lounge bar of his nominated pub. As it happened, I got there first and was well into my second pint of bitter when he finally arrived full of bluster and apologies. It was something that I would get used to when we worked together as he was nearly always late.

Graham outlined his ideas for us to create a touring jousting performance. He explained that Katie's dad Sir Trevor was keen to help with introductions and he thought it would be feasible to do several shows every year similar to the one we had just been part of in the grounds of Battle Abbey. Unbeknown to me at the time, Graham knew the details of all the costs of putting on the Battle Abbey festival and that the stuntmen had charged a fortune for putting on the jousting. They were about five times more expensive than us and I think Graham saw us as a way of making easy money. He would find us lots of high-quality shows, pay us the same as we were charging now but actually charge the shows a similar amount to what the stuntmen had charged. I worked this out further down the line, but for now I was a little star struck and eager to listen to all his great ideas.

After visiting several fashionable bars and an equally fashionable restaurant we made our way home to the new apartment. We turned into a dark side-street that made me feel anxious for our safety and then entered a darkened house from an equally dark back-yard. Graham switched on a light as we entered the property. The light was at the top of the stairs two storeys up and very dim, giving just enough light to make out the narrow twisting staircase. Halfway up on the first floor was a tiny landing, where there was an entrance door to another flat and astonishingly, fitted to the opposite wall was a small gents urinal. Graham pointed this smelly grubby thing out as we squeezed past it commenting "Very handy if you need a pee when somebody is using the bathroom." I just could not believe my eyes. The flat wasn't big enough to swing a cat around, for what he was paying I could have rented a mansion in Nottingham. My love affair with London high life was waning fast!

I visited London many times that Autumn in 1971 sometimes on my own and sometimes with Dad. Dad had made friends with a group of arty-farty people at Battle and we were wined, dined and generally paraded around fashionable gatherings by them. These were great fun and we made many useful contacts. We were even invited to have drinks at one of the great Gentleman's Club complete with leather armchairs and a butler. We had been warned to wear suits for our visit to the club, but I was not wearing a tie as it was fashionable to have an open necked shirt with a suit at that time. At the reception I was discretely taken to one side and handed a tie by a steward who whispered into my ear, "You will need to pop this on Sir, nobody is allowed to enter without a suit and a tie Sir." I have thought long and hard but cannot remember the name of the club only that it was very famous and counted several Prime Ministers as past or present members.

Although we met lots of people who thought we were amazing and what we did was "Absolutely Fabulous" we still didn't have anything to show for it except a depleted bank balance and a grumpy mother who was questioning whether all the time away in London and the expense was worth it. Just before Christmas we had two meetings with Sir Trevor Lloyd-Hughes who told us he had several things in the pipeline and hopefully early in the new year he would be able to give us some positive news but, in the meantime, to get on with upgrading our costumes and equipment. At that period, we were fielding up to ten mounted knights for a show and basically copying the show that the stunt men did. The show was all horsemanship and no sword or any other hand to hand combat. Dad and his stallion were the mainstay of the show.

It was an exciting time, and a time that kept me happy and stimulated. I read everything I could about Jousting and Knights, both fact and fiction. Jousting I discovered spanned over five hundred years, the costumes and equipment changed drastically over that period. So, my first task was to choose a period in history that we were going to represent. During my visits to London I found that one of the first questions I was always asked was, "What period do you represent."

The costumes we that we used up to this point were hired from theatrical costumiers in Nottingham and London, the armour that they supplied was just knitted string sprayed silver to simulate chainmail. We had our own surcoats made in our preferred colours and coat of arms. For our helmets or to be correct helms we had copied the ones worn by the stunt men. Again, the stunt men had hired theirs from a film prop company. Theirs were made of fibre glass but at that time we had no experience of working with fibre glass, so we had made ours out of sheet metal, a material we were used to working with. I had already made what was called a five-plate jousting helm in steel for the Battle tournament and being metal it probably saved me from serious injury when the lance struck my head. After that incident we decided that all our helms in future would be made of steel. The chainmail, five plate barrel helm and the shape of the shields that we used determined that we represented the twelfth century. My biggest discovery during my research was that arms and armour changed very slowly during the whole of the jousting period. Kings and the ultra-wealthy upgraded their equipment all the time to the very latest and best. Lesser Lords and Knights hung onto their old weapons and armour and could be well over fifty years behind the times. This gave me great flexibility when sourcing our costumes and if someone challenged their authenticity, I could easily justify them on the vague slow change theory, anywhere between 1100 AD to 1250 AD.

The Theatrical Costumiers in Nottingham were very small as they only served the two theatres in the city. However, in London there were two huge companies that supplied the numerous theatres and the vibrant film industry that was based close to the city, one was called Angels and the other Burmams and Nathans.

If we were going to be performing at a great number of venues during the next year it made sense to buy rather than rent costumes and so with that in mind, I made appointments with both companies with the view to purchasing a variety of knights and squires costumes. There was no internet or mobile phones in those days, so I made appointments with both companies and got basic directions as to the location of each company. Then armed with an A to Z of London I set out on an adventure of visiting parts of London not usually seen by tourists.

It was a true eye opener to visit these institutions of the film and theatre worlds. Their stock of costumes that started with caveman times right through to modern day left me speechless. Thousands of costumes all labelled with size, era, social class and profession. However big your production was they could easily clothe your whole cast. Despite their huge stocks I could not persuade either company to sell me anything at all, they only hired and never sold any of their costumes. I did however purchase a quart of fake blood and a palette of theatrical grease makeup.

However, my visit to these two theatrical institutions was not in vain. They were very accommodating, and I spent several hours at both companies gleaning lots of valuable information and although they would not sell me anything, they did give me the names and telephone numbers of two people that might be able to help me. This information was given to me with a nod and a wink which led me to believe that some costumes might be being sold to trusted friends out of the back doors.

These two people would become my main suppliers of costumes and weapons for years to come. One was Terry Goulden who I had already met briefly at the Battle Tournament and the other man was Alan Meeks. Alan was the first person I dealt with as he was an Armourer and well established in the film industry. He made some beautiful weapons, swords, spears, axes and halberds and I still have a matching pair of his swords to this day forty-five years later. The jousting troupe also still has examples of his work in their props room.

Alan supplied everything that we couldn't make ourselves. Up until this point we only had fake chainmail head pieces (a Coif) and a knee length coat (a Hauberk) and then knee length leather boots that were not really authentic to our period. Alan was able to supply chainmail leggings with an integral leather soul (Chausses)This was a game changer for us as it put us on a par with the top Knights of the stuntmen's group.

All this of course came at a cost and so as 1971 came to an end, although I had the contacts to source most of what we needed, I didn't have the money or the bookings to proceed.

In mid-January all our bookings came at once, but it was not all good news, despite Sir Trevor getting us shows that were beyond our wildest dreams. It was the beyond our wildest dreams that was the problem, we just had no plans in place to do all these prestigious shows. We didn't have the personnel, horses, equipment or the knowledge of how to manage such an operation.

In the space of three weeks we were offered 117 days' work that amounted to 224 performances and this didn't include small village shows that we had already promised to perform at. To say that we were in a state of shock was an understatement. Graham ever the optimist begged Dad and me not to reject the offers out of hand as Sir Trevor had worked very hard to get these shows and he had put his reputation on the line getting us this stunning work. Not only that but it was a once in a lifetime chance to make it into the big time and it could change all of our lives for the better. Graham firmly nailed his colours to the mast by declaring that he was prepared to give up his very good job at Ford and work with us to make it happen.

The big worry was that one of the offers was to do a summer season at a new Medieval Theme Park in North wales, sixteen weeks two shows per day seven days a week. Graham was up for everything, but it wasn't him having to get his body battered every day, I was excited and scared shitless all at the same time, Dad was against the summer season but liked the idea of doing the other big prestigious shows, however he liked the idea of the of the big money we could earn doing the summer season. It was more than we all earned in a year.

We consulted the rest of the people who jousted with us and they were mainly Dad's age except for Brent Haddon and Brian Hinksman who were a year or two older than me. Everyone except Brian were of the same opinion as Dad. Brian like Graham was willing to give up everything in the pursuit of fame and fortune.

Besides the summer season which was at Gwrych Castle in North Wales, we had been offered a daily slot at the Horse of the Year Show which in those days was held at Wembley Pool in North London, a weekend performing at Syon Park, the London home of the Duke of Northumberland that is a set in 200 acres of parkland with a long frontage along the Thames River. These shows would be held in the park and include two evening performances under flood lights that was a World First for jousting. This was a joint show with Max Diamond and his stunt men. Another show was to travel to Scotland to recreate the famous Eglington Tournament that had been held in the Royal Burgh of Irvine during the mid-Eighteen Hundreds. Finally, there was an appearance at the Preston Guild celebrations, something that is only held once every twenty-five years. Again, this was a ground-breaking performance; the Knights would be part of an outdoor production of Camelot and perform the jousting scenes live in front of the stage at ground level between the stage and the orchestra.

After much argument we agreed that we would take on everything. Dad would run a group of the original founders of the Jousting Association and do the one-off shows and Brian, Graham and myself would form a new jousting group and we would go and run the shows in Wales.

All we needed to make this a reality was twenty new staff eight of which would have to be good enough horsemen to joust and be prepared to do stunt falls, be artistic enough to perform in front of an audience of two thousand and be prepared to give up everything they were doing for the whole of the summer. Writing this now makes me wonder about our sanity, but when you are young everything and anything seems to be possible. We also required eight to ten horses that would joust, costumes and equipment for about thirty people. We were so far out on a limb we couldn't see the tree.

Once we had secured the contracts, I went to see the bank manager about a very large loan. Graham talked me through how the meeting might pan-out. His advice was to go into the meeting quietly confident and chatty, not to mention the loan at all and just talk about the fantastic plans we had for this incredible forthcoming season. He told me to stay nonchalant and to wait until he asked how much money we needed to make this happen. I followed his instructions to the letter and amazingly after nearly half an hour of talking about all the great things that had happened the bank manger looked at his watched and said, "I have another appointment in a few minutes so how much are you looking for?" Graham told me to ask for more than we needed, we needed £8,000 so I asked for £10,000. To my astonishment he agreed and said that I could have another £2,000 flexibility just in case we needed it. As Dad was the only house owner the loan was secured against his house. Although dad readily agreed to using his house as security the consequences if things went wrong weighed heavily on me. Graham had no worries as he was not connected to the loan at all. This was something that would become Graham's trademark as my deals with him progressed, but I never really gave it any thought at that particular time as there were far more important things happening.

It was a crazy time for the next four months; it was like a king preparing to go to war. There were endless planning meetings equipment to source or make, horses to buy and train, people to interview employ and train. It was an endless merry go round always acquiring new skills or knowledge on a daily basis. The adrenalin flow was amazing, I loved every minute of it!

I learnt how to work with glass fibre and resin, where to get steel oil tempered for our swords. I sourced long lengths of bamboo to make our lances and reinforced them with glass fibre resin. I researched English and Welsh Heraldry to ensure that everything was authentic. Not everything was successful and there were as many failures as there was successes, but we kept moving forward, we had no alternative.

Looking back, I think it was this period in my life that got me addicted to working on time scaled projects. Trying to pull endless things together in a small-time frame and meet what seems to be an impossible deadline, gave me an incredible buzz.

My wife and fellow workers would probably say it made me impossible to live or work with! I would work myself to both physical and mental exhaustion. Sometimes I could not speak because my brain had so many things swirling around in it, so many things to complete before that deadline. Whenever a deadline came, there were still many extra things that I would have liked to have completed but deadlines are final, and you just have to go with what you have at that moment. When I watch Master Chef on television it reminds me of those manic days, you know when the Chefs are told "Times up" that they all would have liked just a bit more time to achieve the perfection that they had in their mind.

I thought that when I reached the deadline of moving to Wales that all this pressure would end, but little did I know that our summer season in Wales was going to be constant deadlines and pressure from May through to September. We performed about 200 shows I missed maybe 10 shows due to injury and was general manager of everything except financial matters, which were Graham's Department. Just writing about it now makes me feel ill.

On the good side I earned a lot of money and as soon as her college course finished my girlfriend Louise joined me for the rest of the season. We got our first dog and developed a taste for good food and fine wine. At the end of the season I bought my first new car. A bright yellow Ford Cortina Estate Car.

A lot of what happened at Gwrych Castle is well documented in my First book. The Knights Errant. For this book all I need to say is that I returned home a very different person. We were treated very badly by the locals who in the main refused to speak to us or do business with us. I discovered that big business was ruthless and had no morals. Also, that fame was a poisoned chalice and after basking in the limelight for a few weeks I became almost a recluse, travelling great distances just to have an evening meal in a restaurant where nobody recognised me. I learnt a lot about people and found it hard to trust anyone. I had sort of grown a shell in Wales, always wary of people's motives. I took a step back whenever someone proposed to do something and took time to try and work out the real reason, they wanted to do it, what was their real angle? When I went to Wales, there were many people I called friends. When I came back, I took a very different view, I now had only one or two friends, real friends that I knew I could trust.

The intensity of the shows at Gwrych Castle meant we needed to constantly replace horses as they got sick of the constant jousting and Knights falling off their backs. A lot of the training of new horses fell to me and I probably rode about three hours most days. We were living with our horses every day and like cavalry men before us a great bond developed between horse and rider. It touched my soul and the fact that I was choosing to ride rather than being told to ride by my father made me into a true horseman and I learned many equestrian skills during my time at the Castle and I am still learning to this day.

When I returned home from Wales, I rented a flat in West Bridgford which by coincidence it was almost directly opposite my grandfather's house where I had spent so many happy days during my early childhood. During my childhood it seemed to be such a big house and garden it now looked much smaller than I remembered it. My flat was small and cosy and was the upstairs of a semi-detached house with an outside staircase for access. Its big downside was that it was fully furnished so you couldn't add any personal touches, but the biggest downside was that the owner lived downstairs, and it came with a long list of must do's and do not's.

Although Lou and I had been living together in Wales, her parents were not aware of this and for a few days she had to go home every night until she plucked up the courage to tell her parents. In the end, after formally getting engaged she was allowed to come and live with me. We soon moved to a larger flat with parking and a garden just off Musters Road in West Bridgford. We were still living there when we married in September 1973 almost a year to the day after returning from Wales. Not long after we married, we rented an old farmhouse on the Wysall road at the back of Bunny Park.

Back at the stables Mum and Dad had taken on a manager to run the stables after Dad had his heart attack and although he was recovering well, he now suffered from Angina that left him extremely breathless in cold or windy weather. The manager was a very good instructor but managing the livery, yard staff and farm work was proving a step to far and sections of the business were starting to slide.

Graham offered to do an in-depth analysis of the business and give us a business plan for the future. It was in his interest as well as ours to have a successful riding school if the jousting side of the business was going to continue to grow. Jousting was seasonal and the horses that we used needed to earn their keep all year round.

Graham's proposal shocked the whole family. To an accountant it made sense but to us it was madness. His proposal was that we reduce the size of our classes, sell off half the horses so that all the horses would be used on every ride and therefore double our profitably. Unfortunately, he had failed to notice that they were not industrial widgets and that they came in many different shapes and sizes all with differing temperaments they also tended to go lame on quite a regular basis. For once the family agreed on something and I think that bridge building that had been going on for the past two years was finally complete.

Dad and I rarely agreed on anything because we were complete opposites, we saw everything from a different prospective. I am a Gemini and Dad is an Aquarius and apparently these two, star signs just don't get on. I do not do horoscopes, but I have noticed that people with the same star sign seem to share the same traits. Amazingly Lou is the same star sign as Dad and our marriage has now lasted forty-five years. We do see and feel things very differently but because we both have strong personalities; we sort of temper each other's harsher traits.

Back to Graham's proposals, his other suggestion was that we needed to almost double the price of our livery. Dad rejected the idea calling it madness but looking at Graham's figures it made absolute sense. It had been a bad summer for farmers and hay, straw and grain was all in short supply causing prices to go through the roof. All the aforementioned had more than doubled in price and coupled with an inflation rate that rose from 5% in 1970 up to over 25% by mid-1974 we were keeping our liveries at a substantial loss. The problem was Dad hadn't increased his prices since the late 1960s. The price rise was a terrible bombshell and nearly all our liveries left. Many were Mum and Dads friends, there was a lot of bad blood but as the year wore on, people got used to continuous price rises for everything in all walks of life.

We had to pull together as a family and try and survive. Lou and I were about to get married, Graham realised that neither jousting or riding schools were not going make his fortune and gradually drifted away to find more lucrative work.

I had gone full circle leaving and returning home, but I had learned a lot on that journey. Horses became my life and Lou's. Lou had been at the stables since she was six years old and kept a horse there for many years. She understood the business, its workings, its heart, and its soul.

Horses would take me down many paths and open many doors for me.

Little did I realise that my life was just beginning! Enough to write my final book of the Bunny Hill Chronicles trilogy. My working title is 'Osses and 'Osse People. Hopefully ready to publish in about two years 2020-2021

The End

I do hope you have enjoyed this book; every word has been typed by me using the one finger typing method. Hence the two years to write it.

I hope it gives others hope and encouragement to persevere when things are not going so well in their lives and to think of life as a rollercoaster with lots of ups and downs.

If you enjoyed the read please write a quick review on Amazon and I can be contacted by email: samhumphrey2@gmail.com

As with my other book The Knights-Errant I will be making a donation from each book sale to my chosen charity: Guide Dogs for the Blind.

About the Author

Sam Humphrey was born in West Bridgford, near Nottingham in 1951. The family moved to Bunny Hill, eight miles south of Nottingham, when he was four years old. He has lived or worked on Bunny Hill all his life. Horses and the countryside have always been a major part of his life. Sam married his wife Louise in 1973 when he was 22 years old and Louise just 18 years old. They have two children, Mark born in 1978, and Emma born in 1979, and now also have three granddaughters. Their children have both pursued successful careers in the equestrian world.

Sam was educated at the local village primary school of Costock and then at Rushcliffe Grammar school. He later studied science and management studies at Peoples College, Nottingham and later studied Trade Union Law in the workplace and the History of the English Language at West Bridgford college.

He left school at the age of sixteen to work in the family riding school business, and also spent six months working as a jobbing builder with his future brother-in-law, before joining British Gypsum Research Department at their plant at nearby East Leake. He left British Gypsum in 1971 to take over running the jousting at Gwrych Castle and became managing director of Medieval Entertainments Ltd. In 1973, Lou and Sam formed the School of National Equitation Limited with Sam's parents. Sam was again managing director and Lou was company secretary. They became sole owners of the business in 1991 when they purchased the other half of the business from Sam's parents on their retirement. Sam and Lou have also owned a riding clothes and saddlery shop and been partners in an auction company specializing in selling horses, saddlery, and farm equipment, where Sam was an Auctioneer.

Sam has taught riding all his life, taking his first, class lesson at the age of 10 years, when his father failed to get home in time for the lesson. He has a Diploma in Sports Psychology and uses Bio-mechanics as the foundation for his teaching. Always attracted to the adrenalin side of riding, as a youngster he was a member of the Quorn Hunt Pony Club Prince Philip Cup Team for mounted games, then as a teenager he jumped a string of ponies at county level for a local owner. In the 70's and early 80's he rode in point-to-point races, riding and training his own horses. Later in his racing career, he was granted a National Hunt Amateur License and went onto achieve one of his ambitions of riding in a race at the world-famous Cheltenham Racecourse. He started hunting with the Quorn hunt when he was five, and has hunted with many Fox, Drag and Blood hound packs both in the UK and Ireland, and has been Field Master of three different packs and was a keen participant in Teamchasing since its inception in 1974 until late 1990s.

From the late 1970s until his retirement Sam was involved in many Films and Television programs, providing horses and also appearing on screen which earned him the right to be granted an Actors Equity Card. This led him into training would be film stunt performers, for the horse-riding part of their entrance exam to the stunt register. It always gives Sam great pleasure when he sees the name of one of his pupils appear in the film credits.

Although now officially retired, Sam continues to teach and help his son with the family Riding Centre, which was started in 1955.

Sam plans to write another book about his equine life and the larger than life characters he has met.

The Bunny Hill Chronicles.

When I wrote the Knights-Errant, I had intended it to be a one off! I was fulfilling a drunken pledge to the older members of the Jousting Troupe to put down on paper all the amazing things that happened to us as we toured constantly for nearly twenty years performing in many different countries.

When I came to publish it on Amazon, I had to fill in endless questions about the book. One of the questions was name of series, I suppose I could have written none, but a light bulb moment prompted me to write The Bunny Hill Chronicles. After I had published The Knights-Errant people kept asking, was I going to write anything else and it was then that those words I had written in my light bulb moment came back to me and prompted me to start work on Boy Gone Feral on Bunny Hill and to plan another book dedicated to the horse side of my life: - working title Osse's and Osse People,

The Knights-Errant. Published Amazon 2017

Boy Gone Feral on Bunny Hill. Published Amazon 2019

Contact: - samhumphrey2@gmail.com

Back Cover Photograph

The Author riding Gladstonian (Stable name Oggie) owned by Judge Richard Benson (better known to his friends as Dick), clearing the water jump at Cheltenham in a 3 mile 2 furlong steeple chase.

Made in the USA
Middletown, DE
17 February 2020